EVERYDAY
SLOW
COOKER

EVERYDAY
SLOW
COOKER

130 Modern Recipes, with **40** Gluten-Free Dishes
and **50** Multicooker Variations

BY THE EDITORS OF
CookingLight

Oxmoor
House.

©2018 Time Inc. Books, a division of Meredith Corporation
Published by Oxmoor House, an imprint of Time Inc. Books
225 Liberty Street, New York, NY 10281

Senior Editor: Rachel Quinlivan West, R.D.
Assistant Editor: April Colburn
Project Editor: Lacie Pinyan
Design Director: Melissa Clark
Photo Director: Paden Reich
Designer: AnnaMaria Jacob
Photographers: Antonis Achilleos, Caitlin Bensel, Jennifer Causey,
  Stephen DeVries, Greg DuPree, Alison Miksch, Victor Protasio
Prop Stylists: Cindy Barr, Mary Clayton Carl, Kay E. Clarke,
Missie Neville Crawford, Audrey Davis, Thom Driver, Christine Keely,
Lindsey Lower, Mindi Shapiro Levine
Food Stylists: Mary Claire Britton, Torie Cox, Margaret Monroe Dickey,
  Anna Hampton, Rishon Hanners, Emily Nabors Hall, Chelsea Zimmer
Recipe Developers and Testers: Ann Taylor Pittman, Time Inc. Food Studios,
  Carolyn Williams
Recipe Editor: Julie Christopher
Senior Production Manager: Greg A. Amason
Associate Manager for Project Management and Production: Anna Muñiz
Copy Editors: Dolores Hydock, Jacqueline Giovanelli
Proofreader: Adrienne Davis
Indexer: Mary Ann Laurens
Fellows: Holly Ravazzolo, Hanna Yokeley

ISBN-13: 978-0-8487-5645-1
Library of Congress Control Number: 2018941157

First Edition 2018
Printed in the United States of America
10 9 8 7 6 5 4 3 2 1

We welcome your comments and suggestions
about Time Inc. Books. Please write to us at:
Time Inc. Books
Attention: Book Editors
P.O. Box 62310
Tampa, Florida 33662-2310

Time Inc. Books products may be purchased for business or promotional use.
For information on bulk purchases, please contact Christi Crowley in the
Special Sales Department at (845) 895-9858.

On the cover
Left: Beef-Barley Soup with Red Wine and Pesto, page 214
Center: Umami Chicken and Vegetable Ramen Bowl, page 230
Right: Chile-Rubbed Pork with Corn and Black Beans, page 55

CONTENTS

WELCOME

We all crave food that's easy to make and tastes amazing. Even though the slow cooker is a proven solution when it comes to hands-free, care-free cooking, it often fails to give us the vibrant, creative, and healthy food we want to prepare. But no more! With *Everyday Slow Cooker*, you can now have it all.

This book offers the supereasy slow-cooking process you love with new recipes featuring modern ingredients and global flavors. Try Lemongrass-Coconut Marinated Chicken (page 83) and Indian Lamb and Butternut Squash Stew (page 226) for busy weeknight dinner solutions. Count on tried-and-true favorites such as Easy Jerk Pork Shoulder (page 52) and Brown Rice Pilaf with Cherries and Hazelnuts (page 280) to please any crowd. With big flavor and a beautiful appearance, these slow-cooked dishes will surely impress your dinner guests—they'll never know your slow cooker did all the work. Plus, on more than 50 recipes, we've included directions for cooking the dish in a multicooker, making this book useful for both appliances. Moreover, for your ultimate ease, find cooking advice, a chapter on slow-cooking fundamentals to get you started, and a produce guide to help you shop.

Because these recipes are from *Cooking Light*, they aren't just delicious; they're also good for you—each developed with both satisfaction and health in mind. You'll find fresh fare such as Cod with Tomato-Balsamic Jam (page 125) and Mediterranean Quinoa with Arugula (page 190), as well as comforting dishes such as Barbecue Brisket Sliders (page 36) and Tortellini with Creamy Butternut Sauce (page 166). There are even dozens of gluten-free recipes included, ensuring that there's something here for everyone.

For home cooks ready for updated slow-cooker dishes full of original flavors and an array of nutrients, we invite you to start here. Your slow cooker is waiting.

—the editors of *Cooking Light*

1 THE BASICS

WHY USE A SLOW COOKER?

The slow cooker truly is a life-changing appliance. It's the nearly magical kitchen tool that allows you to toss together ingredients, walk away for hours, and return to a hot, ready-to-eat meal. Who doesn't love that? The slow cooker undeniably helps make home-cooking hassle free and approachable—we've listed our favorite perks below to prove it. However, the slow cooker isn't just a resource for when you have little time and energy to cook; it's also the anytime solution for making mouthwateringly tender foods full of flavor. In this section, you'll learn how your slow cooker works to make the delicious, satisfying food you crave, plus you'll get tips for making the most of the handiest kitchen appliance you own.

In addition to making delicious food, here are other benefits that your slow cooker offers:

- **SAVES PREP TIME AND EFFORT.** The vast majority of recipes here limit hands-on prep time to 20 minutes or less. Often, there are just a few simple steps to complete before food goes into the slow cooker, and we promise they're worth it for maximum flavor. Plus, we've made them as quick and efficient as possible.
- **ELIMINATES THE NEED TO TEND FOOD WHILE IT COOKS.** Once you cover the cooker and set the temperature, you can walk away—even leave home—for hours until the food is ready.
- **USES ENERGY EFFICIENTLY.** Slow cookers use very little energy, approximately the same amount as a single light bulb.

- **KEEPS YOUR KITCHEN FROM GETTING HOT.** Unlike an oven, slow cookers release only a small amount of heat around them, containing most of the heat within their vessels.
- **SAVES MONEY.** Slow-cooking is one of the easiest and most time-efficient ways to cook—even the busiest people can manage to make home-cooked meals using this method. When you cook at home and don't spend precious dollars eating out, your wallet will show it. Also, cheaper cuts of meat are actually better for slow-cooking (more on that on page 16).
- **HELPS YOU BE HEALTHY.** Fat will rise to the top of your slow cooker as food cooks. Just scoop it off at the end and toss it. Furthermore, restaurants often load dishes with sodium, calories, and saturated fat. By slow-cooking at home, you can control how much of these nutrients go into your food. Bonus: Because these recipes are from *Cooking Light*, you can trust that they've been developed with the perfect balance of flavor, satisfaction, and health in mind.
- **MAKES FOOD EASY TO TRANSPORT AND KEEP WARM.** Instead of transferring hot food to another dish when taking food to a dinner party, potluck, tailgate, etc., you can carry the insulated slow cooker. Just unplug the slow cooker and use the handles or oven mitts to carefully move it. When you arrive, plug the cooker back in, set it on WARM, and effortlessly maintain food temperature for hours. The appliance does double duty as the serving vessel.

HOW SLOW COOKERS WORK

Slow cookers are comprised of three main parts: base, vessel, and lid. The base contains the heating element. The vessel, usually made of ceramic, stoneware, or metal, is where food is placed. In some slow cookers, the vessel is built into the base, while in others the vessel is a removable insert. The heavier the vessel material, the more even the heat distribution from the heat element will be, and that's what you want—even heat surrounding the bottom and sides of the food. The lid keeps the heat and moisture locked inside the cooker, a crucial part of slow-cooking.

These three parts work together to make the tender slow-cooked foods you love. As the heating element warms the food, the food releases moisture as steam. Any liquid added to the vessel will also partially evaporate as steam. The steam creates a slight vacuum seal on the lid that allows virtually none of the moisture to escape. As steam builds inside the slow cooker, it cranks up the temperature even more and helps cook the food. The steam also keeps the food moist, allowing it to cook for long periods of time without drying out.

The two main cooking techniques that slow cookers employ are braising and poaching. In braising, food is browned, and then cooked with liquid over a long time. This method works best for tough, thick cuts of meat, such as a roast. In poaching, food is not initially browned. It's cooked submerged in simmering liquid for a shorter amount of time. This method works best for tender, lean meats and fish.

Slow cookers have three basic settings: HIGH, LOW, and WARM. The exact temperatures of each will slightly vary between slow cookers depending on type and wear-and-tear, but these ranges generally hold true:

HIGH	212°F to 300°F
LOW	170°F to 200°F
WARM	165°F

The WARM setting keeps food just warm enough to be eaten without being overcooked. It also eliminates the need to reheat the food later. Never cook food on WARM; only switch to it after the food is completely cooked. This setting will help keep dips and sauces from drying out.

SELECTING THE RIGHT SLOW COOKER

Because of the many perks that slow cookers provide, we implore you to get one ASAP! "But which one?" you might ask. Here are some helpful factors to consider when choosing the best slow cooker for you:

SIZE: Slow cookers come in various sizes, most commonly ranging from 1 to 8½ quarts. Each of the recipes in this book lists the specific size of slow cooker needed. The majority call for a 5- to 6-quart slow cooker, though a few call for a smaller 3- to 4-quart size. If you find yourself in doubt with other recipes, here are general guidelines to help you know what slow cooker size is best:

- For 1-3 people, use a 3- to 4-quart slow cooker.
- For 4-9 people, use a 5- to 6-quart slow cooker.
- For 10+ people, a 7- to 8½-quart slow cooker may be best depending on the food.

If you want leftovers, using a larger slow cooker than you need is the way to go: Larger cookers will make enough food for reheated meals throughout the week. If you enjoy entertaining, it may be beneficial to have multiple slow cookers in different sizes. Smaller slow cookers are ideal for party dips, and larger ones help you feed a crowd. Some slow cookers come with multiple inserts in different sizes, giving you several slow cookers in one. If you buy only one slow cooker, though, we suggest the 5- to 6-quart variety; it's the most versatile size.

SHAPE: Slow cookers come in round, oval, and rectangular shapes. The benefit of oval or rectangular varieties is that large pieces of meat like ribs or a whole chicken or inserts used to bake breads or desserts fit better. For this reason, most large slow cookers are oval or rectangular, while small slow cookers are often round.

TIMER: Many slow cookers allow you to set a timer that changes the setting to WARM when the cook time is over. This ensures that food doesn't dry out or burn if you aren't there to manually adjust the setting. You can also set the timer to move the temperature from LOW to HIGH and vice versa at the appropriate times.

INSPECT YOUR SLOW COOKER FOR PROPER FUNCTIONING

You may need to check that your slow cooker is heating properly, especially if you are using an older one. To do this, fill the slow cooker between ½ and ⅔ of the way full with lukewarm water. Secure the lid, and set the slow cooker on the LOW setting. Leave the cooker untouched for 8 hours—it's essential that you do not lift the lid during this time. At the end of 8 hours, remove the lid and immediately check the water temperature using a food thermometer. The water should be 185°F. If the temperature is higher, know that you need to reduce the cooking time when using your slow cooker so that foods don't burn or dry out. If the temperature is lower than 185°F, you should purchase a new slow cooker since yours doesn't heat food fast enough to be considered safe.

FOOD SAFETY

Always check food for doneness after cooking and before eating. Insert a food thermometer into the thickest portion of the food, and use this information from the USDA to determine if the food is ready to be eaten or if it needs more cook time:

SAFE MINIMUM INTERNAL TEMPERATURES	
Beef, Lamb, Pork, Veal	145°F
Ground Meats	160°F
Ham	145°F
Poultry	165°F
Eggs	160°F
Fish, Shellfish	145°F
Leftovers	165°F

The "danger zone" for the internal temperature of foods is between 40°F and 140°F. In this range of temperatures, harmful bacteria can easily and rapidly breed. To avoid this, hot foods should be kept at or above 140°F and cold foods should be kept at or below 40°F. Be sure to refrigerate cooked foods within two hours of cooking.

6 SAFETY TIPS

• Don't add frozen ingredients to the slow cooker. They will heat up too slowly, lingering in the "danger zone" too long and giving harmful bacteria time to grow.
• Don't store uncooked food in the vessel (or insert) in the refrigerator, and then transfer it all to the base and immediately start cooking. The chilled vessel, and consequently the food, won't heat quickly enough to ward off bacteria.
• Don't store hot, just-cooked food in the vessel (or insert) in the refrigerator. It will take the food too long to safely cool down inside the thick container. You also risk cracking the vessel as it adjusts too rapidly from hot to cold.
• Cut or arrange meat in the slow cooker in a way that allows it to cook through. If cooking a whole chicken, be sure that your slow cooker is large enough for the entire bird to fit inside when the lid is closed.
• Move the slow cooker away from anything that could catch fire. Although fire risk is minimal since slow cookers are made to retain their heat, it's wise to clear loose papers, kitchen towels, or other combustible objects from the area near the slow cooker base, especially if the cooker will be unattended.
• Never put the slow cooker base in water. You run the risk of damaging its wiring and worse—personal injury.

PREP SECRETS

Save time by doing these tasks the day or night before revving up your slow cooker. (Be sure to store prepped foods in separate, sealable containers in the refrigerator until ready to use.)
• Trim and discard unwanted fat from meat and poultry.
• Wash, peel, and chop vegetables.
• Measure out dry ingredients.
• Cut meat and poultry into smaller pieces if needed to fit inside the slow cooker or if the recipe calls for smaller pieces.
• Brown meat and poultry.
• Prepare sauces or rubs.
• Gather and lay out all needed supplies such as knives, mixing bowls, cooking spray, spices, etc.

COOKING TIPS FOR SUCCESS

FILL PROPERLY

It's important not to overfill or underfill your slow cooker. Overfilling with food will keep it from cooking properly, and overfilling with liquid is a surefire way to achieve the mushy mess you don't want. On the other hand, add too little food or liquid and you risk drying out your dinner. Fill the cooker about ½ to ⅔ of the way full. Check the manufacturer's instructions for directions specific to your slow cooker. Added liquid should come no further than halfway up the vegetables and meat. Because virtually none of the liquid will evaporate, don't worry about adding more liquid throughout cooking. In fact, because all food releases some moisture as it cooks, you'll end up with more liquid in the cooker than you start with.

PICK THE RIGHT MEATS

The fattier the meat, the more liquid it releases and the less added liquid is needed to cook it in. Large, fatty cuts of meat such as rump, shanks, short ribs, and shoulder, which are usually the cheaper cuts, perform best in the slow cooker, as their fat keeps them tender over the long cook time. Furthermore, these fattier cuts are often found in the animal's most-used muscles and,

consequently, are tougher. Tough meat is an advantage in slow-cooking since meat must remain intact and slowly break down over several hours. Leaner cuts of meat are often more expensive and get dry and tough with the lengthy cook time. Nevertheless, it's smart to trim excess fat from meat before cooking. There's plenty of fat within the meat to keep it moist, and any excess fat will melt into the dish, giving it an oily texture.

MAXIMIZE FLAVOR

Many of these recipes pack as much pleasing flavor as possible into their dishes by browning meats or poultry before they go into the cooker. Sure, this requires a bit of extra hands-on time—and on days when you can't afford that, skip the browning and don't fret it—but lightly searing meat truly transforms the flavor of the whole dish by infusing it with savory, smoky flavor. Likewise, using the reserved pan drippings from the meat to sauté any vegetables further amps up the flavor. Here's how:

IMAGE 1: Start by heating oil in a skillet, and when it's hot add the meat or poultry. Lightly brown the meat on both sides. Your goal isn't to cook the meat through but to create a light caramelization on the outside. Once

there's a golden brown color on each side, transfer the meat to the slow cooker, reserving the leftover oil, meat juices, and charred browned bits in the skillet.

IMAGE 2: Next, add the vegetables the recipe calls for, such as onion and garlic, to the reserved drippings in the hot skillet and stir often until they soften. Occasionally scrape the bottom of the skillet to loosen any browned bits. The savory drippings will not only tenderize the vegetables the way that pure oil will but also will infuse them with a more complex flavor.

When the vegetables are tender, transfer them along with the pan drippings to the slow cooker, where the drippings will further flavor the dish as it cooks. Some recipes may call for briefly cooking wine or stock in the pan after the food is removed, and then transferring it to the slow cooker. This is to ensure that all the flavorful browned bits get transferred to the slow cooker.

DON'T OVERCOOK INGREDIENTS

Tender vegetables, such as kale and cabbage, may become mushy if cooked too long. Consider adding them to the slow cooker at the end of the cook time so that they wilt but don't disintegrate. **Pasta**, too, will turn mushy if overcooked, so be sure to follow recipe times exactly. If **seafood** is cooked for too long it will become rubbery. Shrimp and scallops as well as delicate and lean fish varieties such as bass, cod, and swordfish

should be cooked for only about 20 minutes or less, while fattier fish such as salmon and tuna and tough seafood such as octopus can handle an hour or more of cooking. At the end of the cook time, add **fresh herbs** or a splash of **vinegar** or **citrus juice** to brighten the dish and cut through the rich flavor that has been building. You can add these ingredients at the beginning, but expect their flavor to be diluted. **Citrus zest**, on the other hand, can sometimes make the dish bitter if added at the beginning of the cook time, so that may be best added towards the end. **Dried herbs** and **spices** are ideal for slow cooking, but don't overadd them at the beginning because their flavors will intensify over the cooking time. Finally, **dairy** such as milk, cheese, yogurt, and sour cream should be added at the end or it will curdle during cooking.

UTILIZE THE COOKING LIQUID

Don't toss the liquid from your slow cooker! Often, it can be transformed into a delicious sauce for the dish. After removing the food from the slow cooker, skim off any fat from the surface of the liquid that remains. (You may also need to strain the liquid to remove herbs or other unwanted substances.) Add a bit of cornstarch mixed with water to the liquid and stir until it thickens, or heat the remaining liquid until it thickens. Drizzle the resulting sauce over the dish for added flavor and moisture. (Note: Not every recipe will produce or benefit from a sauce.)

DON'T LIFT THE LID

It may be tempting to uncover the slow cooker to check the progress of the dish, but don't! Lifting the lid releases the steam that's so crucial to producing tender, moist slow-cooker food. Each time you lift the lid the temperature within decreases and the time needed to fully cook the dish increases. Purchase a slow cooker with a transparent lid so you can monitor the food as it cooks without affecting the cook time.

MAKE CLEANUP A CINCH

No one wants to spend time scrubbing their slow cooker and scratching off hardened, dried bits of food. To avoid doing so, coat the slow cooker with cooking spray before filling it with food. Better yet, use a disposable slow-cooker liner (shown in the image to the left), which you can find near the aluminum foil and ziplock plastic bags at your supermarket. Using liners will not only prevent food from sticking to the slow cooker, it will eliminate the need to clean the cooker at all. Just discard the liner, and the cooker is ready to be used again or stored.

SLOW-COOKER HACKS

Use your slow cooker in these ways to maximize its value.

- **FONDUE POT:** Melt cheese, chocolate, or candy inside and let guests dip into the slow cooker. The WARM setting keeps the food at the right dipping consistency.
- **PUNCH BOWL:** Make, transport, and serve beverages directly from the slow cooker.
- **VEGETABLE STEAMER:** Stack bamboo or lemongrass or use coils of aluminum foil to create a platform in your slow cooker. Place the food that you want to steam on top. Add water to the bottom of the slow cooker, and turn it on.
- **DOUBLE BOILER:** Place a heatproof bowl in the center of the slow cooker, and add water around the bowl. Add the food you wish to boil to the bowl, secure the slow cooker lid, and turn on the slow cooker.
- **BAKING VESSEL:** Place a heatproof pan on the bottom of the slow cooker or rest it on the edges. Add the batter or dough to the pan, cover the cooker, and turn it on.
- **PORTION CONTROLLER:** Make individual portions of a dish by placing ramekins inside the slow cooker— ideal for desserts, lasagna, or other casseroles. Fill the ramekins with food, place them on the bottom of the slow cooker, secure the lid, and turn on the slow cooker.

MULTICOOKER VARIATIONS

In addition to slow-cooker recipes, we've included more than 50 recipe conversions for multicookers to make these the most versatile recipes you have. You'll find multicooker instructions labeled on all the applicable recipes. There are a variety of multicookers on the market that you can use; however, for simplicity, we've based each multicooker variation here on an Instant Pot®. If using a different brand of multicooker, consult your instruction manual to see how your multicooker, and, thus the multicooker directions, might be different. For first-time multicooker users, no matter the brand, it's crucial to read the instruction manual. Here are a few pointers to keep in mind if you're using an Instant Pot®.

On SLOW COOK, the pot cooks at a lower heat and, thus, requires a longer cook time than many slow cookers, so the times listed in the multicooker directions are at the upper end of the times in the original recipes. (If food is not done to your liking, add more time.) The cooker works similarly to electric cooktops, not gas ones: When you turn the cooker off, residual heat continues to cook the food. When using the SAUTÉ function, do not use the lid or the food will boil over and can ruin the pot. When in SAUTÉ mode, the pot cycles on and off. Stir often until you get used to how your pot heats; adjust to a lower heat setting if food is boiling too vigorously. Follow the instructions for venting the pressure valve, which is necessary to prevent pressure build-up. If using another multicooker variety, refer to your manual for specifics regarding its SLOW COOK and SAUTÉ functions and how they might impact the cooking times given here.

CHUCK ROAST WITH POTATOES AND CARROTS

HANDS-ON: 35 MINUTES **TOTAL:** 9 HOURS, 55 MINUTES **SERVES** 12

This dish is winter comfort food at its finest. A bright, slightly sweet sauce balances the rich and tender braised beef. You can substitute multi-colored baby potatoes (halved) for the Yukon variety and fresh fennel fronds for the parsley, if desired.

2¼ pounds boneless chuck roast, trimmed

1½ teaspoons kosher salt

3 tablespoons olive oil

1 pound carrots, peeled and cut into 3-inch pieces

4 medium Yukon Gold potatoes (about 1½ pounds), quartered

1 small head cabbage, cored and quartered

1¼ cups unsalted beef stock

3 tablespoons apple cider vinegar

3 tablespoons light brown sugar

2 tablespoons stone-ground mustard

2 garlic cloves, minced (about 2 teaspoons)

¾ teaspoon black pepper

3 tablespoons roughly chopped fresh flat-leaf parsley

1 Sprinkle the roast with 1 teaspoon of the salt. Heat the oil in a large skillet over medium-high; add the roast, and cook until browned, about 4 minutes on each side. Transfer the roast to a 5- to 6-quart slow cooker. Place the carrots, potatoes, and cabbage on and around the roast.

2 Stir together the beef stock, vinegar, brown sugar, mustard, garlic, pepper, and remaining ½ teaspoon salt in a bowl, and pour the mixture over the vegetables and roast. Cover and cook on LOW until the roast and vegetables are tender, about 9 hours. Turn off the slow cooker, and remove the roast, reserving the cooking liquid and vegetables in the slow cooker. Cover the slow cooker to keep the cooking liquid and the vegetables warm. Let the roast rest 20 minutes; slice the roast across the grain. Remove the cabbage from the slow cooker, and cut the cabbage into slices. Place the cabbage, potatoes, and carrots on a serving platter; top with the sliced meat. Sprinkle with the parsley, and serve with the reserved cooking liquid.

(SERVING SIZE: 1½ cups beef and vegetables, about 3 tablespoons sauce): CALORIES 242; FAT 7g (sat 2g, unsat 5g); PROTEIN 22g; CARB 23g; FIBER 4g; SUGARS 9g (added sugars 3g); SODIUM 418mg; CALC 11% DV; POTASSIUM 18% DV

MULTICOOKER DIRECTIONS

IN STEP 1, sprinkle the roast with 1 teaspoon of the salt. Remove the lid of a 6-quart multicooker. Place the oil in the inner pot. Press SAUTÉ [Normal], and heat, swirling to coat the bottom of the pot. Add the roast, and cook until browned on each side. Turn off the cooker. Place the vegetables on and around the roast. **IN STEP 2,** pour the beef stock mixture over the roast and vegetables. Lock the lid; turn Pressure Valve to "Venting." Cook on SLOW COOK [Normal] until the roast and vegetables are tender, about 9 hours. Remove the roast from the pot, reserving the cooking liquid and vegetables in the pot. Turn off the cooker. Replace the lid; press KEEP WARM. **FINISH STEP 2.**

KOREAN BEEF IN CABBAGE LEAVES

HANDS-ON: 20 MINUTES   **TOTAL:** 8 HOURS, 20 MINUTES   **SERVES** 8

Rice vinegar, sesame seeds, and brown sugar make this simple sauce irresistible! One-fourth cup of sesame seeds may sound like a lot, but it's the perfect amount to give the sauce its nutty, earthy flair. Serve with hot cooked rice and garnish with thinly sliced red and green jalapeño peppers, if desired.

¼ cup all-purpose flour

2 pounds boneless chuck roast, trimmed and cut into 2-inch cubes

1½ tablespoons sesame oil

Cooking spray

8 garlic cloves, crushed

½ cup rice vinegar

¼ cup sesame seeds

3 tablespoons lower-sodium soy sauce

3 tablespoons light brown sugar

2 tablespoons Sriracha chili sauce

1 tablespoon minced fresh ginger

¾ teaspoon kosher salt

16 medium-sized savoy cabbage leaves (from 1 head)

16 small scallions (green parts only), sliced diagonally

1 Place the flour and beef in a large ziplock plastic freezer bag; seal and shake to coat. Heat the oil in a large nonstick skillet over medium-high. Add half of the beef to the skillet, and cook, stirring occasionally, until browned on all sides, about 6 minutes. Transfer the beef to a 5- to 6-quart slow cooker coated with cooking spray, reserving the drippings in the skillet. Repeat the procedure with the remaining beef. Add the garlic to the reserved drippings in the skillet, and cook, stirring occasionally, until fragrant, about 1 minute. Add the garlic to the slow cooker.

2 Stir together the vinegar, sesame seeds, soy sauce, brown sugar, Sriracha, ginger, and salt in a small bowl, and pour over the beef in the slow cooker. Cover and cook on LOW until the beef is very tender, 8 to 9 hours.

3 Remove the beef from the slow cooker, reserving the cooking liquid. Pour the cooking liquid through a fine wire-mesh strainer into a bowl, discarding the solids. Divide the beef among the cabbage leaves; sprinkle with the scallions, and drizzle each serving with ¼ cup of the cooking liquid.

(SERVING SIZE: 2 filled cabbage leaves): CALORIES 255; FAT 10g (sat 2g, unsat 6g); PROTEIN 28g; CARB 13g; FIBER 2g; SUGARS 6g (added sugars 5g); SODIUM 575mg; CALC 6% DV; POTASSIUM 14% DV

HERB-AND-MUSHROOM-BRAISED BEEF

HANDS-ON: 35 MINUTES **TOTAL:** 8 HOURS, 35 MINUTES **SERVES** 8

With its comforting flavors contributed by savory meat, mushrooms, onions, carrots, and fresh herbs, this stew-style dish is a wonderful supper on cold-weather days. Consider freezing it into portions for busy weeknight meals. You could also shred the meat and serve it on sandwiches.

3 pounds boneless chuck roast, trimmed and cut into 2-inch cubes

¼ cup all-purpose flour

2 teaspoons minced garlic (from 2 garlic cloves)

2 teaspoons chopped fresh thyme, plus more for garnish

1 teaspoon chopped fresh rosemary, plus more for garnish

1 teaspoon chopped fresh oregano

1½ teaspoons kosher salt

¼ cup olive oil

2 (8-ounce) packages fresh cremini mushrooms, quartered

¾ cup dry red wine

2 cups frozen pearl onions, thawed (from 1 [14.4-ounce] package)

1½ cups unsalted beef stock

5 medium carrots, peeled and cut diagonally into 2-inch pieces (about 2 cups)

1 tablespoon sherry vinegar

Fresh oregano leaves (optional)

1 Place the beef cubes, flour, garlic, thyme, rosemary, oregano, and ½ teaspoon of the salt in a large ziplock plastic freezer bag; seal and toss to coat the beef. Remove the beef from the bag, reserving the flour mixture in the bag. Heat 2 tablespoons of the oil in a large nonstick skillet over medium-high; add the beef, in batches if necessary. Cook until browned on all sides, 10 to 12 minutes. Transfer the beef to a 5- to 6-quart slow cooker, reserving the drippings in the skillet.

2 Add the mushrooms and remaining 2 tablespoons oil to the reserved drippings in the skillet, and cook, stirring occasionally, until the mushrooms are deep brown and all of the moisture has evaporated from the skillet, 6 to 8 minutes. Add the red wine, stirring to loosen any browned bits from the bottom of the skillet. Add the mushroom mixture to the slow cooker. Add the pearl onions, beef stock, carrots, reserved flour mixture, and remaining 1 teaspoon salt to the slow cooker, and stir until combined. Cover and cook on LOW until the beef is very tender, about 8 hours. Skim the fat from the cooking liquid, and stir in the vinegar. Garnish with the additional chopped fresh thyme and rosemary and the oregano leaves, if desired.

(SERVING SIZE: 1½ cups): CALORIES 363; FAT 14g (sat 4g, unsat 9g); PROTEIN 40g; CARB 13g; FIBER 2g; SUGARS 5g (added sugars 0g); SODIUM 550mg; CALC 6% DV; POTASSIUM 28% DV

MULTICOOKER DIRECTIONS

IN STEP 1, transfer the browned beef to the inner pot of a 6-quart multicooker, reserving the drippings in the skillet. **IN STEP 2,** add the cooked mushroom mixture to the pot. Add the pearl onions, beef stock, carrots, reserved flour mixture, and remaining 1 teaspoon salt to the pot; stir until combined. Lock the lid; turn Pressure Valve to "Venting." Cook on SLOW COOK [Normal] until the beef is very tender, about 8 hours. **FINISH STEP 2.**

CLASSIC POT-AU-FEU

HANDS-ON: 20 MINUTES   **TOTAL:** 8 HOURS, 20 MINUTES   **SERVES** 8

This French dish boasts succulent meats—both chuck roast and short ribs—hearty vegetables, and a rich broth. The leeks and celery become tender and slightly chewy over the long roasting time, giving the dish varied textures.

2 pounds boneless chuck roast, trimmed

1½ pounds lean bone-in beef short ribs, trimmed

2 tablespoons olive oil

1¾ teaspoons kosher salt

½ teaspoon black pepper

4½ cups water

5 fresh thyme sprigs

3 bay leaves

1 garlic head, cut in half crosswise

2 leeks (white and light green parts only), halved lengthwise

4 celery stalks (about 8 ounces), cut into 2-inch pieces

4 Yukon Gold potatoes (about 1 pound), cut into 2-inch pieces

4 carrots (about 1 pound), peeled and cut into 2-inch pieces (or 1 pound baby carrots, tops trimmed)

1 rutabaga (about 1 pound), cut into 2-inch pieces

¼ cup crème fraîche

2 tablespoons thinly sliced fresh chives

Cornichons

Dijon mustard

Prepared horseradish

1 Rub the roast and the ribs with the olive oil; sprinkle with the salt and pepper. Heat a large nonstick skillet over medium-high. Cook the roast in the hot skillet, turning to brown on all sides, 5 minutes. Transfer the roast to a 6-quart slow cooker, reserving the drippings in the skillet. Add the ribs to the reserved drippings in the hot skillet, and cook, turning to brown on all sides, 6 minutes. Transfer the ribs to the slow cooker, reserving the drippings in the skillet. Add ½ cup of the water to the reserved drippings in the hot skillet, stirring to loosen the browned bits from the bottom of the skillet; pour into the slow cooker. Add the thyme, bay leaves, garlic, and remaining 4 cups water to the slow cooker. Cover and cook on LOW 5 hours.

2 Add the leek halves, celery, potatoes, carrots, and rutabaga to the slow cooker. Cover and cook on LOW until the beef and vegetables are tender, about 3 hours. Remove the roast, ribs, and vegetables from the slow cooker, reserving the cooking liquid in the slow cooker; discard the garlic, thyme sprigs, and bay leaves. Pour the reserved cooking liquid through a cheesecloth-lined colander into an 8-cup glass measuring cup, discarding the solids. Skim the fat from the surface of the cooking liquid.

3 Slice the roast thinly. Remove the meat from the ribs, discarding the bones, fat, and gristle. Arrange the roast, rib meat, leek halves, celery, potatoes, carrots, and rutabaga on a serving platter. Drizzle with the desired amount of the cooking liquid, and serve with the crème fraîche, chives, cornichons, Dijon mustard, horseradish, and the remaining cooking liquid.

(SERVING SIZE: 1½ cups): CALORIES 354; FAT 15g (sat 5g, unsat 8g); PROTEIN 34g; CARB 21g; FIBER 4g; SUGARS 6g (added sugars 0g); SODIUM 577mg; CALC 8% DV; POTASSIUM 25% DV

ASIAN SHORT RIBS

HANDS-ON: 20 MINUTES   **TOTAL:** 8 HOURS, 20 MINUTES   **SERVES** 4

These beef short ribs are fall-off-the-bone tender with extra umami flavor from the mushrooms, garlic, and soy sauce. The brown sugar tempers the ultra savoriness and makes the ribs sticky and scrumptious. The recipe will work just as well with a boneless chuck roast cut into 2-inch chunks, if that's what you have on hand. Garnish with fresh cilantro leaves and additional crushed red pepper, if desired.

8 lean bone-in beef short ribs (about
   2½ pounds), trimmed
⅝ teaspoon kosher salt
½ teaspoon black pepper
1½ tablespoons canola oil
2 cups sliced fresh shiitake mushroom caps
   (about 4 ounces)
1 tablespoon finely chopped garlic (about
   3 garlic cloves)

2 teaspoons finely chopped fresh ginger
½ cup unsalted beef stock
¼ cup packed light brown sugar
¼ cup rice vinegar
1½ tablespoons lower-sodium soy sauce
1 teaspoon crushed red pepper

1 Sprinkle the ribs with the salt and pepper. Heat 1 tablespoon of the oil in a large skillet over medium-high. Add half of the ribs to the skillet; cook, turning occasionally, until browned on all sides, about 8 minutes. Transfer the ribs to a 6-quart slow cooker, discarding the drippings in the skillet. (Don't wipe the skillet clean.) Repeat the procedure with the remaining ribs. Add the remaining ½ tablespoon oil to the skillet; stir in the mushrooms, garlic, and ginger. Cook, stirring often, until the mushrooms soften slightly, about 4 minutes; transfer the mushroom mixture to the slow cooker. Add the beef stock, brown sugar, vinegar, soy sauce, and crushed red pepper to the slow cooker. Cover and cook on LOW until the ribs are tender, about 8 hours.

2 Transfer the ribs to a serving platter, reserving the cooking liquid in the slow cooker. Skim the fat from the surface of the cooking liquid. Drizzle the ribs with the cooking liquid.

(**SERVING SIZE:** 2 short ribs, 4 tablespoons sauce): **CALORIES** 334; **FAT** 19g (sat 6g, unsat 11g); **PROTEIN** 24g; **CARB** 16g; **FIBER** 1g; **SUGARS** 14g (added sugars 13g); **SODIUM** 583mg; **CALC** 3% DV; **POTASSIUM** 11% DV

RED CHILE-BEEF TACOS

HANDS-ON: 20 MINUTES   **TOTAL:** 8 HOURS, 20 MINUTES   **SERVES** 10

The sauce in this dish is smoky and rich from the chiles, onion, fire-roasted tomatoes, and beef. Toast the tortillas, if you'd like (see the tip on page 129 for directions).

1¼ cups unsalted beef stock
3 dried guajillo chiles, stems and seeds
  removed
3 dried ancho chiles, stems and seeds
  removed
1 roughly chopped white onion (about
  6 ounces)
1 teaspoon ground cumin
1 (14.5-ounce) can fire-roasted diced
  tomatoes, undrained

5 garlic cloves, crushed
3 pounds skirt steak, cut into 4 pieces
2¼ teaspoons kosher salt
½ teaspoon black pepper
20 (6-inch) corn tortillas
1 cup loosely packed fresh cilantro leaves
¾ cup thinly sliced radishes (about 4 radishes)
10 lime wedges

1 Place the beef stock in a microwavable bowl, and microwave on HIGH 2 minutes. Stir together the chiles, hot beef stock, onion, cumin, tomatoes, and garlic in a 5-quart slow cooker. Sprinkle the steak with the salt and pepper; nestle into the chile mixture in the slow cooker. Cover and cook on LOW until the beef is tender, about 8 hours.

2 Transfer the steak to a plate, reserving the chile mixture in the slow cooker; shred the steak with 2 forks. Skim the fat from the surface of the chile mixture, and transfer the chile mixture to a blender. Remove the center piece of the blender lid (to allow steam to escape); secure the lid on the blender. Place a clean towel over the opening in the lid (to avoid splatters). Process until smooth. Pour the mixture into a saucepan; cook over medium-high, stirring occasionally, until the sauce has thickened, about 15 minutes.

3 Combine 2 cups of the sauce and the shredded beef in a large bowl, tossing to coat. Reserve the remaining sauce for another use. Divide the beef mixture evenly among the tortillas. Top evenly with the cilantro and radishes, and serve with the lime wedges.

(SERVING SIZE: 2 tacos): CALORIES 408; FAT 14g (sat 4g, unsat 8g); PROTEIN 34g; CARB 40g; FIBER 7g; SUGARS 4g (added sugars 0g); SODIUM 576mg; CALC 8% DV; POTASSIUM 23% DV

MULTICOOKER DIRECTIONS

IN STEP 1, place the beef stock in the inner pot of a 6-quart multicooker. With the lid off, press SAUTÉ [Normal]; cook until just simmering. Turn off the cooker. Stir in the chiles, onion, cumin, tomatoes, and garlic. Sprinkle the steak with the salt and pepper; nestle into the chile mixture in the pot. Lock the lid; turn Pressure Valve to "Venting." Cook on SLOW COOK [Normal] until the beef is tender, about 8 hours. Turn off the cooker. **IN STEP 2,** return the blended mixture to the inner pot. With the lid off, press SAUTÉ [Normal]; cook, uncovered, until the sauce has thickened, stirring often to prevent scorching. Turn off the cooker. **COMPLETE STEP 3.**

BRISKET AND ONIONS OVER BUTTERY MASHED POTATOES

HANDS-ON: 20 MINUTES   **TOTAL:** 8 HOURS, 20 MINUTES   **SERVES** 10

This brisket is seasoned with tangy mustard, sweet turbinado sugar, and pungent garlic. Substitute brown sugar for the turbinado, if desired, and use the tube variety of tomato paste so any leftovers stay fresh longer.

3 tablespoons whole-grain mustard
2 tablespoons turbinado sugar
3 garlic cloves, minced (about 1 tablespoon)
2 tablespoons olive oil
2½ pounds beef brisket, trimmed
1 teaspoon kosher salt
1 teaspoon black pepper
2 medium-sized red onions (6 to 8 ounces each), each cut into 8 wedges

1 cup unsalted beef stock
2 tablespoons tomato paste
1 fresh rosemary sprig
1 (24-ounce) package frozen steam-and-mash potatoes (such as Ore-Ida Steam n' Mash Cut Russet Potatoes)
2 tablespoons unsalted butter, cut into pieces
¼ cup chopped fresh flat-leaf parsley

1 Stir together the mustard, sugar, and garlic in a small bowl, forming a paste; set aside.

2 Heat the oil in a large nonstick skillet over medium-high. Sprinkle the beef with the salt and pepper. (If needed, cut the beef into 2 pieces to fit in the skillet and slow cooker.) Add the beef to the hot skillet; cook until browned, about 4 minutes on each side. Transfer the beef to a 5- to 6-quart slow cooker, reserving the drippings in the skillet. Spread the paste over the brisket.

3 Add the onions to the reserved drippings in the skillet; cook, turning once, until the onions are lightly browned, about 4 minutes. Place the onions on the top of the beef in the slow cooker, reserving the drippings in the skillet. Whisk together the beef stock and tomato paste in a medium bowl; add the stock mixture to the reserved drippings in the skillet, and cook, stirring to loosen the browned bits from the bottom of the skillet, about 30 seconds. Pour the stock mixture over the onions and beef in the slow cooker. Add the rosemary sprig. Cover and cook on LOW until very tender and the beef is beginning to fall apart, about 8 hours. Transfer the beef to a cutting board, reserving the cooking liquid in the slow cooker. Discard the rosemary sprig. Let the beef rest 10 minutes.

4 Meanwhile, prepare the potatoes according to the package directions. Transfer to a serving bowl, and stir in the 2 tablespoons butter until melted.

5 Thinly slice or coarsely shred the beef. Serve the beef and onions over the mashed potatoes; sprinkle with the parsley, and serve with the reserved cooking liquid.

(SERVING SIZE: ⅓ cup potatoes, 3 ounces beef, ⅓ cup sauce): CALORIES 335; FAT 16g (sat 6g, unsat 9g); PROTEIN 26g; CARB 18g; FIBER 2g; SUGARS 4g (added sugars 3g); SODIUM 628mg; CALC 6% DV; POTASSIUM 17% DV

MEATS

BARBECUE BRISKET SLIDERS

HANDS-ON: 15 MINUTES **TOTAL:** 8 HOURS, 15 MINUTES **SERVES** 8

Serve these brisket sliders when company's coming—perhaps to watch the big game—for an easy, crowd-pleasing dish. The crisp, tangy coleslaw is the perfect pairing for the tender, rich brisket. Serve with chips, crudités, and cold beer to round out the meal.

2 chipotle chiles in adobo sauce, minced (about 2 tablespoons)
1½ tablespoons light brown sugar
3 garlic cloves, grated (about 1 tablespoon)
1 teaspoon ground cumin
1½ tablespoons olive oil
1 teaspoon kosher salt
¾ teaspoon black pepper

2 pounds beef brisket, trimmed
¾ cup water
⅓ cup no-salt-added ketchup
2 tablespoons lower-sodium Worcestershire sauce
3 tablespoons apple cider vinegar
4 cups shredded multicolored coleslaw mix
16 whole-wheat slider buns

1 Stir together the minced chipotle chiles, brown sugar, garlic, cumin, ½ tablespoon of the olive oil, ¾ teaspoon of the salt, and ½ teaspoon of the pepper in a small bowl. Rub all of the mixture over the brisket. Place the brisket in a 5- to 6-quart slow cooker.

2 Whisk together the water, ketchup, Worcestershire, and 2 tablespoons of the vinegar in a small bowl; pour over the brisket in the slow cooker. Cover and cook on LOW until the brisket is very tender, about 8 hours.

3 Transfer the brisket to a cutting board, reserving the sauce in the slow cooker. Shred the brisket with 2 forks into bite-sized pieces. Return the shredded meat to the reserved sauce in the slow cooker, stirring to combine.

4 Just before serving, whisk together the remaining 1 tablespoon each olive oil and vinegar and remaining ¼ teaspoon each salt and pepper in a medium bowl. Add the coleslaw mix, and toss to coat. Divide the brisket and slaw evenly among the slider buns.

(SERVING SIZE: 2 sliders): CALORIES 412; FAT 11g (sat 2g, unsat 6g); PROTEIN 35g; CARB 44g; FIBER 3g; SUGARS 13g (added sugars 3g); SODIUM 648mg; CALC 12% DV; POTASSIUM 13% DV

FLANK STEAK AU JUS SANDWICHES

HANDS-ON: 20 MINUTES **TOTAL:** 7 HOURS, 20 MINUTES **SERVES** 8

Juicy flank steak, beefy sauce, and caramelized onions come together easily to create this delectable hoagie sandwich. The flank steak is tender, moist, and flavor-packed, making it a great base recipe not only for these sandwiches but also for any recipe that calls for shredded beef, such as Italian sandwiches or chili.

1½ tablespoons olive oil
2 tablespoons dark brown sugar
¾ teaspoon kosher salt
1 teaspoon ground cumin
1 teaspoon paprika
1 teaspoon black pepper
3 garlic cloves, grated (about 1 tablespoon)
2 pounds flank steak, trimmed
1 large onion (about 13⅜ ounces), cut into thin slices

1 (12-ounce) bottle beer (such as Yuengling Lager)
2 tablespoons lower-sodium soy sauce
1 bay leaf
1 teaspoon fresh thyme leaves
2 teaspoons cornstarch
1 teaspoon water
8 small whole-wheat hoagie rolls, split and toasted

1 Stir together the olive oil, brown sugar, salt, cumin, paprika, pepper, and garlic, forming a paste; rub the paste into both sides of the steak, using all of the mixture. Place the onion slices in a 5- to 6-quart slow cooker; top with the steak. Pour the beer and soy sauce over the steak. Add the bay leaf and thyme. Cover and cook on LOW until the steak is tender, 7 to 8 hours.

2 Transfer the steak and onions to a platter, reserving the cooking liquid in the slow cooker; cover the steak and onions with aluminum foil to keep warm.

3 Pour the reserved cooking liquid through a wire-mesh strainer into a medium saucepan, discarding the solids. Bring to a boil over high, and boil until the sauce is reduced to about 1½ cups, about 12 minutes. Stir together the cornstarch and water in a small bowl; drizzle into the sauce, and whisk until blended. Reduce the heat to medium-high, and simmer, stirring often, until thickened, about 1 minute. Shred the steak with 2 forks. Divide the steak and onions among the toasted rolls. Pour the sauce into dipping bowls, and serve with the sandwiches.

(SERVING SIZE: ½ cup steak, ¼ cup onions, about 2 tablespoons sauce, 1 hoagie roll): CALORIES 402; FAT 12g (sat 3g, unsat 7g); PROTEIN 31g; CARB 41g; FIBER 5g; SUGARS 9g (added sugars 3g); SODIUM 729mg; CALC 11% DV; POTASSIUM 17% DV

MULTICOOKER DIRECTIONS

IN STEP 1, rub the paste evenly into both sides of the steak. Place the onion slices in the inner pot of a 6-quart multicooker; top with the steak. Pour the beer and soy sauce over the steak. Add the bay leaf and thyme. Lock the lid; turn Pressure Valve to "Venting." Cook on SLOW COOK [Normal] until the steak is tender, about 8 hours. **COMPLETE STEPS 2 AND 3.**

ROPA VIEJA

HANDS-ON: 10 MINUTES **TOTAL:** 8 HOURS, 10 MINUTES **SERVES** 8

Ropa Vieja is a Cuban dish of meat, peppers, and onions. Literally translated it means "old clothes," a reference to the colorful pieces of red and yellow peppers and tomatoes in the dish. Garnish with additional fresh oregano leaves, if desired.

1 medium-sized red bell pepper (about 5⅛ ounces), roughly chopped

1 medium-sized yellow onion (about 8 ounces), roughly chopped

4 medium-sized plum tomatoes (about 1 pound, 3 ounces), roughly chopped

2 garlic cloves

2 tablespoons fresh oregano leaves

1 teaspoon ground cumin

½ cup unsalted beef stock

2 tablespoons no-salt-added ketchup

2 pounds flank steak, trimmed and cut crosswise into 2-inch pieces

2 tablespoons extra-virgin olive oil

½ teaspoon black pepper

1¾ teaspoons kosher salt

⅓ cup roughly chopped pimiento-stuffed green olives (about 3 ounces)

2 (15-ounce) cans no-salt-added black beans, drained and rinsed

2 (8.8-ounce) packages precooked microwavable brown rice (such as Uncle Ben's Ready Rice)

1 Place the bell pepper, onion, tomatoes, garlic, oregano, and cumin in a food processor; pulse until finely chopped, 5 to 6 times. Transfer the bell pepper mixture to a 5- or 6-quart slow cooker; stir in the beef stock and ketchup. Place the steak, oil, black pepper, and 1 teaspoon of the salt in a medium bowl, and toss to coat. Submerge the steak in the bell pepper mixture in the slow cooker. Cover and cook on LOW until the meat is very tender, about 8 hours.

2 Transfer the steak to a large bowl, reserving the sauce in the slow cooker. Shred the steak pieces with 2 forks. Toss the shredded steak with 1 cup of the reserved sauce in the bowl, and stir in the chopped green olives.

3 Stir together the beans and ¼ teaspoon of the salt in a medium saucepan, and cook over medium until heated through, about 5 minutes. Keep warm. Prepare the rice according to the package directions, and season with the remaining ½ teaspoon salt. Serve the shredded steak mixture with the rice, beans, and remaining reserved sauce from the slow cooker.

(SERVING SIZE: ½ cup steak, about ¼ cup beans, about ¼ cup rice, about 1 cup sauce): CALORIES 400; FAT 13g (sat 3g, unsat 7g); PROTEIN 33g; CARB 38g; FIBER 7g; SUGARS 3g (added sugars 0g); SODIUM 700mg; CALC 9% DV; POTASSIUM 23% DV

MULTICOOKER DIRECTIONS

IN STEP 1, transfer the finely chopped bell pepper mixture to the inner pot of a 6-quart multicooker; stir in the beef stock and ketchup. Place the steak, oil, black pepper, and 1 teaspoon of the salt in a medium bowl; toss to coat. Submerge the steak in the bell pepper mixture in the pot. Lock the lid; turn Pressure Valve to "Venting." Cook on SLOW COOK [Normal] until the meat is very tender, about 8 hours. Turn off the cooker. Press KEEP WARM. **IN STEP 2,** transfer the steak to a large bowl, reserving the sauce in the pot. Shred the steak with 2 forks. Add 1 cup of the reserved sauce to the shredded steak, reserving the remaining sauce in the pot; toss well and stir in the chopped green olives. **COMPLETE STEP 3.**

PORK SAUSAGE BOLOGNESE

HANDS-ON: 20 MINUTES   **TOTAL:** 8 HOURS, 35 MINUTES   **SERVES** 8

Here's the meaty, saucy pasta that we all crave. If you have any leftovers, freeze them and reheat on a cold night when you're in need of a hot, comforting dish. Serve with a simple, crisp salad and crusty bread. For the prettiest appearance, sprinkle with whole fresh basil leaves instead of chopped oregano.

1 pound lean ground pork

8 ounces mild Italian pork sausage, casings removed

1 (26.46-ounce) package strained tomatoes (such as Pomi)

2 cups chopped yellow onion (from 1 onion)

1 cup finely chopped carrots (from 3 carrots)

¼ cup tomato paste

¼ cup dry red wine

1 teaspoon kosher salt

½ teaspoon black pepper

3 garlic cloves, minced (about 1 tablespoon)

16 ounces uncooked whole-wheat penne pasta

2 ounces Parmesan cheese, grated (about ½ cup)

¼ cup loosely packed fresh basil leaves, torn

2 tablespoons chopped fresh oregano

1 Heat a large nonstick skillet over medium-high. Add the ground pork and sausage to the hot skillet; cook the pork and sausage, stirring to crumble, until browned, about 7 minutes. Drain well; transfer the pork mixture to a 5- to 6-quart slow cooker. Stir in the tomatoes, onion, carrots, tomato paste, red wine, salt, pepper, and garlic. Cover and cook on LOW until the sauce is thickened slightly and the vegetables are very tender, about 8 hours.

2 Prepare the pasta according to the package directions, omitting the salt and fat. Serve the meat sauce over the hot cooked pasta, and sprinkle with the cheese, basil, and oregano.

(SERVING SIZE: 1 cup pasta, scant 1 cup sauce): CALORIES 490; FAT 18g (sat 6g, unsat 8g); PROTEIN 26g; CARB 56g; FIBER 8g; SUGARS 9g (added sugars 0g); SODIUM 659mg; CALC 11% DV; POTASSIUM 15% DV

MULTICOOKER DIRECTIONS

IN STEP 1, transfer the browned pork mixture to the inner pot of a 6-quart multicooker. Stir in the tomatoes, onion, carrots, tomato paste, red wine, salt, pepper, and garlic. Lock the lid; turn Pressure Valve to "Venting." Cook on SLOW COOK [Normal] until the sauce is thickened slightly and the vegetables are very tender, about 8 hours. Turn off the cooker. **COMPLETE STEP 2.**

SPICY PLUM-GLAZED MEATBALLS

HANDS-ON: 25 MINUTES **TOTAL:** 2 HOURS **SERVES** 4

Tender, tangy, spicy, sweet—these meatballs might become your new go-to dish. They cook in the slow cooker for only about an hour and a half, so they're a great dinner solution on days when you don't have much time for dinner prep. Consider wearing gloves when shaping the meatballs to make cleanup a cinch.

1 pound lean ground pork
½ cup panko (Japanese-style breadcrumbs)
1 large egg, lightly beaten
3 tablespoons finely chopped scallions (from 2 scallions), plus more for garnish
¼ teaspoon black pepper
Cooking spray

⅓ cup plum sauce
¼ cup water
2½ tablespoons lower-sodium soy sauce
1 tablespoon Sriracha chili sauce
2 teaspoons minced fresh ginger
2 tablespoons rice vinegar, plus more to taste
2 cups hot cooked jasmine rice

1 Gently stir together the pork, panko, egg, scallions, and pepper in a large bowl until blended. Shape the mixture into 24 (1-inch) meatballs. Place the meatballs in a 5- to 6-quart slow cooker coated with cooking spray.

2 Stir together the plum sauce, water, soy sauce, Sriracha, and ginger in a small bowl, and pour over the meatballs. Cover and cook on HIGH until the meatballs are firm and a thermometer inserted into 3 to 4 meatballs registers 145°F, about 1 hour and 30 minutes. Transfer the meatballs to a platter with a slotted spoon, reserving the sauce mixture in the slow cooker. Cover the meatballs with aluminum foil to keep warm.

3 Pour the sauce mixture through a wire-mesh strainer into a large skillet, discarding the solids. Bring the sauce mixture to a boil over high, stirring occasionally. Cook, stirring occasionally, until the glaze is reduced to about ⅓ cup, about 4 minutes. Stir in the rice vinegar. Add the meatballs to the skillet, and stir to coat. Add more rice vinegar to taste.

4 Serve the meatballs and sauce over the hot cooked rice; garnish with the additional scallions, if desired.

(SERVING SIZE: ½ cup rice, 6 meatballs, ¼ cup sauce): CALORIES 415; FAT 12g (sat 4g, unsat 7g); PROTEIN 28g; CARB 47g; FIBER 2g; SUGARS 6g (added sugars 1g); SODIUM 677mg; CALC 3% DV; POTASSIUM 4% DV

NOTE

Plum sauce is a Chinese-style sweet and sour condiment that's made with plums and other ingredients such as vinegar, ginger, and garlic. Traditionally, it's a dipping sauce, but here it coats the meatballs. Find plum sauce in the international foods aisle of your supermarket.

WHITE BEAN–AND–SAUSAGE CASSOULET

HANDS-ON: 20 MINUTES **TOTAL:** 3 HOURS, 50 MINUTES **SERVES** 4

This dish comes together quickly without fuss. Mashing some of the beans makes the broth creamier, while a topping of toasted panko adds contrasting crunchiness. Serve with a crusty baguette to sop up every last drop of the sauce. Garnish with fresh thyme sprigs, if desired.

6 ounces Italian pork sausage, casings removed
¾ cup chopped yellow onion (from 1 onion)
¼ cup chopped celery (from 1 celery stalk)
¼ cup matchstick carrots
2 tablespoons, plus 1 teaspoon chopped fresh thyme
2 tablespoons tomato paste
1 (14.5-ounce) can no-salt-added fire-roasted diced tomatoes, undrained

¾ teaspoon black pepper
⅛ teaspoon kosher salt
1 cup unsalted chicken stock
2 (15-ounce) cans no-salt-added Great Northern or cannellini beans, drained and rinsed
2 teaspoons olive oil
⅓ cup panko (Japanese-style breadcrumbs)

1 Cook the sausage in a large nonstick skillet over medium-high, stirring to crumble the sausage, until the oil begins to release, about 2 minutes. Add the onion, celery, carrots, and 2 tablespoons of the thyme to the skillet; cook, stirring occasionally, 5 minutes. Stir in the tomato paste; cook, stirring constantly, 1 minute. Stir in the tomatoes, pepper, and salt; bring to a boil over medium-high.

2 Transfer the sausage mixture to a 6-quart slow cooker; stir in the chicken stock. Mash ½ cup of the rinsed beans. Add the mashed and whole beans to the slow cooker. Cover and cook on LOW until the vegetables are tender, 3 hours and 30 minutes to 4 hours.

3 Heat the oil in a small skillet over medium. Add the panko, and cook, stirring constantly, until golden brown, 3 to 4 minutes. Stir the remaining 1 teaspoon thyme into the panko. Divide the sausage mixture among 4 bowls; top with the toasted panko mixture, and serve immediately.

(SERVING SIZE: 1¾ cups): CALORIES 404; FAT 18g (sat 5g, unsat 11g); PROTEIN 19g; CARB 42g; FIBER 11g; SUGARS 8g (added sugars 0g); SODIUM 570mg; CALC 10% DV; POTASSIUM 20% DV

MULTICOOKER DIRECTIONS

IN STEP 1, place the sausage in the inner pot of a 6-quart multicooker. With the lid off, press SAUTÉ [Normal], and cook uncovered, stirring often, until the oil begins to release. Add the onion, celery, carrots, and 2 tablespoons of the thyme; cook uncovered, stirring often, 5 minutes. Stir in the tomato paste; cook, stirring constantly, until blended. Stir in the tomatoes, pepper, and salt; bring to a boil. Turn off the cooker. Stir in the chicken stock. Mash ½ cup of the rinsed beans. Add the mashed and whole beans to the pot. Lock the lid; turn Pressure Valve to "Venting." Cook on SLOW COOK [Normal] until the vegetables are tender, about 4 hours. **COMPLETE STEP 3.**

PORK RAGOUT OVER CASARECCE PASTA

HANDS-ON: 25 MINUTES   **TOTAL:** 7 HOURS, 45 MINUTES   **SERVES** 12

You'll want this dish on a fall or winter evening when you're hosting a crowd for dinner. Substitute beef brisket or chuck roast, if you'd like—you'll just need to cook it for an additional hour or two. Garnish with fresh rosemary and oregano leaves, if desired.

2 pounds boneless pork shoulder roast (Boston butt), trimmed
1 teaspoon black pepper
1 tablespoon kosher salt
2 tablespoons canola oil
6 medium shallots, halved lengthwise
2 tablespoons minced fresh garlic
1½ tablespoons chopped fresh rosemary
1½ tablespoons chopped fresh oregano
¼ cup unsalted tomato paste

1 cup dry red wine
⅔ cup unsalted chicken stock
2 tablespoons Dijon mustard
1 (28-ounce) can unsalted whole peeled plum tomatoes, undrained
3 cups chopped Lacinato kale
1 tablespoon red wine vinegar
2 pounds uncooked casarecce or cavatappi pasta

1 Rub the pork with the pepper and 2 teaspoons of the salt. Heat the oil in a large skillet over medium-high; add the pork, and cook until browned on all sides, about 2 minutes per side. Transfer to a 5- to 6-quart slow cooker, reserving the drippings in the skillet.

2 Reduce the heat to medium, and add the shallots, garlic, rosemary, and oregano to the skillet. Cook, stirring occasionally, until the shallots are softened and the garlic is fragrant, about 3 minutes. Add the tomato paste, and cook, stirring constantly, until darkened, about 1 minute. Add the red wine, and bring to a boil; cook until reduced by half, about 5 minutes. Whisk together the chicken stock and mustard in a measuring cup until smooth. Add to the skillet, and return to a boil. Transfer the contents of the skillet to the slow cooker.

3 Add the tomatoes to the slow cooker, and stir to mash the whole tomatoes. Cover and cook on LOW until the pork is cooked through and tender when pierced with a fork, about 7 hours. Transfer the pork to a plate, and shred with 2 forks.

4 Increase the slow-cooker heat to HIGH. Stir in the shredded pork, kale, and remaining 1 teaspoon salt. Cover and cook until the kale is tender, about 5 minutes. Stir in the vinegar.

5 Cook the pasta according to the package directions. Serve the ragout over the pasta.

(SERVING SIZE: ¾ cup pasta, ⅔ cup sauce): CALORIES 461; FAT 9g (sat 3g, unsat 5g); PROTEIN 27g; CARB 65g; FIBER 5g; SUGARS 7g (added sugars 0g); SODIUM 668mg; CALC 5% DV; POTASSIUM 19% DV

SOY-GLAZED PORK IN LETTUCE CUPS

HANDS-ON: 20 MINUTES   **TOTAL:** 8 HOURS, 45 MINUTES   **SERVES** 8

Bright flavors highlight this creative spin on weeknight dinner. Pickled carrots and radishes lend tartness to the dish while the orange peels and cinnamon add citrus and spice. You can make the pickled vegetables up to 5 days ahead.

½ cup unsalted chicken stock
¼ cup lower-sodium soy sauce
2 tablespoons Asian chili-garlic sauce
½ teaspoon black pepper
¼ teaspoon kosher salt
4 garlic cloves, smashed
2 (1-inch-wide) orange peel strips
1 cinnamon stick
2½ pounds boneless pork shoulder roast (Boston butt), trimmed

½ cup white wine vinegar
1 tablespoon granulated sugar
½ teaspoon crushed red pepper
½ cup matchstick carrots
½ cup very thinly sliced radishes (about 4 radishes)
16 Boston lettuce leaves
Fresh cilantro leaves (optional)

1 Stir together the chicken stock, soy sauce, chili-garlic sauce, black pepper, salt, garlic, orange peel strips, and cinnamon stick in a 5- to 6-quart slow cooker. Add the pork shoulder, turning to coat on all sides. Cover and cook on LOW until tender when pierced, about 8 hours.

2 Transfer the pork to a cutting board, reserving the cooking liquid in the slow cooker. Let the pork rest 5 minutes. Shred the pork with 2 forks into bite-sized pieces.

3 Skim the fat from the top of the cooking liquid in the slow cooker, if desired. Remove and discard the garlic cloves, orange peel strips, and cinnamon stick. Transfer the cooking liquid to a medium skillet, and bring to a boil over high. Boil until the sauce is syrupy and reduced to about ¼ cup, about 10 minutes. Toss the shredded pork with the sauce.

4 Stir together the vinegar, sugar, and red pepper in a small saucepan; bring to a boil over high. Add the carrots and radishes. Remove from the heat, and let stand 15 minutes. Drain the pickled vegetables, discarding the liquid.

5 Spoon about ¼ cup of the pork mixture onto each lettuce leaf, and top with 1 tablespoon of the pickled vegetables. Garnish with the cilantro leaves, if desired.

(SERVING SIZE: 2 lettuce cups): CALORIES 226; FAT 10g (sat 4g, unsat 6g); PROTEIN 29g; CARB 3g; FIBER 1g; SUGARS 1g (added sugars 1g); SODIUM 525mg; CALC 3% DV; POTASSIUM 16% DV

MULTICOOKER DIRECTIONS

IN STEP 1, stir together the chicken stock, soy sauce, chili-garlic sauce, black pepper, salt, garlic, orange peel strips, and cinnamon stick in the inner pot of a 6-quart multicooker. Add the pork, turning to coat. Lock the lid; turn Pressure Valve to "Venting." Cook on SLOW COOK [Normal] until the pork is tender, about 8 hours. Turn off the cooker. **COMPLETE STEPS 2 THROUGH 5.**

EASY JERK PORK SHOULDER

HANDS-ON: 15 MINUTES **TOTAL:** 8 HOURS, 25 MINUTES **SERVES** 8

The name of this recipe says it all: It's an easy, mostly hands-off jerk pork dish that comes together in a snap. The cayenne provides a little heat, but mostly the pork gets its flavor from the cinnamon and allspice. The bright salsa-pineapple topping cools the dish off and gives it a pretty, dinner-party–worthy appearance. Serve the meat alone, or pile it on buns for sandwiches or shredded atop nachos. Garnish with fresh thyme sprigs, if desired.

1 tablespoon dark brown sugar
2 teaspoons chopped fresh thyme
1¾ teaspoons kosher salt
1½ teaspoons garlic powder
1½ teaspoons onion powder
1 teaspoon cayenne pepper
½ teaspoon ground allspice
¼ teaspoon ground cinnamon

3 pounds lean bone-in pork shoulder roast (Boston butt), trimmed
2 tablespoons canola oil
2 cups chopped yellow onion (from 1 onion)
½ cup fresh orange juice (from 2 oranges)
¾ cup fresh salsa or pico de gallo
⅓ cup finely chopped fresh pineapple

1 Stir together the brown sugar, thyme, salt, garlic powder, onion powder, cayenne, allspice, and cinnamon in a small bowl. Rub the pork with the oil, and rub the spice mixture all over the pork. Place the pork in a 5- to 6-quart slow cooker. Add the onion and orange juice to the slow cooker. Cover and cook on LOW until the pork is tender, about 8 hours. Transfer the pork to a platter, reserving the cooking liquid in the slow cooker. Let the pork rest 10 minutes. Skim the fat from the reserved cooking liquid. Break the pork into large pieces, and toss with the reserved cooking liquid.

2 Stir together the salsa and pineapple in a small bowl; serve over the pork.

(SERVING SIZE: ¾ cup pork, 2 tablespoons salsa): **CALORIES** 236; **FAT** 11g (sat 3g, unsat 7g); **PROTEIN** 21g; **CARB** 11g; **FIBER** 1g; **SUGARS** 6g (added sugars 2g); **SODIUM** 559mg; **CALC** 4% DV; **POTASSIUM** 14% DV

NOTE

In cooking context, the term "jerk" refers to a blend of spices, predominately allspice, that's used to marinate meat before it's cooked. Here, the allspice—which tastes like cinnamon, cloves, and nutmeg—strongly flavors the pork to give it the classic jerk flavor before the pork is braised in the slow cooker.

CHILE-RUBBED PORK WITH CORN AND BLACK BEANS

HANDS-ON: 15 MINUTES   **TOTAL:** 2 HOURS, 55 MINUTES   **SERVES** 8

With minimal hands-on prep and only a couple hours in the slow cooker, you end up with incredibly flavorful, spice-rubbed pork and a bean-and-corn side dish, which easily converts to a next-day salsa.

4 ears fresh corn, husks removed
½ cup unsalted chicken stock
2 tablespoons dark brown sugar
1 tablespoon chipotle chile powder
2 teaspoons unsweetened cocoa
1 teaspoon black pepper
2 teaspoons kosher salt
2 (1-pound) pork tenderloins, trimmed

3 tablespoons olive oil
2 (15-ounce) cans no-salt-added black beans, drained and rinsed
⅓ cup chopped fresh cilantro
⅓ cup finely chopped red onion (from 1 onion)
3 tablespoons fresh lime juice (from 2 limes), plus 1 whole lime
Fresh cilantro leaves (optional)

1 Place the corn and chicken stock in a 5- to 6-quart slow cooker.

2 Stir together the brown sugar, chile powder, cocoa, black pepper, and 1½ teaspoons of the salt in a small bowl. Rub the tenderloins evenly with 1 tablespoon of the olive oil, and rub the spice mixture all over the tenderloins. Place the pork on top of the corn in the slow cooker. Cover and cook on LOW until a thermometer inserted in the thickest part of the tenderloins registers 140°F and the corn is tender, 2 hours and 30 minutes to 3 hours.

3 Transfer the pork to a cutting board; let rest 10 minutes. Remove the corn from the slow cooker, discarding the cooking liquid. Cut the kernels from the cobs, and place the kernels in a medium bowl; stir in the beans, cilantro, red onion, lime juice, and remaining 2 tablespoons olive oil and ½ teaspoon salt.

4 Cut the remaining lime into 8 wedges. Slice the pork. Divide the corn mixture and sliced pork among 8 plates; serve with the lime wedges. Garnish with the cilantro leaves, if desired.

(SERVING SIZE: 4 to 5 pork slices, ½ cup corn mixture): **CALORIES** 322; **FAT** 9g (sat 2g, unsat 6g); **PROTEIN** 32g; **CARB** 29g; **FIBER** 6g; **SUGARS** 7g (added sugars 3g); **SODIUM** 600mg; **CALC** 6% DV; **POTASSIUM** 24% DV

NOTE

Chipotle chile powder is readily available in most grocery stores, but don't confuse it with chili powder. Chipotle chile powder is dried, smoked jalapeño peppers, and this spice is known for its smoky taste. Chili powder is a spice blend containing cumin, garlic, and other spices of which chile pepper is only one ingredient.

HONEY-LIME PORK NACHOS

HANDS-ON: 15 MINUTES **TOTAL:** 2 HOURS, 28 MINUTES **SERVES** 8

Serve these nachos at your next party—they'll vanish! Tossing the cubed pork back into the slow cooker with the honey, lime, and garlic gives it extra-tangy sweetness. For the prettiest appearance, use whole cilantro leaves instead of chopped.

1½ pounds boneless pork loin, trimmed

1¼ teaspoons kosher salt

3 tablespoons honey

3 tablespoons fresh lime juice (from 2 limes)

1 tablespoon sliced garlic (from 3 garlic cloves)

8 ounces baked multigrain tortilla chips

4 ounces pepper Jack cheese, shredded (about 1 cup)

½ cup diced tomato (from 1 tomato)

⅓ cup thinly sliced red onion (from 1 onion)

¼ cup chopped fresh cilantro

⅓ cup reduced-fat sour cream

2 tablespoons whole milk

8 lime wedges

1 Sprinkle the pork with 1 teaspoon of the salt, and place in a 5- to 6-quart slow cooker. Drizzle with the honey and lime juice; top with the garlic slices. Cover and cook on LOW until a thermometer inserted in the thickest part of the pork registers 140°F, 2 to 3 hours. Transfer the pork to a cutting board, reserving the drippings in the slow cooker; let the pork rest 10 minutes. Cut the pork into small cubes, and toss with the reserved drippings in the slow cooker.

2 Preheat the broiler to high with the oven rack 6 inches from the heat.

3 Arrange the chips in an even layer on a rimmed baking sheet. Sprinkle with the pork and cheese. Broil until the cheese is melted, 3 to 5 minutes. Top with the tomato, onion, cilantro, and remaining ¼ teaspoon salt. Whisk together the sour cream and milk in a small bowl, and drizzle over the nachos. Serve with the lime wedges.

(SERVING SIZE: 1 cup): CALORIES 349; FAT 15g (sat 5g, unsat 9g); PROTEIN 25g; CARB 28g; FIBER 3g; SUGARS 10g (added sugars 6g); SODIUM 561mg; CALC 18% DV; POTASSIUM 12% DV

PORK LOIN WITH PORT AND ROSEMARY SAUCE

HANDS-ON: 25 MINUTES   **TOTAL:** 3 HOURS, 43 MINUTES   **SERVES** 12

Garlic-seasoned pork loin, port-and-tomato-based sauce, and creamy mashed potatoes all made with less than 30 minutes of hands-on prep—who could ask for more? Garnish with additional fresh rosemary sprigs, if desired.

3 pounds boneless pork loin, trimmed
8 garlic cloves, halved lengthwise
2¼ teaspoons kosher salt
1 teaspoon black pepper
1 tablespoon olive oil
2 teaspoons anchovy paste
2 fresh rosemary sprigs
½ cup port

1 (28-ounce) can no-salt-added crushed tomatoes, undrained
1 (24-ounce) package frozen steam-and-mash potatoes (such as Ore-Ida Steam n' Mash Cut Russet Potatoes)
6 tablespoons crème fraîche
6 tablespoons half-and-half
4 tablespoons unsalted butter

1 Cut 16 small pockets around the outside of the pork loin, and stuff the garlic into the pockets. Sprinkle the pork with 1 teaspoon of the salt and ½ teaspoon of the pepper.

2 Heat the oil in a large nonstick skillet over medium-high until shimmering, about 1 minute. Add the pork loin, and cook, turning to brown on all sides, 10 minutes. Transfer the pork to a 5- to 6-quart slow cooker, reserving the drippings in the skillet.

3 Add the anchovy paste and rosemary to the reserved drippings in the skillet. Reduce the heat to medium, and cook, stirring often, until aromatic, about 1 minute. Add the port, and bring to a boil, stirring to loosen the browned bits from the bottom of the skillet. Transfer the mixture to the slow cooker, and add the tomatoes and ½ teaspoon of the salt. Cover and cook on LOW until a thermometer inserted in the thickest portion of the pork registers 140°F, about 3 hours. Transfer the pork to a cutting board or serving platter, reserving the cooking liquid in the slow cooker; let the pork rest 10 minutes. Discard the rosemary sprigs.

4 Transfer the reserved cooking liquid to a medium saucepan. Bring to a boil over medium-high; boil, stirring occasionally, until the sauce is reduced to about 3 cups, about 8 minutes.

5 Meanwhile, prepare the potatoes according to the package directions, omitting the milk and butter. Add the crème fraîche, half-and-half, 2 tablespoons of the butter, and the remaining ¾ teaspoon salt and ½ teaspoon pepper to the steamed potatoes; mash to the desired consistency.

6 Stir the remaining 2 tablespoons of the butter into the reduced sauce until melted. Slice the pork, and serve with the potatoes and reduced sauce.

(SERVING SIZE: 3 ounces pork, ⅓ cup potatoes, ⅛ cup tomato sauce): **CALORIES** 296; **FAT** 11g (sat 5g, unsat 4g); **PROTEIN** 27g; **CARB** 18g; **FIBER** 3g; **SUGARS** 2g (added sugars 0g); **SODIUM** 664mg; **CALC** 4% DV; **POTASSIUM** 16% DV

MEATS

BRAISED LAMB SHANKS WITH GARLIC GREMOLATA

HANDS-ON: 30 MINUTES **TOTAL:** 6 HOURS, 40 MINUTES **SERVES** 6

With the glamour of a fancy entrée yet all the ease of slow-cooker prep, this is ideal to serve to dinner guests or family for Sunday supper. Let the lamb and sauce be the star of the meal, and serve with blanched beans or roasted carrots.

3 cups chopped yellow onion (from 2 onions)
1 cup chopped carrots (from 1 carrot)
5 garlic cloves, smashed
3 (20-ounce) lamb shanks, trimmed
1½ teaspoons kosher salt
1½ teaspoons black pepper
1 tablespoon canola oil

2 cups dry red wine
1 garlic head
¼ cup panko (Japanese-style breadcrumbs)
5 tablespoons extra-virgin olive oil
¼ cup finely chopped fresh flat-leaf parsley
2 teaspoons lemon zest (from 1 lemon)

1 Stir together the onion, carrots, and smashed garlic cloves in a 5- to 6-quart slow cooker.

2 Sprinkle the lamb with 1 teaspoon each of the salt and pepper. Heat a large nonstick skillet over medium-high. Add the canola oil to the skillet; swirl to coat. Add the lamb shanks; cook, in batches if necessary, turning to brown on all sides, 6 minutes. Transfer the lamb to the slow cooker, discarding the drippings in the skillet. (Don't wipe the skillet clean.) Add the wine to the skillet, stirring to loosen the browned bits from the bottom of the skillet. Pour the wine mixture over the lamb in the slow cooker. Wrap the garlic head tightly in aluminum foil, and place in the slow cooker. Cover and cook on LOW until the lamb is tender, 6 to 7 hours. Transfer the lamb to a platter, discarding the cooking liquid; let the lamb rest 10 minutes.

3 Toss the panko with 1 tablespoon of the olive oil, and place in a medium skillet over medium-high. Cook, stirring often, until the panko is golden brown, 2 to 3 minutes. Remove the garlic head from the slow cooker, and unwrap the garlic, discarding the foil. Squeeze the garlic into a medium bowl, and add the remaining ¼ cup olive oil and ½ teaspoon each salt and pepper. Stir in the panko, parsley, and lemon zest.

4 Remove the lamb meat from the bones; discard the bones. Divide the lamb among 6 plates; top with the garlic mixture.

(SERVING SIZE: about 4 ounces lamb, 1½ tablespoons gremolata): CALORIES 418; FAT 24g (sat 5g, unsat 17g); PROTEIN 43g; CARB 5g; FIBER 1g; SUGARS 1g (added sugars 0g); SODIUM 590mg; CALC 3% DV; POTASSIUM 17% DV

TIP
Wrapping the garlic in foil and slow cooking it with the meat rather than roasting it on a baking sheet saves time and another pan.

LAMB WITH POMEGRANATE AND CILANTRO-MINT SAUCE

HANDS-ON: 20 MINUTES **TOTAL:** 7 HOURS, 20 MINUTES **SERVES** 6

Both the meat and the sauce are versatile and could work in other applications: Use the lamb for a stew or drizzle the sauce on grilled chicken. If mint is polarizing for your crowd, use parsley. A salad and couscous with toasted sliced almonds make nice accompaniments. Garnish with additional fresh mint leaves, if desired.

2 teaspoons ground turmeric

1½ teaspoons kosher salt

3 (20-ounce) lamb shanks, trimmed

3 cups sliced yellow onion (from 2 onions)

⅓ cup unsalted beef stock

½ cup loosely packed fresh mint leaves

½ cup loosely packed fresh cilantro leaves

2 tablespoons hot water

¼ cup extra-virgin olive oil

2 tablespoons apple cider vinegar

1 garlic clove

½ cup pomegranate arils

1 Sprinkle the turmeric and 1 teaspoon of the salt evenly over the lamb shanks. Place the lamb shanks, thick (meaty) side down, in a 5- to 6-quart slow cooker. Add the onion and stock. Cover and cook on LOW until the lamb is tender, 7 to 8 hours.

2 Place the mint and cilantro in a mini food processor; pour the hot water over the herbs. Add the oil, vinegar, garlic, and remaining ½ teaspoon salt; process until the herb mixture is smooth, about 20 seconds.

3 Transfer the lamb and onion to a platter, discarding the cooking liquid in the slow cooker. Remove the lamb meat from the bones, and discard the bones. Drizzle the herb mixture over the lamb, and sprinkle with the pomegranate arils.

(**SERVING SIZE:** about 4 ounces lamb, 1½ tablespoons sauce, 4 teaspoons pomegranate arils): CALORIES 400; FAT 19g (sat 5g, unsat 13g); PROTEIN 43g; CARB 12g; FIBER 2g; SUGARS 4g (added sugars 0g); SODIUM 592mg; CALC 4% DV; POTASSIUM 19% DV

LAMB, BARLEY, AND APRICOT TAGINE

HANDS-ON: 30 MINUTES **TOTAL:** 8 HOURS, 30 MINUTES **SERVES** 8

A tagine is a North African dish of spiced, braised meat. Our version features lamb slow cooked with apricots, cinnamon, and barley and topped with cilantro and golden raisins just before serving. The result is a dish brimming with varied flavors, textures, and colors. Garnish with fresh cilantro and crushed red pepper, if desired.

3 cups unsalted beef stock
2½ cups chopped white onion (from 2 onions)
1 cup uncooked whole-grain hulled barley
   (not pearled; about 7½ ounces)
1 cup dried apricot halves (about 6 ounces)
3 tablespoons tomato paste
2 teaspoons kosher salt
1½ teaspoons ground cumin
1 teaspoon ground coriander

½ teaspoon cayenne pepper
8 garlic cloves, minced (about 2 tablespoons)
2 cinnamon sticks
2 pounds lamb shoulder or lamb leg, trimmed
   and cut into 2-inch cubes
½ cup chopped fresh cilantro
½ cup golden raisins
1 tablespoon fresh lemon juice (from 1 lemon)

1 Stir together the stock, onion, barley, apricots, tomato paste, salt, cumin, coriander, cayenne, garlic, and cinnamon sticks in a 5- to 6-quart slow cooker.

2 Heat a large nonstick skillet over medium-high. Cook the lamb in 2 batches, turning occasionally, until browned on all sides, about 8 minutes. Add the browned lamb to the slow cooker. Cover and cook on LOW until the lamb is tender, about 8 hours. Discard the cinnamon sticks.

3 Turn off the slow cooker; stir in the cilantro, raisins, and lemon juice just before serving.

(SERVING SIZE: about 1 cup): CALORIES 436; FAT 18g (sat 7g, unsat 9g); PROTEIN 27g; CARB 43g; FIBER 8g; SUGARS 18g (added sugars 0g); SODIUM 647mg; CALC 7% DV; POTASSIUM 20% DV

MULTICOOKER DIRECTIONS

IN STEP 1, add the stock mixture to the inner pot of a 6-quart multicooker. **IN STEP 2,** add the browned lamb to the pot. Lock the lid; turn Pressure Valve to "Venting." Cook on SLOW COOK [Normal] 8 hours. Discard the cinnamon sticks. **COMPLETE STEP 3.**

MIDDLE EASTERN MEATBALLS WITH RAITA

HANDS-ON: 25 MINUTES **TOTAL:** 2 HOURS, 25 MINUTES **SERVES** 6

This meal features dense and tender lamb meatballs, creamy and refreshing cucumber raita—a traditional Indian sauce made with yogurt and vegetables—and whole-wheat couscous, a grain-like pasta that can be found at most supermarkets. Garnish with fresh dill sprigs, and serve with lightly toasted pita, if desired.

⅔ cup panko (Japanese-style breadcrumbs)

3 tablespoons 2% reduced-fat milk

1½ pounds lean ground lamb

2 tablespoons chopped fresh mint

1 tablespoon chopped fresh oregano

1 tablespoon finely chopped garlic (from 3 garlic cloves)

1½ teaspoons ground cumin

½ teaspoon black pepper

½ cup, plus 2 tablespoons finely chopped yellow onion (from 1 onion)

1½ teaspoons kosher salt

Cooking spray

¼ cup unsalted beef stock

½ cup shredded English cucumber (from 1 cucumber)

½ cup plain whole-milk yogurt

1 tablespoon chopped fresh dill

2 teaspoons fresh lemon juice (from 1 lemon)

1½ cups uncooked whole-wheat couscous

1 Place the breadcrumbs and milk in a large bowl, stirring with a fork until moistened. Add the lamb, mint, oregano, garlic, cumin, pepper, ½ cup of the onion, and 1 teaspoon of the salt, stirring gently with a fork until combined. Shape the lamb mixture into 24 (1¼-inch) meatballs. Place the meatballs in a 6-quart slow cooker coated with cooking spray. Top with the beef stock. Cover; cook on LOW until a thermometer inserted in 3 to 4 meatballs registers 145°F, 2 to 3 hours.

2 Squeeze the cucumber in a clean kitchen towel to remove the excess water. Whisk together the cucumber, yogurt, dill, lemon juice, and remaining 2 tablespoons onion and ½ teaspoon salt in a medium bowl until blended.

3 Prepare the couscous according to the package directions, omitting the salt and fat. Divide the couscous and meatballs among 6 plates; top with the yogurt mixture.

(SERVING SIZE: ½ cup couscous, 4 meatballs, about 1 tablespoon raita): CALORIES 447; FAT 16g (sat 6g, unsat 9g); PROTEIN 33g; CARB 46g; FIBER 7g; SUGARS 4g (added sugars 0g); SODIUM 591mg; CALC 9% DV; POTASSIUM 13% DV

POULTRY

3

LEMON, GARLIC, AND SAGE CHICKEN

HANDS-ON: 20 MINUTES **TOTAL:** 5 HOURS, 30 MINUTES **SERVES** 4

When slow-cooking a whole chicken, it's best to buy a better-quality chicken such as one from a farm stand. The flavor and texture of the bird will hold up best over the long cook time. Also, leaving the skin on during cooking will ensure that the chicken stays moist. If you have leftover chicken, use it for a chicken soup or in a chicken salad sandwich. For a beautiful presentation, serve the chicken surrounded by fresh sage leaves and roasted, halved lemons and garlic heads.

2 tablespoons unsalted butter, softened
2 tablespoons chopped fresh sage
¾ teaspoon kosher salt
½ teaspoon black pepper
2 garlic cloves, minced (about 2 teaspoons)
1 (3½-pound) whole chicken

15 fresh flat-leaf parsley sprigs
Cooking spray
1 tablespoon cornstarch
1 tablespoon water
1 teaspoon fresh lemon juice (from 1 lemon)

1 Stir together the butter, sage, salt, pepper, and garlic in a small bowl. Remove and discard the giblets and neck from the chicken. Trim the excess fat. Starting at the neck cavity, loosen the skin from the breasts and drumsticks with your fingers, without totally detaching the skin. Rub half of the butter mixture under the skin, and carefully replace the skin. Rub the remaining butter mixture over the outside of the chicken. Tuck the wingtips under the chicken. Place 12 of the parsley sprigs into the chicken cavity.

2 Place the chicken, breast side up, on a small rack coated with cooking spray. Place the rack inside a 6-quart slow cooker. Cover and cook on LOW until a thermometer inserted into the meaty part of the thigh and not touching the bone registers 165°F, 5 to 6 hours.

3 Remove the chicken from the slow cooker, reserving the cooking liquid in the slow cooker. Let the chicken rest 10 minutes. Discard the skin and the 12 parsley sprigs, and cut the chicken into 8 pieces.

4 Skim the fat from the surface of the cooking liquid. Pour the cooking liquid into a saucepan; bring to a boil over high. Whisk together the cornstarch and water in a small bowl; whisk into the cooking liquid. Boil, whisking often, until the sauce thickens, about 1 minute. Stir in the lemon juice. Remove the leaves from the remaining 3 parsley sprigs. Chop the parsley leaves, and stir into the sauce. Serve the chicken with the sauce.

(SERVING SIZE: 2 pieces chicken, about ¼ cup sauce): CALORIES 289; FAT 11g (sat 5g, unsat 5g); PROTEIN 42g; CARB 3g; FIBER 0g; SUGARS 0g (added sugars 0g); SODIUM 515mg; CALC 4% DV; POTASSIUM 15% DV

CHICKPEA-AND-TOMATO STEWED CHICKEN

HANDS-ON: 20 MINUTES **TOTAL:** 3 HOURS, 20 MINUTES **SERVES** 4

Cooking the chicken in the butter ups the poultry's succulent flavor. Using the drippings that remain in the pan to cook other ingredients—onion, garlic, and tomatoes—builds even more deliciously complex flavor into the dish. Garnish with additional fresh rosemary sprigs, if desired.

1 (3-pound) whole chicken, skinned
1 teaspoon kosher salt
1 teaspoon black pepper
2 tablespoons unsalted butter
2 tablespoons canola oil
2 cups chopped white onions (from 2 large onions)

3 garlic cloves, minced (about 1 tablespoon)
2 (14.5-ounce) cans no-salt-added fire-roasted diced tomatoes, undrained
2 (15-ounce) cans no-salt-added chickpeas (garbanzo beans), drained and rinsed
1 (2-inch) fresh rosemary sprig

1 Remove and discard the giblets and neck from the chicken. Cut the chicken into 4 pieces. Season the chicken pieces on all sides with the salt and pepper. Melt the butter with the oil in a large skillet over medium-high. Cook the chicken pieces, in batches, turning often, until browned on all sides, 5 to 7 minutes per batch. Transfer the chicken to a 6-quart slow cooker, reserving the drippings in the skillet.

2 Pour off all but 1 tablespoon of the drippings from the skillet. Add the onions to the reserved drippings in the skillet, and cook, stirring often, until softened, about 3 minutes. Add the garlic and cook, stirring often, until fragrant, about 30 seconds. Add the tomatoes, and bring to a boil, stirring to loosen any browned bits from the bottom of the skillet. Stir in the chickpeas and rosemary sprig.

3 Pour the chickpea mixture over the chicken in the slow cooker. Cover and cook on LOW until the chicken is tender, 3 to 4 hours. Discard the rosemary sprig. Divide the chickpea mixture among 4 shallow bowls; top with the chicken.

(SERVING SIZE: ¾ cup chickpea mixture, 1 piece of chicken): CALORIES 542; FAT 19g (sat 5g, unsat 12g); PROTEIN 47g; CARB 42g; FIBER 11g; SUGARS 10g (added sugars 0g); SODIUM 710mg; CALC 17% DV; POTASSIUM 25% DV

TIP

To save time and effort if you aren't a knife-wielding pro, ask your butcher to trim a whole chicken into 4 pieces, or buy separate pieces.

CHICKEN AND HONEY-GLAZED ROOT VEGETABLES

HANDS-ON: 20 MINUTES **TOTAL:** 4 HOURS, 20 MINUTES **SERVES** 6

This beautiful dish should be a standby for day-of decisions to host dinner. In the spring, substitute baby white turnips and baby carrots for the regular varieties.

Cooking spray
2 medium turnips, peeled and chopped (about 1 pound)
4 carrots, diagonally cut into 1-inch pieces (about 1 pound)
3 parsnips, diagonally cut into 1-inch pieces about (1 pound)
1 yellow onion, cut into thin wedges (about 8 ounces)
4 fresh thyme sprigs

1 tablespoon honey
2 tablespoons olive oil
1 teaspoon kosher salt
1 teaspoon black pepper
4 bone-in, skinless chicken thighs (about 1¼ pounds)
4 chicken drumsticks, skinned (about 1 pound)
3 tablespoons red wine vinegar
¼ cup dry Marsala wine
Fresh thyme sprigs (optional)

1 Coat a 5- to 6-quart slow cooker with cooking spray. Arrange the turnips, carrots, parsnips, onions, and thyme in the slow cooker. Whisk together the honey, 1 tablespoon of the oil, and ¼ teaspoon each of the salt and pepper in a small bowl; pour over the vegetables in the slow cooker, and toss gently to coat.

2 Sprinkle the chicken thighs and drumsticks evenly with ½ teaspoon of the salt and the remaining ¾ teaspoon pepper. Heat the remaining 1 tablespoon oil in a large nonstick skillet over medium-high. Add the chicken thighs to the skillet; cook, turning once, until golden brown, about 2 minutes per side. Place the thighs on top of the vegetables in the slow cooker. Add the drumsticks to the skillet; cook, turning to brown on all sides, 3 to 4 minutes. (Do not wipe the skillet clean.) Place the drumsticks on top of the vegetables in the slow cooker. Add the vinegar and wine to the skillet, and cook, stirring and scraping to loosen the browned bits from the bottom of the skillet, about 30 seconds. Pour over the chicken in the slow cooker.

3 Cover and cook on LOW until the chicken and vegetables are tender, about 4 to 5 hours. Transfer the chicken and vegetables to a serving platter, reserving the cooking liquid in the slow cooker. Sprinkle the chicken and vegetables with the remaining ¼ teaspoon salt. Serve with the reserved cooking liquid from the slow cooker. If desired, garnish with the fresh thyme sprigs.

(SERVING SIZE: 1¼ pieces chicken, ¾ cup vegetables): CALORIES 370; FAT 11.5g (sat 2g, unsat 8g); PROTEIN 36g; CARB 29g; FIBER 7g; SUGARS 14g (added sugars 3g); SODIUM 581mg; CALC 8% DV; POTASSIUM 24% DV

TIP
To reduce prep time, cut the vegetables the night before; refrigerate.
Place in the slow cooker with the browned chicken the next day.

SPICY CHICKEN QUARTERS WITH SWEET POTATOES

HANDS-ON: 20 MINUTES **TOTAL:** 4 HOURS, 20 MINUTES **SERVES** 4

The quick-rub on the chicken quarters creates a spicy, sweet crust once the chicken is browned, which helps flavor the entire dish. Adding cornstarch to the sauce at the end will thicken it, giving you a nice, syrupy glaze topping.

2 large sweet potatoes (about 1½ pounds), peeled and cut into 2-inch pieces
1 teaspoon kosher salt
½ teaspoon black pepper
1 tablespoon light brown sugar
1 teaspoon chili powder
½ teaspoon cayenne pepper
¼ teaspoon ground cinnamon

4 chicken leg quarters (about 2¾ pounds), skinned
2 tablespoons olive oil
¾ cup unsalted chicken stock
1 tablespoon cornstarch
1 tablespoon water
Fresh cilantro leaves (optional)

1 Place the sweet potatoes in an even layer in a 5- to 6-quart slow cooker; sprinkle evenly with ¼ teaspoon each of the salt and black pepper.

2 Stir together the brown sugar, chili powder, cayenne, cinnamon, and remaining ¾ teaspoon salt and ¼ teaspoon black pepper in a small bowl. Rub the spice mixture all over the chicken.

3 Heat the oil in a large nonstick skillet over medium-high. Add the chicken, and cook until browned on both sides, 2 to 3 minutes per side. Remove the chicken from the skillet, reserving the drippings in the skillet. Place the chicken in a single layer, with the pieces slightly overlapping, on the sweet potatoes in the slow cooker.

4 Add the stock to the reserved drippings in the skillet, and cook, stirring and scraping to loosen the browned bits from the bottom of the skillet, about 2 minutes. Pour the stock mixture over the chicken. Cover and cook on LOW until the chicken and sweet potatoes are tender, about 4 hours.

5 Transfer the chicken and sweet potatoes to a serving platter, reserving the cooking liquid in the slow cooker. Skim and discard the fat from the cooking liquid, and transfer the cooking liquid to a medium saucepan. Bring to a boil over high. Whisk together the cornstarch and water in a small bowl; whisk the cornstarch mixture into the boiling cooking liquid, and cook, whisking constantly, until thickened, about 1 minute. Serve the sauce with the chicken and sweet potatoes, and, if desired, garnish with the cilantro leaves.

(SERVING SIZE: 1 leg quarter, ½ cup sweet potatoes, ¼ cup sauce): CALORIES 407; FAT 14g (sat 3g, unsat 10g); PROTEIN 37g; CARB 31g; FIBER 4g; SUGARS 9g (added sugars 3g); SODIUM 763mg; CALC 6% DV; POTASSIUM 25% DV

CHARRED CHILE VERDE CHICKEN

HANDS-ON: 20 MINUTES **TOTAL:** 4 HOURS, 20 MINUTES **SERVES** 4

Chile verde is a Mexican green chile sauce made with tomatillos, garlic, and hot peppers. Here, the sauce is poured over chicken quarters and infuses them with a sweet spice as the dish slowly cooks. Don't skip charring the vegetables—it's key to opening up their bold flavors and giving the sauce its iconic dark green color.

Garnish with thinly sliced jalapeño chiles and fresh thyme sprigs, if desired.

Cooking spray
1 pound tomatillos, husks removed
3 garlic cloves
1 poblano chile (about 6 ounces), stemmed and seeded
1 jalapeño chile, stemmed and seeded
1 small white onion, quartered
½ cup unsalted chicken stock

2 tablespoons fresh oregano leaves
¾ teaspoon kosher salt
1 teaspoon ground cumin
½ teaspoon black pepper
4 small chicken leg quarters (about 2¼ pounds), skinned
2 cups hot cooked brown rice

1 Preheat the broiler with the oven rack 6 inches from the heat. Line a rimmed baking sheet with aluminum foil. Lightly coat the foil with cooking spray.

2 Place the tomatillos, garlic, poblano, jalapeño, and onion quarters on the prepared pan; broil until well charred and blistered, 8 to 10 minutes, turning the vegetables halfway through. Process the charred vegetables, any pan juices, stock, oregano, salt, cumin, and pepper in a blender until smooth, about 2 minutes.

3 Coat a 5- to 6-quart slow cooker with cooking spray, and add the chicken; pour the tomatillo mixture over the chicken. Cover and cook on LOW until the chicken is tender, about 4 hours. Serve the chicken and tomatillo mixture over the rice.

(SERVING SIZE: ½ cup rice, 1 chicken leg quarter, ¼ cup sauce): **CALORIES** 362; **FAT** 9g (sat 2g, unsat 5g); **PROTEIN** 33g; **CARB** 38g; **FIBER** 5g; **SUGARS** 6g (added sugars 0g); **SODIUM** 524mg; **CALC** 5% DV; **POTASSIUM** 23% DV

NOTE

Don't confuse tomatillos with green tomatoes. Green tomatoes are simply unripe tomatoes, while tomatillos, though also green, are an entirely different fruit. Tomatillos are covered in a husk that should be removed before cooking. Many supermarkets carry tomatillos, but if you have trouble finding them there, you can always find them in Latin food stores.

STICKY SESAME CHICKEN DRUMSTICKS

HANDS-ON: 20 MINUTES   **TOTAL:** 3 HOURS, 50 MINUTES   **SERVES** 4

Skip the takeout and make amazing Chinese food at home! Broiling the drumsticks after they slow-cook caramelizes their glaze and gives them their satisfying sticky, sweet quality. To make this recipe gluten free, use gluten-free soy sauce.

8 chicken drumsticks (about 2 pounds), skinned
1 tablespoon toasted sesame oil
⅛ teaspoon kosher salt
¼ teaspoon black pepper
¼ cup unsalted chicken stock
3 tablespoons honey
2 tablespoons lower-sodium soy sauce

2 garlic cloves, minced (about 2 teaspoons)
Cooking spray
1 tablespoon rice vinegar
2 teaspoons cornstarch
2 bunches scallions, green parts only, cut into 1½-inch pieces (about 1 ounce)
2 teaspoons toasted sesame seeds

1 Rub the chicken with the sesame oil; sprinkle with the salt and pepper. Place in a 5- to 6-quart slow cooker. Whisk together the stock, honey, soy sauce, and garlic in a small bowl; pour over the chicken in the slow cooker. Cover and cook on LOW until the chicken is tender, about 3 hours and 30 minutes.

2 Preheat the broiler to high with the rack 6 inches from the heat. Lightly coat a rimmed baking sheet with cooking spray. Transfer the chicken from the slow cooker to the baking sheet, reserving the cooking liquid in the slow cooker. Broil the chicken, turning once, until lightly caramelized, about 3 minutes on each side. Transfer the chicken to a serving platter.

3 Pour the reserved cooking liquid from the slow cooker into a small saucepan. Whisk together the vinegar and cornstarch in a small bowl; whisk the cornstarch mixture into the cooking liquid. Bring to a boil over medium-high, whisking often, and cook, whisking constantly, until thickened, about 1 minute. Drizzle the sauce over the chicken; sprinkle with the scallions and sesame seeds.

(SERVING SIZE: 2 drumsticks, ¼ cup scallions, ½ teaspoon sesame seeds): CALORIES 275; FAT 9g (sat 2g, unsat 6g); PROTEIN 28g; CARB 20g; FIBER 2g; SUGARS 14g (added sugars 13g); SODIUM 519mg; CALC 6% DV; POTASSIUM 14% DV

LEMONGRASS-COCONUT MARINATED CHICKEN

HANDS-ON: 20 MINUTES **TOTAL:** 15 HOURS, 50 MINUTES, INCLUDING 8 HOURS MARINATING **SERVES** 6

In this recipe, minimal effort produces big flavor, making it the perfect starter recipe for anyone learning to cook their own Thai food. If you can't find wide rice noodles, any rice noodle can be substituted.

3¾ pounds bone-in, skinless chicken thighs (about 8)

3 tablespoons finely chopped lemongrass

2 tablespoons sambal oelek (ground fresh chile paste)

1¼ cups canned light coconut milk

¾ cup unsalted chicken stock

6 garlic cloves, crushed

2 large yellow onions, quartered

2 large carrots, each cut into 4 pieces

1 (2-inch) piece fresh ginger, peeled and sliced

2 tablespoons reduced-sodium soy sauce

5 teaspoons Vietnamese fish sauce

1 tablespoon fresh lime juice

½ teaspoon granulated sugar

8 ounces uncooked wide rice noodles

2 cups thinly sliced English cucumber

½ cup loosely packed fresh cilantro leaves

¼ cup chopped unsalted peanuts

1 Place the chicken, lemongrass, sambal oelek, and ¾ cup of the coconut milk in a large ziplock plastic freezer bag. Seal and turn to coat; chill 8 to 24 hours.

2 Place the stock, garlic, onions, carrots, and ginger in a 6-quart slow cooker. Remove the chicken from the marinade, and discard the marinade. Arrange the chicken on top of the onion mixture. Cover and cook on LOW until the chicken is tender, about 7 hours and 30 minutes. Remove the chicken from the slow cooker, and discard the bones. Shred the chicken into bite-sized pieces.

3 Pour the cooking liquid through a colander over a bowl; discard the solids. Stir together the strained cooking liquid, soy sauce, fish sauce, lime juice, sugar, and remaining ½ cup coconut milk in a saucepan. Bring to a boil; stir until the sugar dissolves. Remove from the heat.

4 Prepare the noodles according to the package directions. Divide the noodles among 6 bowls. Top with the chicken, cucumber, and cilantro. Pour the coconut broth over each bowl, and sprinkle evenly with the peanuts.

(SERVING SIZE: ½ cup noodles, 3½ ounces chicken, ⅓ cup cucumber, 4 teaspoons cilantro, ⅓ cup coconut broth): **CALORIES** 439; **FAT** 16g (sat 4g, unsat 9g); **PROTEIN** 40g; **CARB** 35g; **FIBER** 1g; **SUGARS** 1g (added sugars 0g); **SODIUM** 671mg; **CALC** 3% DV; **POTASSIUM** 14% DV

TIP

For quickest day-of meal prep, make the chicken and coconut broth a day in advance and refrigerate. When ready to eat, simply reheat them, cook the noodles, and serve.

CHIPOTLE CHICKEN TACOS WITH AVOCADO CREMA

HANDS-ON: 20 MINUTES **TOTAL:** 4 HOURS, 20 MINUTES **SERVES** 6

A rich, creamy topping made of mashed avocado, sour cream, lime juice, and salt takes these spicy chicken tacos to the next level. Lightly toast the tortillas, if desired (see the tip on page 129 for directions). Use any leftover avocado cream as a chip dip, and serve with tortilla chips.

1 cup frozen fire-roasted corn, thawed

1 cup frozen bell pepper medley, thawed (such as Birds Eye Recipe Ready Tri Color Pepper & Onion Blend)

2 (15-ounce) cans no-salt-added black beans, drained and rinsed

1 canned chipotle chile in adobo sauce, minced

1 tablespoon canned adobo sauce

1¼ pounds bone-in, skinless chicken thighs (about 6)

½ teaspoon black pepper

1¼ teaspoons kosher salt

1 tablespoon olive oil

1 large ripe avocado, chopped

1 tablespoon fresh lime juice (from 1 lime)

1 tablespoon reduced-fat sour cream

12 (6-inch) corn tortillas

½ cup thinly sliced red onions (from 1 onion)

Fresh cilantro leaves

1 Stir together the corn, pepper medley, beans, chile, and adobo sauce in a 5- to 6-quart slow cooker. Sprinkle the chicken with the black pepper and 1 teaspoon of the salt. Heat the oil in a large skillet over medium-high. Cook the chicken, turning once, until browned on both sides, about 3 minutes per side. Place the chicken on the vegetables in the slow cooker. Cover and cook on LOW until the chicken is tender, about 4 hours. Transfer the chicken from the slow cooker to a cutting board, reserving the vegetable mixture in the slow cooker. Shred the chicken into bite-sized pieces, discarding the bones. Return the chicken to the slow cooker, and stir to combine.

2 Combine the avocado, lime juice, sour cream, and remaining ¼ teaspoon salt in a small bowl; mash with a fork until almost smooth. Heat the tortillas according to the package directions. Divide the chicken mixture evenly among the tortillas using a slotted spoon, and top with the avocado mixture. Sprinkle evenly with the red onions and cilantro.

(SERVING SIZE: 2 tortillas, about 1 cup meat and vegetables, 1 tablespoon crema): CALORIES 490; FAT 15g (sat 2g, unsat 9g); PROTEIN 31g; CARB 62g; FIBER 13g; SUGARS 5g (added sugars 0g); SODIUM 566mg; CALC 12% DV; POTASSIUM 21% DV

CHICKEN-AND-RICE BOWLS

HANDS-ON: 15 MINUTES **TOTAL:** 3 HOURS, 45 MINUTES **SERVES** 8

A bowl of tender shredded chicken, hot cooked rice, and slightly spicy black beans served with fresh toppings is a meal that will satisfy anytime. Make this dish on the weekend and reheat throughout the week for easy at-work lunches or dinner at the end of a long day. For a variation, swap the brown rice for a grain medley.

8 bone-in, skinless chicken thighs (about 3 pounds)

2 teaspoons ground cumin

1 teaspoon black pepper

½ teaspoon ground coriander

¾ teaspoon kosher salt

½ cup unsalted chicken stock

2 (8.8-ounce) packages precooked microwavable brown rice (such as Uncle Ben's Ready Rice)

2 (15-ounce) cans no-salt-added black beans, drained and rinsed

1 tablespoon olive oil

¼ teaspoon cayenne pepper

2 cups fresh pico de gallo

¾ cup thinly sliced radishes (about 5 radishes)

2 ripe avocados, sliced

Fresh cilantro leaves (optional)

1 Sprinkle the chicken with the cumin, black pepper, coriander, and ½ teaspoon of the salt. Place the chicken in a 5- to 6-quart slow cooker. Add the stock; cover and cook on LOW until the chicken is tender, about 3 hours and 30 minutes. Transfer the chicken from the slow cooker to a cutting board, reserving the cooking liquid in the slow cooker. Shred the chicken into bite-sized pieces, discarding the bones. Toss the chicken with ½ cup of the reserved cooking liquid from the slow cooker and the remaining ¼ teaspoon salt.

2 Prepare the rice according to the package directions. Stir together the beans, oil, and cayenne in a small microwavable bowl; microwave on HIGH until thoroughly heated, 1 to 2 minutes. Divide the chicken, rice, beans, and pico among 8 shallow bowls; top evenly with the radishes and avocado. Garnish with the cilantro leaves, if desired.

(SERVING SIZE: about ½ cup chicken, ½ cup rice, ¼ cup beans, ¼ cup pico): CALORIES 470; FAT 17g (sat 3g, unsat 11g); PROTEIN 40g; CARB 40g; FIBER 11g; SUGARS 1g (added sugars 0g); SODIUM 615mg; CALC 7% DV; POTASSIUM 25% DV

TIP

Look for fresh pico de gallo—a salsa made primarily of tomatoes, onions, and cilantro—packaged in a clear plastic tub in the produce, deli, or prepared foods section of your supermarket.

MOROCCAN CHICKEN, VEGETABLES, AND COUSCOUS

HANDS-ON: 25 MINUTES **TOTAL:** 4 HOURS, 25 MINUTES **SERVES** 8

Loaded with chicken, onion, butternut squash, apricots, chickpeas, and couscous, this dish is not only bursting with color and texture, but it's also packed with protein and a host of vitamins and even contains a dose of fiber.

½ teaspoon ground cumin
½ teaspoon ground ginger
½ teaspoon black pepper
¼ teaspoon ground cinnamon
¼ teaspoon cayenne pepper
1¼ teaspoons kosher salt
8 bone-in, skinless chicken thighs (about 3 pounds)
1 tablespoon olive oil
1 cup refrigerated prechopped yellow onions (about 4 ounces)

3 cups refrigerated prechopped peeled butternut squash (about 16 ounces)
1 cup unsalted chicken stock
½ cup dried apricots, halved (about 3 ounces)
1 (15-ounce) can no-salt-added chickpeas (garbanzo beans), drained and rinsed
1¾ cups uncooked whole-wheat couscous
¼ cup toasted sliced almonds
Fresh cilantro leaves (optional)

1 Stir together the cumin, ginger, black pepper, cinnamon, cayenne, and ¾ teaspoon of the salt in a small bowl. Rub the spice mixture all over the chicken. Heat the oil in a large nonstick skillet over medium-high. Add the chicken to the skillet, and cook on 1 side until well browned, about 6 minutes; turn the chicken over, and cook 1 minute. Transfer the chicken to a 5- to 6-quart slow cooker. Add the onions to the skillet, and cook, stirring often, until tender, about 4 minutes. Spoon the onions around the chicken in the slow cooker.

2 Stir the squash, stock, apricots, chickpeas, and remaining ½ teaspoon salt into the slow cooker. Cover and cook on LOW until the chicken is cooked through and the vegetables are tender, about 4 hours.

3 Prepare the couscous according to the package directions, omitting the salt and fat. Divide the couscous among 8 bowls. Top with the chicken mixture; sprinkle evenly with the almonds. Garnish with the cilantro leaves, if desired.

(**SERVING SIZE:** about ½ cup couscous, about 1 cup chicken mixture): **CALORIES** 496; **FAT** 15g (sat 3g, unsat 12g); **PROTEIN** 43g; **CARB** 49g; **FIBER** 7g; **SUGARS** 7g (added sugars 0g); **SODIUM** 453mg; **CALC** 7% DV; **POTASSIUM** 12% DV

CHICKEN-AND-TOMATO RAGOUT OVER POLENTA

HANDS-ON: 20 MINUTES **TOTAL:** 3 HOURS, 50 MINUTES **SERVES** 8

Cooking the polenta in chicken stock infuses it with robust savoriness, and melting the Parmesan cheese into the polenta further adds a salty, nutty quality. It's the perfect balance to the acidic, tomato-forward sauce. And while this dish is fancy enough to serve to guests at a dinner party, the use of presliced mushrooms and quick-cooking polenta keeps the hands-on time to a minimum. Garnish with fresh oregano and basil leaves, if desired.

3 tablespoons olive oil

1 (8-ounce) package sliced fresh cremini mushrooms

1 cup chopped celery (from 2 celery stalks)

1 cup chopped yellow onions (from 1 large onion)

2 tablespoons chopped fresh oregano

2 tablespoons chopped fresh basil

1 tablespoon minced garlic (from 3 garlic cloves)

¾ teaspoon kosher salt

½ teaspoon black pepper

Cooking spray

1 (14.5-ounce) can no-salt-added diced tomatoes, undrained

8 bone-in, skinless chicken thighs (about 2¾ pounds)

4 cups unsalted chicken stock

2 cups water

1½ cups uncooked quick-cooking polenta

4 ounces Parmesan cheese, grated (about 1 cup)

1 Heat 1 tablespoon of the oil in a large nonstick skillet over medium-high. Add the mushrooms, celery, and onions to the skillet; cook, stirring often, until the liquid evaporates and the vegetables are tender-crisp, about 6 minutes. Stir in the oregano, basil, garlic, and ¼ teaspoon each of the salt and pepper. Transfer the mushroom mixture to a 5- to 6-quart slow cooker coated with cooking spray. (Do not wipe the skillet clean.) Stir the tomatoes into the mushroom mixture in the slow cooker.

2 Heat the remaining 2 tablespoons oil in the skillet over medium-high. Sprinkle the chicken with the remaining ½ teaspoon salt and ¼ teaspoon pepper. Add the chicken to the skillet; cook, turning once, until browned, about 3 minutes per side. Place the chicken on top of the vegetable mixture in the slow cooker. Cover and cook on LOW until a thermometer inserted into the thickest portion of the chicken reads 165°F, 3 hours and 30 minutes to 4 hours.

3 Bring the stock and water to a boil in a large saucepan over high. Whisk in the polenta; reduce the heat to medium-low, and cook, whisking often, until the liquid is absorbed, 5 to 6 minutes. Whisk in ½ cup of the cheese. Divide the polenta evenly among 8 shallow bowls; top evenly with the chicken, vegetable mixture, and remaining ½ cup cheese.

(SERVING SIZE: 1¼ cups): CALORIES 446; FAT 20g (sat 6g, unsat 14g); PROTEIN 40g; CARB 24g; FIBER 4g; SUGARS 3g (added sugars 0g); SODIUM 625mg; CALC 15% DV; POTASSIUM 7% DV

LEMON-PEPPER CHICKEN THIGHS WITH BROCCOLINI

HANDS-ON: 10 MINUTES **TOTAL:** 3 HOURS, 40 MINUTES **SERVES** 4

What if you could have fall-off-the-bone-tender chicken thighs and tender-crisp Broccolini to feed 4 with 10 minutes of hands-on time and 8 common ingredients? Now, you can, and here's the recipe to prove it. Garnish with fresh oregano leaves and additional kosher salt and black pepper, if desired.

1 tablespoon black pepper
1 tablespoon lemon zest, plus 3 tablespoons fresh juice (from 2 lemons)
1 tablespoon chopped fresh oregano
¾ teaspoon kosher salt
8 bone-in, skinless chicken thighs (about 2 pounds)

½ cup unsalted chicken stock
8 lemon slices (from 1 lemon)
1 pound fresh Broccolini, trimmed (about 3 bunches)

Stir together the pepper, lemon zest, oregano, and ½ teaspoon of the salt in a small bowl. Rub the chicken with the lemon-pepper mixture. Place in a 5- to 6-quart slow cooker. Add the stock and lemon juice to the slow cooker. Top evenly with the lemon slices. Cover and cook on LOW 1 hour and 30 minutes. Uncover the slow cooker and place the Broccolini on top of the chicken. Sprinkle with the remaining ¼ teaspoon salt. Cover and cook until the chicken and vegetables are tender, about 2 more hours.

(SERVING SIZE: 2 chicken thighs, 1½ cups Broccolini): CALORIES 292; FAT 11g (sat 3g, unsat 7g); PROTEIN 37g; CARB 10g; FIBER 2g; SUGARS 3g (added sugars 0g); SODIUM 548mg; CALC 11% DV; POTASSIUM 21% DV

TIP

If you cannot find bone-in, skinless chicken thighs, ask your butcher to remove the skin from bone-in, skin-on thighs for you.

ROSEMARY-MUSHROOM CHICKEN OVER LINGUINE

HANDS-ON: 20 MINUTES **TOTAL:** 4 HOURS, 25 MINUTES **SERVES** 4

The classic pairing of shallots and mushrooms gives this easy entrée a timeless quality that's sure to please everyone at your table. Swirling the stock and flour together at the beginning is a pro tip for creating a thick sauce that moistens the final dish and helps all the ingredients come together.

1 cup unsalted chicken stock
2½ tablespoons all-purpose flour
1 cup sliced shallots (from 4 shallots)
8 ounces sliced fresh cremini mushrooms
4 ounces sliced fresh shiitake mushrooms
⅓ cup dry Marsala wine
2 teaspoons chopped fresh rosemary

8 boneless, skinless chicken thighs (about 1½ pounds)
¾ teaspoon kosher salt
½ teaspoon black pepper
8 ounces uncooked whole-wheat linguine
2 tablespoons whole fresh flat-leaf parsley leaves

1 Whisk together the stock and flour in a 5- to 6-quart slow cooker until blended. Place the shallots, mushrooms, Marsala, and rosemary in the slow cooker. Sprinkle the chicken with the salt and pepper; arrange the chicken in the slow cooker, nestling it among the vegetables and liquid. Cover and cook on LOW until the chicken is tender and the sauce has thickened, about 4 hours.

2 Transfer the chicken from the slow cooker to a serving platter, reserving the cooking liquid and vegetables in the slow cooker. Transfer the cooking liquid and vegetables to a 2-quart saucepan; bring to a boil over medium-high. Boil, stirring occasionally, until the sauce is reduced to 2 cups, about 5 minutes.

3 Cook the linguine according to the package directions, omitting the salt and fat; drain. Divide the linguine among 4 bowls; serve the chicken over the pasta. Top with the sauce. Sprinkle evenly with the parsley.

(SERVING SIZE: ½ cup pasta, 2 chicken thighs, ¼ cup sauce): **CALORIES** 463; **FAT** 9g (sat 3g, unsat 5g); **PROTEIN** 49g; **CARB** 53g; **FIBER** 7g; **SUGARS** 7g (added sugars 0g); **SODIUM** 551mg; **CALC** 7% DV; **POTASSIUM** 12% DV

MULTICOOKER DIRECTIONS

IN STEP 1, whisk together the stock and flour in the inner pot of a 6-quart multicooker until blended; add the shallots, mushrooms, Marsala, and rosemary. Sprinkle the chicken with the salt and pepper; arrange the chicken in the pot, nestling it among the vegetables and liquid. Lock the lid; turn Pressure Valve to "Venting." Cook on SLOW COOK [Normal] until the chicken is tender and the sauce has thickened, about 4 hours. Turn off the cooker. **IN STEP 2,** transfer the chicken to a serving platter, reserving the cooking liquid and vegetables in the pot. With the lid off, press SAUTÉ [Normal]. Bring to a boil; cook uncovered, stirring often, until the sauce is reduced to 2 cups. **COMPLETE STEP 3.**

CHICKEN MOLE WITH CILANTRO RICE

HANDS-ON: 25 MINUTES **TOTAL:** 4 HOURS **SERVES** 8

Mole sauce is a Mexican condiment primarily composed of fruit, chile pepper, nuts, and spices. In our rendition, these ingredients take the form of raisins and tomatoes; ancho chiles; smoked almonds; and cocoa, cumin, and cinnamon. The rich mixture coats the browned chicken thighs in the slow cooker, and doubles as a topping on the final dish. Garnish with fresh cilantro leaves, if desired.

- 4 dried ancho chiles, stemmed and seeded (about 1 ounce)
- 2 tablespoons olive oil
- 12 boneless, skinless chicken thighs (about 3 pounds)
- ⅓ cup smoked almonds (about 1 ounce)
- ⅓ cup raisins (about 1¾ ounces)
- 2 tablespoons unsweetened cocoa
- 1 teaspoon ground cumin
- ½ teaspoon ground cinnamon
- 1½ teaspoons kosher salt
- 2 large tomatoes (about 1½ pounds), roughly chopped
- 1 large white onion, roughly chopped (about 10 ounces)
- 3 garlic cloves
- 2 (8.8-ounce) packages precooked microwavable brown rice (such as Uncle Ben's Ready Rice)
- ½ cup finely chopped fresh cilantro

1 Place the chiles in a bowl; add boiling water to cover. Let stand 10 minutes; drain well, reserving the chiles and discarding the liquid.

2 Heat 1 tablespoon of the oil in a large nonstick skillet over medium-high. Add half of the chicken thighs to the skillet, and cook on 1 side until browned, about 5 minutes. Turn the chicken over, and cook 1 minute. Transfer the chicken to a 5- to 6-quart slow cooker. Repeat the procedure with the remaining oil and chicken.

3 Place the chiles, almonds, raisins, cocoa, cumin, cinnamon, salt, tomatoes, onions, and garlic in a blender; process until smooth, 1 to 2 minutes. Pour the chile mixture over the chicken in the slow cooker. Cover and cook on LOW until the chicken is tender, about 3 hours and 30 minutes.

4 Prepare the rice according to the package directions; stir in the cilantro. Divide the rice among 8 bowls. Serve the chicken and sauce over the rice.

(SERVING SIZE: about ⅓ cup rice, about 5 ounces chicken, ½ cup sauce): CALORIES 420; FAT 17g (sat 3g, unsat 11g); PROTEIN 41g; CARB 31g; FIBER 5g; SUGARS 7g (added sugars 0g); SODIUM 562mg; CALC 5% DV; POTASSIUM 11% DV

TIP
You can find dried ancho chiles in the international food aisle at most supermarkets and definitely at Latin food stores.

SWEET-AND-SPICY GLAZED CHICKEN

HANDS-ON: 15 MINUTES **TOTAL:** 3 HOURS, 30 MINUTES **SERVES** 6

You can fully indulge in the sticky-sweetness this dish offers when you know that calories, saturated fat, carbs, and sugar are in check.

⅓ cup no-salt-added ketchup

3 tablespoons Sriracha chili sauce, plus more for serving

2½ tablespoons oyster sauce

1 tablespoon lower-sodium Worcestershire sauce

½ cup, plus 2 teaspoons water

2 pounds boneless, skinless chicken thighs, cut into 1½-inch pieces

1 red bell pepper, cut into 1-inch pieces (about 8 ounces)

½ teaspoon black pepper

¼ teaspoon kosher salt

2 teaspoons cornstarch

¾ cup chopped scallions (about 1 ounce)

½ cup fresh cilantro leaves

2 (8.8-ounce) packages precooked microwavable brown rice (such as Uncle Ben's Ready Rice)

2 teaspoons sesame seeds

Sliced scallions (optional)

1 Whisk together the ketchup, Sriracha, oyster sauce, Worcestershire sauce, and ½ cup of the water in a medium bowl until blended. Place the chicken and bell pepper in a 5- to 6-quart slow cooker. Sprinkle the chicken and bell pepper evenly with the black pepper and salt. Pour the ketchup mixture over the chicken. Cover and cook on LOW until the chicken is tender, about 3 hours.

2 Whisk together the cornstarch and remaining 2 teaspoons water. Uncover the slow cooker, and whisk the cornstarch mixture into the chicken mixture in the slow cooker. Cover and cook on HIGH until the chicken mixture has thickened slightly, about 15 minutes. Stir in the chopped scallions and cilantro.

3 Meanwhile, prepare the rice according to the package directions. Divide the rice among 6 bowls. Serve the chicken mixture over the rice, and sprinkle evenly with the sesame seeds. Drizzle with the additional Sriracha and garnish with the sliced scallions, if desired.

(SERVING SIZE: ½ cup rice, 1 cup chicken mixture): **CALORIES** 380; **FAT** 9g (sat 2g, unsat 6g); **PROTEIN** 33g; **CARB** 35g; **FIBER** 2g; **SUGARS** 5g (added sugars 1g); **SODIUM** 617mg; **CALC** 4% DV; **POTASSIUM** 15% DV

MULTICOOKER DIRECTIONS

IN STEP 1, whisk together the ketchup, Sriracha, oyster sauce, Worcestershire sauce, and ½ cup of the water in a medium bowl until blended. Place the chicken and bell pepper in the inner pot of a 6-quart multicooker. Sprinkle the chicken and bell pepper with the pepper and salt. Pour the ketchup mixture over the chicken; stir. Lock the lid; turn Pressure Valve to "Venting." Cook on SLOW COOK [Normal] until the chicken is tender, about 3 hours. Turn off the cooker. **IN STEP 2,** stir the cornstarch mixture into the chicken mixture. With the lid off, press SAUTÉ [Normal]; cook uncovered, stirring often, until the chicken mixture has thickened slightly. Stir in the chopped scallions and cilantro. **COMPLETE STEP 3.**

MEDITERRANEAN LEMON CHICKEN WITH ORZO

HANDS-ON: 20 MINUTES   **TOTAL:** 4 HOURS, 20 MINUTES   **SERVES** 6

Let your slow cooker do the bulk of the work and end up with a meal that fulfills all your Mediterranean-food cravings. The mix of onions, tomatoes, kalamata olives, oregano, and parsley adds pleasing acidity to the browned chicken, while toasted pine nuts lend interest to the orzo.

2 teaspoons lemon zest, plus 3 tablespoons fresh juice (from 1 lemon)

1¾ cups roughly chopped yellow onions (from 2 medium onions)

1 (14.5-ounce) can no-salt-added diced tomatoes, drained

¼ cup pitted kalamata olives, halved (about 12 olives)

3 tablespoons chopped fresh oregano

3 tablespoons chopped fresh flat-leaf parsley

3 pounds bone-in, skinless chicken breasts (about 4 large breasts)

1 teaspoon black pepper

1 teaspoon kosher salt

2 tablespoons olive oil

1¼ cups uncooked whole-wheat orzo pasta

¼ cup pine nuts, toasted

1 Place the lemon zest in a bowl; cover and refrigerate. Stir together the lemon juice, onions, tomatoes, olives, and 2 tablespoons each oregano and parsley in a 5- to 6-quart slow cooker.

2 Sprinkle the chicken with the pepper and ¾ teaspoon of the salt. Heat a large nonstick skillet over medium-high. Add the oil to the skillet; swirl to coat. Add the chicken to the skillet; cook, turning once, until browned, about 3 minutes per side. Transfer the chicken to the slow cooker. Cover and cook on LOW until the chicken is cooked through, about 4 hours.

3 Meanwhile, prepare the orzo according to the package directions, omitting the salt and fat; drain. Stir the pine nuts and remaining ¼ teaspoon salt into the orzo.

4 Remove the chicken from the slow cooker, reserving the cooking liquid in the slow cooker. Shred the chicken, discarding the bones. Stir the chicken and lemon zest into the cooking liquid. Divide the orzo among 6 bowls. Serve the chicken mixture over the orzo, and sprinkle with the remaining 1 tablespoon each oregano and parsley.

(SERVING SIZE: ½ cup orzo, 1 cup shredded chicken mixture): CALORIES 480; FAT 16g (sat 2g, unsat 11g); PROTEIN 47g; CARB 35g; FIBER 8g; SUGARS 4g (added sugars 0g); SODIUM 534mg; CALC 6% DV; POTASSIUM 25% DV

CHICKEN WITH POTATOES, CARROTS, AND HERB SAUCE

HANDS-ON: 20 MINUTES **TOTAL:** 4 HOURS, 20 MINUTES **SERVES** 4

Impress the in-laws, neighbors, or any other dinner guests with this pretty dish. It's a slow-cooker meal that actually looks and tastes like it was oven-roasted. To save time, prep the vegetables a day ahead or in the morning, and then refrigerate until ready to brown the meat and start the slow cooker.

1¼ cups ½-inch-thick carrot slices (about 7 ounces)

1 pound small (about 2-inch-diameter) red potatoes, each cut into eighths

1½ cups sliced yellow onions (about 6 ounces)

1 tablespoon chopped fresh oregano

1 tablespoon chopped garlic (from 3 garlic cloves)

3 tablespoons chopped fresh flat-leaf parsley

¾ teaspoon kosher salt

½ teaspoon black pepper

Cooking spray

4 bone-in, skinless chicken breasts (about 2 pounds)

1 tablespoon olive oil

¾ cup unsalted chicken stock

¼ cup dry white wine

2 tablespoons all-purpose flour

1 Place the carrot slices, potatoes, onions, oregano, garlic, 2 tablespoons of the parsley, and ¼ teaspoon each of the salt and pepper in a 5- to 6-quart slow cooker evenly coated with cooking spray.

2 Sprinkle the chicken with the remaining ½ teaspoon salt and ¼ teaspoon pepper. Heat the oil in a large nonstick skillet over medium-high. Add the chicken to the skillet, meaty side down, and cook until well browned, about 6 minutes. Turn the chicken over, and cook 1 minute. Place the chicken on top of the vegetables in the slow cooker. (Do not wipe the skillet clean.) Whisk together the stock, wine, and flour. Add the stock mixture to the skillet; bring to a boil, and boil 1 minute, scraping to loosen any browned bits from the bottom of the skillet. Pour the stock mixture over the chicken in the slow cooker. Cover and cook on LOW until the chicken is cooked through, about 4 hours. Serve the chicken and vegetables with the sauce, and sprinkle evenly with the remaining 1 tablespoon chopped fresh parsley.

(SERVING SIZE: 1 breast, about 1 cup vegetables, about ¼ cup sauce): CALORIES 409; FAT 9g (sat 2g, unsat 5g); PROTEIN 46g; CARB 35g; FIBER 4g; SUGARS 6g (added sugars 0g); SODIUM 511mg; CALC 6% DV; POTASSIUM 42% DV

SMOKED CHICKEN SAUSAGE WITH CABBAGE AND APPLES

HANDS-ON: 20 MINUTES **TOTAL:** 6 HOURS, 20 MINUTES **SERVES** 6

The cabbage comes out tender without being mushy and gives the dish a slightly sweet flavor. A splash of vinegar at the end perks up the whole meal with a bit of acidic brightness. There are several varieties of smoked chicken sausage from which you can choose. We recommend using an apple-flavored smoked sausage to complement the apples and vinegar.

1 medium-sized green cabbage head, cored and cut into 16 wedges (about 2 pounds)

2 Granny Smith apples, cored and cut into 1-inch-thick wedges (about 20 ounces)

¼ teaspoon kosher salt

½ teaspoon smoked paprika

½ teaspoon black pepper

2½ tablespoons olive oil

1 (13-ounce) package smoked chicken sausage, cut diagonally into 2-inch pieces

3 tablespoons apple cider vinegar, plus more for serving

¼ cup unsalted chicken stock

Fresh flat-leaf parsley leaves (optional)

1 Toss together the cabbage, apples, salt, paprika, pepper, and 1½ tablespoons of the olive oil in a 5- to 6-quart slow cooker. Cover and cook on HIGH until the vegetables are tender, 5 to 6 hours.

2 Heat the remaining 1 tablespoon oil in a large nonstick skillet over medium-high. Add the sausage, and cook, turning to brown on all sides, about 4 minutes. Remove from the heat; add 3 tablespoons of the vinegar. Return to the heat, and cook until most of the liquid evaporates, about 30 seconds. Add the stock to the skillet; bring to a boil, scraping to loosen the browned bits from the bottom of the skillet. Spoon over the vegetable mixture in the slow cooker. Cover and cook on HIGH until the flavors come together, about 1 hour. Garnish with the fresh parsley leaves, if desired, and serve with a splash of apple cider vinegar.

(SERVING SIZE: 4 to 5 sausage slices [about ⅔ cup], 1½ cups vegetables): CALORIES 250; FAT 11g (sat 2g, unsat 8g); PROTEIN 11g; CARB 25g; FIBER 7g; SUGARS 16g (added sugars 0g); SODIUM 605mg; CALC 10% DV; POTASSIUM 13% DV

TURKEY THIGHS WITH HERB GRAVY

HANDS-ON: 15 MINUTES   **TOTAL:** 4 HOURS, 45 MINUTES   **SERVES** 6

Those who love tender, moist dark meat will love these turkey thighs. If turkey thighs aren't available, ask your butcher to cut up a whole turkey and give you the bone-in thighs. Feel free to substitute an equal weight of chicken thighs for the turkey thighs, if desired. This pairs well with a simple side of steamed green beans.

1 tablespoon olive oil
4 bone-in, skinless turkey thighs (about 3 pounds)
¾ teaspoon coarsely ground black pepper
1 teaspoon kosher salt
¼ cup finely chopped shallots (from 1 large shallot)

2 tablespoons sliced garlic (from 6 cloves)
2 tablespoons chopped fresh thyme
1½ cups unsalted chicken stock
2 tablespoons all-purpose flour
1 tablespoon unsalted butter, softened
2 tablespoons chopped fresh flat-leaf parsley

1 Heat the oil in a large nonstick skillet over medium-high. Sprinkle the turkey with the pepper and ¾ teaspoon of the salt. Cook the turkey in the skillet in batches, turning once, until well browned, about 4 minutes per side. Transfer the turkey to a 5- to 6-quart slow cooker. (Do not wipe the skillet clean.)

2 Add the shallots, garlic, and 1 tablespoon of the thyme to the skillet; cook over medium-high, stirring constantly, 30 seconds. Add the stock to the skillet; bring to a boil, stirring and scraping to loosen the browned bits from the bottom of the skillet. Transfer the stock mixture to the slow cooker. Cover and cook on LOW until the turkey is very tender and falling off the bones, about 4 hours and 30 minutes. Transfer the turkey from the slow cooker to a cutting board, and remove the meat from the bones, discarding the bones. Place the turkey on a serving platter, and cover with aluminum foil to keep warm.

3 Pour the cooking liquid from the slow cooker through a wire-mesh strainer into a 2-quart saucepan, discarding the solids. Stir together the flour and butter in a small bowl to form a smooth paste; gradually whisk the flour mixture into the cooking liquid in the saucepan. Bring to a boil over medium-high, whisking constantly; boil, whisking occasionally, until thickened, 3 to 4 minutes. Remove from the heat, and whisk in the parsley and remaining 1 tablespoon thyme and ¼ teaspoon salt. Serve the turkey with the gravy.

(SERVING SIZE: 3 ounces turkey, ⅛ cup gravy): CALORIES 325; FAT 13g (sat 3g, unsat 6g); PROTEIN 48g; CARB 5g; FIBER 1g; SUGARS 1g (added sugars 0g); SODIUM 525mg; CALC 2% DV; POTASSIUM 19% DV

NOTE
Creating a dough-like paste with flour and butter, and whisking it into the cooking liquid—a technique called *beurre manié*—gives the herb gravy a creamy texture that's perfect for spooning over the turkey.

MAPLE-MUSTARD GLAZED TURKEY BREAST

HANDS-ON: 20 MINUTES   **TOTAL:** 4 HOURS   **SERVES** 12

Depart from the expected roasted whole turkey for Thanksgiving dinner, and serve this succulent turkey breast instead. You'll delight guests with a new dish and also save yourself hands-on time and effort. As a bonus on Turkey Day, this recipe leaves your oven free for stuffing and casseroles. If whole turkey breast isn't available, ask your butcher to cut up a whole turkey and give you the whole turkey breast. To make this recipe gluten free, use gluten-free Dijon. For a pretty presentation, serve with fresh thyme and cilantro sprigs.

1 cup apple cider	½ cup unsalted chicken stock
3 fresh thyme sprigs	¼ teaspoon black pepper
⅓ cup pure maple syrup	5 teaspoons cornstarch
2 tablespoons Dijon mustard	2 tablespoons water
1 (6-pound) whole bone-in turkey breast	1 tablespoon apple cider vinegar
1 teaspoon kosher salt	Fresh thyme leaves (optional)

1 Bring the apple cider and thyme sprigs to a boil in a small saucepan over medium-high; cook until the cider is reduced to about ½ cup, about 10 minutes; discard the thyme sprigs. Stir in the maple syrup and mustard.

2 Place the turkey, breast side up, in a 6-quart slow cooker. Loosen the skin from the turkey breast without totally detaching the skin; rub ¾ teaspoon of the salt under the skin. Replace the skin. Pour the apple cider mixture over the turkey in the slow cooker. Cover and cook on HIGH until a meat thermometer inserted in the thickest part of the breast and not touching the bone registers 165°F, about 3 hours and 30 minutes. Remove the turkey from the slow cooker, reserving the cooking liquid in the slow cooker. Let the turkey rest 10 minutes. Remove the skin from the turkey, discarding the skin.

3 Meanwhile, pour the cooking liquid through a wire-mesh strainer into a 2-quart saucepan, discarding the solids. Skim the fat from the surface of the cooking liquid. Stir in the stock, pepper, and remaining ¼ teaspoon salt. Whisk together the cornstarch and water in a small bowl; whisk into the cooking liquid mixture. Bring to a boil over medium-high, whisking constantly; boil, whisking constantly, until thickened, about 10 minutes. Stir in the vinegar. Slice the turkey thinly, discarding the bone; serve with the gravy. Garnish with the thyme leaves, if desired.

(SERVING SIZE: 4 ounces turkey, 3 tablespoons sauce): CALORIES 251; FAT 3g (sat 1g, unsat 2g); PROTEIN 43g; CARB 10g; FIBER 0g; SUGARS 5g (added sugars 5g); SODIUM 367mg; CALC 2% DV; POTASSIUM 11% DV

SALSA TURKEY NACHOS

HANDS-ON: 15 MINUTES **TOTAL:** 3 HOURS, 15 MINUTES **SERVES** 6

Host a cocktail party or game night and serve guests these tasty turkey nachos. The turkey picks up smoky flavor from the chili powder and cumin, and the chips and toppings give the dish varied textures. Serve with margaritas or cold beer and fresh lime wedges, if desired.

1½ pounds bone-in, skinless turkey breast
½ teaspoon black pepper
2 tablespoons fresh lime juice (from 1 lime)
2 tablespoons chili powder
1 teaspoon ground cumin
1 tablespoon honey

3 garlic cloves, minced (about 1 tablespoon)
1½ cups pico de gallo
½ cup chopped fresh cilantro
6 ounces multigrain baked tortilla chips
2 ounces queso fresco (fresh Mexican cheese), crumbled (about ½ cup)

1 Season the turkey with the pepper, and place in a 5- to 6-quart slow cooker. Add the lime juice, chili powder, cumin, honey, garlic, 1 cup of the pico de gallo, and ¼ cup of the cilantro. Cover and cook on LOW until a meat thermometer inserted in the thickest part of the breast and not touching the bone registers 165°F, 3 to 4 hours.

2 Turn the slow cooker to WARM. Using 2 forks, shred the turkey in the slow cooker; discard the bones. Arrange the tortilla chips on a serving platter. Sprinkle the turkey mixture evenly over the tortilla chips using a slotted spoon. Top with the cheese and remaining ½ cup pico de gallo and ¼ cup cilantro.

(SERVING SIZE: ⅙ of the nachos): **CALORIES** 297; **FAT** 9g (sat 2g, unsat 5g); **PROTEIN** 29g; **CARB** 26g; **FIBER** 5g; **SUGARS** 5g (added sugars 3g); **SODIUM** 600mg; **CALC** 11% DV; **POTASSIUM** 7% DV

TURKEY FLORENTINE MEATBALLS OVER ORZO

HANDS-ON: 20 MINUTES **TOTAL:** 3 HOURS, 20 MINUTES **SERVES** 6

Turkey meatballs are a refreshing departure from typical beef meatballs. The chunky marinara sauce and tender orzo will put this entrée on your list of easy weeknight favorites. Garnish with crushed red pepper, if desired.

1 (24.5-ounce) jar lower-sodium marinara sauce (such as Amy's Light in Sodium Premium Organic Pasta Sauce)

1 (14.5-ounce) can no-salt-added fire-roasted diced tomatoes, undrained

1 pound 93/7 lean ground turkey

1 (10-ounce) package frozen chopped spinach, thawed, drained, and squeezed very dry

½ cup whole-wheat panko (Japanese-style breadcrumbs)

1 ounce pecorino Romano cheese, grated (about ¼ cup)

2 tablespoons finely chopped fresh flat-leaf parsley

1 tablespoon finely chopped garlic (from 3 garlic cloves)

2 teaspoons chopped fresh thyme

½ teaspoon kosher salt

½ teaspoon black pepper

12 ounces uncooked whole-wheat orzo pasta

Chopped fresh parsley or basil (optional)

1 Stir together the marinara sauce and diced tomatoes in a 5- to 6-quart slow cooker. Using your hands, combine the turkey, spinach, panko, cheese, parsley, garlic, thyme, salt, and pepper in a large bowl until blended. Shape into 24 (1½-inch) meatballs, and place in the sauce mixture in the slow cooker. Cover and cook on LOW until the meatballs are cooked through, 3 to 4 hours.

2 Meanwhile, prepare the pasta according to the package directions, omitting the salt and fat; drain. Divide the orzo among 6 bowls. Serve the meatballs and sauce over the orzo. Garnish with the chopped fresh parsley or basil, if desired.

(SERVING SIZE: about ⅔ cup orzo, 4 meatballs, about ⅔ cup sauce): CALORIES 434; FAT 8g (sat 3g, unsat 4g); PROTEIN 34g; CARB 62g; FIBER 9g; SUGARS 7g (added sugars 0g); SODIUM 654mg; CALC 17% DV; POTASSIUM 9% DV

MUTICOOKER DIRECTIONS

IN STEP 1, stir together the marinara sauce and diced tomatoes in the inner pot of a 6-quart multicooker. Prepare the meatballs; place in the sauce mixture in the pot. Lock the lid; turn Pressure Valve to "Venting." Cook on SLOW COOK [Normal] until the meatballs are cooked through, about 4 hours. **COMPLETE STEP 2.**

CORNMEAL-TOPPED TURKEY CHILI PIE

HANDS-ON: 20 MINUTES **TOTAL:** 4 HOURS, 50 MINUTES **SERVES** 8

Use your slow cooker to make hearty, slightly spicy chili and to bake a layer of thick, tender cornbread over it. You can substitute any no-salt-added beans for the black beans. Serve with a crisp, green salad, if desired.

6 tablespoons canola oil

1½ pounds 93/7 lean ground turkey

1 large onion, chopped (about 2 cups)

2 garlic cloves, minced (about 2 teaspoons)

2 tablespoons chili powder

1½ teaspoons kosher salt

Cooking spray

2 (14.5-ounce) cans no-salt-added diced fire-roasted tomatoes, undrained

1 cup unsalted chicken stock

1 (15-ounce) can no-salt-added black beans, drained and rinsed

¾ cup (about 3¼ ounces) all-purpose flour

¾ cup (about 4⅛ ounces) fine yellow cornmeal

2 teaspoons baking powder

1 large egg, beaten

¾ cup 2% reduced-fat milk

4 ounces sharp Cheddar cheese, shredded (about 1 cup)

Fresh cilantro leaves (optional)

1 Heat 2 tablespoons of the oil in a large skillet over medium-high. Add the turkey and onions; cook, stirring to crumble the turkey, until browned, about 7 minutes. Add the garlic, chili powder, and 1 teaspoon of the salt, and cook, stirring often, until fragrant, about 1 minute. Transfer to a 5- to 6-quart slow cooker coated with cooking spray. Stir in the tomatoes, stock, and beans until blended.

2 Whisk together the flour, cornmeal, baking powder, and remaining ½ teaspoon salt in a large bowl until well blended. Stir in the egg, milk, cheese, and remaining 4 tablespoons canola oil. Pour the cornmeal batter over the turkey mixture in the slow cooker, gently spreading to cover completely. Cover and cook on LOW until the chili is hot and the crust is lightly browned and cooked through, about 4 hours and 30 minutes. Sprinkle each serving with the cilantro leaves, if desired.

(SERVING SIZE: about 1¼ cups): CALORIES 488; FAT 24g (sat 6g, unsat 15g); PROTEIN 29g; CARB 39g; FIBER 5g; SUGARS 6g (added sugars 0g); SODIUM 629mg; CALC 39% DV; POTASSIUM 8% DV

TIP
To get neat squares of cornbread, use a knife to cut the cornbread before scooping it out.

ITALIAN TURKEY SAUSAGE– AND-SQUASH LASAGNA

HANDS-ON: 20 MINUTES **TOTAL:** 4 HOURS, 20 MINUTES **SERVES** 10

Kids will love this lasagna—and parents will love that it's packed with vitamin-rich zucchini and squash! The veggies also add moisture to the slow cooker, which keeps the lasagna from drying out. Serve with garlic toast, if desired.

16 ounces hot or sweet Italian turkey sausage, casings removed
2 cups chopped yellow onions (from 1 large)
5 garlic cloves, minced (about 5 teaspoons)
½ teaspoon black pepper
1 (24.5-ounce) jar lower-sodium marinara sauce (such as Amy's Light in Sodium Premium Organic Pasta Sauce)
1 cup water
½ cup chopped fresh basil, plus more for garnish
¼ cup chopped fresh flat-leaf parsley

16 ounces part-skim ricotta cheese (about 2 cups)
6 ounces part-skim mozzarella cheese, shredded (about 1½ cups)
Cooking spray
12 uncooked lasagna noodles (about 11¼ ounces)
12 ounces fresh zucchini, cut into ½-inch-thick slices (about 2 cups)
12 ounces fresh yellow squash, cut into ½-inch-thick-slices (about 2 cups)

1 Heat a large skillet over medium-high. Add the sausage to the skillet; cook, stirring to crumble, just until browned, 4 to 6 minutes. Add the onions, garlic, and pepper; cook, stirring occasionally, until the onions are soft, about 8 minutes. Remove the skillet from the heat.

2 Stir together the marinara sauce, water, basil, and parsley in a bowl. Stir together the ricotta and 1 cup of the shredded mozzarella in a separate bowl.

3 Coat a 5- to 6-quart slow cooker with cooking spray. Spoon ¾ cup of the marinara mixture evenly into the bottom of the slow cooker. Top with 4 of the noodles in a single layer, breaking the noodles to fit. Layer half of the sausage mixture, all of the zucchini slices, and half of the ricotta mixture over the noodles; top with ¾ cup of the marinara mixture. Arrange 4 of the noodles over the marinara mixture; top with the remaining sausage mixture, all of the yellow squash slices, and remaining ricotta mixture. Arrange the remaining 4 noodles over the ricotta mixture; top with 2 cups of the marinara mixture, reserving ½ cup remaining marinara mixture. Refrigerate the reserved marinara mixture until 15 minutes before ready to use.

4 Cover and cook on LOW until the pasta is tender, 3 hours and 45 minutes. Remove the lid; spoon the reserved ½ cup marinara mixture over the surface, and sprinkle with the remaining ½ cup shredded mozzarella. Cover and cook 15 minutes. Sprinkle with the additional chopped basil, if desired.

(SERVING SIZE: about 1¼ cups): CALORIES 382; FAT 15g (sat 5g, unsat 7g); PROTEIN 24g; CARB 40g; FIBER 4g; SUGARS 8g (added sugars 0g); SODIUM 627mg; CALC 30% DV; POTASSIUM 10% DV

SEAFOOD

POACHED SEA BASS WITH TOMATO-FENNEL RELISH

HANDS-ON: 30 MINUTES **TOTAL:** 2 HOURS, 45 MINUTES **SERVES** 4

Poaching fish is a smart use for your slow cooker. The wine mixture cooks in the slow cooker for 2 hours to get hot and mingled before the fish is added for 15 to 25 minutes. The relish, with its slightly acidic tomatoes, briney capers, and crunchy fennel, is a great complement for the bass. This dish also makes a fantastic topper for salad greens. Garnish with additional fresh thyme sprigs, if desired.

2 medium shallots
1 cup dry white wine
1 cup water
½ cup fresh lemon juice (from 4 lemons)
2 tablespoons brined caper liquid from jar
1 teaspoon cracked black pepper
1 teaspoon fennel seeds
6 fresh thyme sprigs

4 tablespoons extra-virgin olive oil
10 ounces halved multicolored cherry tomatoes
½ cup thinly sliced fennel bulb (from 1 bulb)
2 tablespoons drained and rinsed capers
4 (6-ounce) skin-on sea bass fillets (about 2 inches thick)
½ teaspoon kosher salt

1 Cut 1 shallot into quarters. Stir together the quartered shallots, wine, water, lemon juice, caper liquid, pepper, fennel seeds, 4 of the thyme sprigs, and 2 tablespoons of the oil in a 3- to 4-quart slow cooker. Cover and cook on LOW until mixture is well incorporated, 2 hours.

2 Finely chop the leaves from the remaining 2 thyme sprigs. Thinly slice the remaining shallot. Stir together the chopped thyme, sliced shallots, cherry tomatoes, sliced fennel, capers, and remaining 2 tablespoons oil in a bowl. Stir 1 tablespoon of the wine mixture from the slow cooker into the relish.

3 Add the sea bass to the slow cooker, skin side up, and nestle into the wine mixture. Cover and cook on LOW until a thermometer inserted in the fillets registers 140°F and the fish flakes easily with a fork, 15 to 25 minutes. Transfer the fish to a platter, discarding the wine mixture in the slow cooker. Sprinkle the fish with the salt, and serve with the tomato-fennel relish.

(SERVING SIZE: 1 fillet, about 1½ cups relish): CALORIES 291; FAT 12g (sat 2g, unsat 10g); PROTEIN 33g; CARB 8g; FIBER 2g; SUGARS 4g (added sugars 0g); SODIUM 577mg; CALC 4% DV; POTASSIUM 21% DV

NOTE

Fennel is a cool-weather vegetable with a crunchy texture and a slightly sweet flavor similar to licorice or star anise. It's composed of a bulb, stalks, feathery fronds, and seeds. This recipe makes use of two parts: fennel seeds to flavor the poaching liquid and sliced fennel bulb as the base for the relish.

SEAFOOD

THAI COCONUT-CURRY FLOUNDER

HANDS-ON: 15 MINUTES **TOTAL:** 3 HOURS, 20 MINUTES **SERVES** 6

This dish boasts delicate, flaky flounder and a sweet, fragrant curry made with rich coconut milk, tender sweet potatoes, and brown rice. The flounder—which can be substituted with tilapia, if desired—cooks well on top of the curry, and adding it to the slow cooker for the last 20 minutes allows it to steam without overcooking. For the prettiest appearance, substitute whole fresh basil leaves for the sliced basil.

2 small sweet potatoes (about 14 ounces), peeled and cut into ½-inch chunks

1 cup uncooked brown jasmine rice

2 tablespoons canola oil

1 (14.5-ounce) can no-salt-added diced tomatoes, undrained

1½ cups water

1 cup chopped green bell pepper (from 1 bell pepper)

2 tablespoons minced garlic (from 6 garlic cloves)

1 cup canned light coconut milk

2½ tablespoons Thai red curry paste

1½ pounds skinless flounder fillets

¼ teaspoon kosher salt

¼ cup thinly sliced fresh basil

1 Microwave the sweet potatoes in a medium-sized microwavable bowl on HIGH until slightly softened, 5 to 6 minutes, stopping to stir after 3 minutes.

2 Add the rice to a 6-quart slow cooker, and drizzle with the oil, stirring to coat evenly. Add the tomatoes, water, bell pepper, garlic, and sweet potatoes, stirring to combine. Cover and cook on HIGH until the rice is tender and the liquid is mostly absorbed, 2 hours and 30 minutes to 3 hours.

3 Gently stir the coconut milk and curry paste into the rice mixture. Cover and cook on HIGH until the liquid is mostly absorbed, about 15 minutes. Place the fish on top of the rice mixture; sprinkle with the salt. Cover and cook on HIGH until the fish flakes easily with a fork, about 20 minutes. Serve the fish with the rice mixture, and sprinkle evenly with the basil.

(SERVING SIZE: 1 cup rice mixture, 3¼ ounces flounder): CALORIES 322; FAT 10g (sat 3g, unsat 6g); PROTEIN 18g; CARB 40g; FIBER 4g; SUGARS 5g (added sugars 0g); SODIUM 635mg; CALC 6% DV; POTASSIUM 14% DV

TIP

To save prep time, purchase a package of prepeeled, prechopped sweet potatoes, such as the 16-ounce steam-in-bag package from Archer Farms, and use 14 ounces from it. Whether using the prechopped variety or not, microwaving the sweet potatoes gives them a head start on cooking, cutting down on the overall cook time.

COD WITH TOMATO-BALSAMIC JAM

HANDS-ON: 15 MINUTES **TOTAL:** 4 HOURS, 40 MINUTES **SERVES** 4

Mellow, slightly sweet, and devoid of the overt fishy flavor that's polarizing for so many, cod is a widely favored fish that's perfect for pairing with a show-stopping sauce or topping like this tomato-balsamic jam. Diced pancetta provides a salty counterpart to the sweet onion, tomatoes, vinegar, and honey and gives the jam complexity. Garnish with fresh thyme sprigs, if desired.

3 ounces diced pancetta (about ½ cup diced)

1 cup chopped sweet onion (from 1 onion)

1 pint cherry tomatoes, halved

1 tablespoon balsamic vinegar

1 tablespoon honey

1 teaspoon fresh thyme leaves

½ teaspoon black pepper

4 (6-ounce) skinless cod fillets

¼ cup fresh flat-leaf parsley leaves (optional)

1 Cook the pancetta in a nonstick skillet over medium, stirring occasionally, until crisp, about 5 minutes. Transfer the pancetta and drippings to a 5-quart slow cooker. Add the onion, tomatoes, vinegar, and honey, stirring to combine. Partially cover, and cook on HIGH until the mixture is syrupy and jam-like, about 4 hours.

2 Stir together the thyme and black pepper in a small bowl. Sprinkle over the cod fillets. Place the fish on the tomato mixture in the slow cooker; cover completely, and cook on LOW until the fish flakes easily with a fork, about 25 minutes. Serve the cod with the tomato jam; sprinkle with the parsley, if desired.

(SERVING SIZE: 1 fillet, ¼ cup jam): CALORIES 243; FAT 8g (sat 4g, unsat 3g); PROTEIN 30g; CARB 11g; FIBER 1g; SUGARS 8g (added sugars 4g); SODIUM 470mg; CALC 3% DV; POTASSIUM 18% DV

TIP

Typically, fully covering the slow cooker during cooking is necessary since the lid locks in moisture and keeps the food from drying out. However, when making the jam, letting the moisture out by only partially covering the cooker is what gives the mixture its thick, syrup-like consistency.

BRAISED SWORDFISH IN RICH TOMATO SAUCE

HANDS-ON: 20 MINUTES   **TOTAL:** 3 HOURS, 35 MINUTES   **SERVES** 4

Cooking swordfish in a slow cooker ensures an uber-moist steak. Be sure to remove the bloodline—a particularly strong-flavored muscle—from the fish as well as any skin and dark meat, or better yet, have your fishmonger do it for you. Garnish with fresh oregano sprigs and leaves, if desired.

1 (28-ounce) can no-salt-added fire-roasted diced tomatoes, drained
1 cup thinly sliced red onion (from 1 onion)
¼ cup pitted and chopped kalamata olives (about 8 olives)
1 tablespoon chopped fresh oregano
2 garlic cloves, finely chopped (about 2 teaspoons)

½ teaspoon granulated sugar
½ teaspoon kosher salt
2 tablespoons tomato paste
¼ cup loosely packed fresh basil leaves, cut into thin strips
4 (6-ounce) swordfish steaks (1¼ inches thick), bloodline removed
1 tablespoon sherry vinegar

Stir together the tomatoes, onion, olives, oregano, garlic, sugar, salt, tomato paste, and half of the basil in a 5- to 6-quart slow cooker. Cover and cook on HIGH until the vegetables are tender, about 3 hours. Stir the tomato mixture, and nestle the fish steaks into the tomato mixture. Cover and cook until the fish is cooked through or a thermometer inserted into the steaks registers 140°F, 15 to 25 minutes. Transfer the fish to a platter, reserving the sauce in the slow cooker; stir the vinegar into the sauce. Spoon the sauce and vegetables over the fish, and sprinkle with the remaining basil.

(SERVING SIZE: 1 swordfish steak, ¾ cup sauce): CALORIES 338; FAT 13g (sat 3g, unsat 9g); PROTEIN 36g; CARB 14g; FIBER 3g; SUGARS 7g (added sugars 1g); SODIUM 542mg; CALC 9% DV; POTASSIUM 25% DV

NOTE

Swordfish, one of the meatiest foods in the sea, is almost sirloin-like in consistency. It contains omega-3 fatty acids that have many health benefits including support for brain, eye, and heart health.

MAHI-MAHI TACOS

HANDS-ON: 15 MINUTES   **TOTAL:** 1 HOUR, 45 MINUTES   **SERVES** 4

This colorful meal requires only 15 minutes of hands-on prep to whip together, making it a home cook's hero. The balance of cooked fish, tomatoes, and onions with the raw cabbage and cilantro gives the dish a light, fresh feel. If desired, lightly toast the tortillas (see the tip below) before filling and garnish the tacos with crushed red pepper. Serve with hot sauce, if desired.

2 teaspoons paprika

1 teaspoon garlic powder

1 teaspoon dried oregano

¾ teaspoon kosher salt

½ teaspoon black pepper

2 tablespoons olive oil

1 pound wild-caught skin-on mahi-mahi fillets

1¼ cups cherry tomatoes, halved (about 7 ounces)

1¼ cups thinly sliced red onion (from 1 onion)

Cooking spray

8 (6-inch) corn tortillas

¾ cup reduced-fat sour cream

1 cup finely shredded cabbage (from 1 small head or 1 [10-ounce] package)

½ cup fresh cilantro leaves

1 lime, cut into wedges (optional)

1 Stir together the paprika, garlic powder, oregano, salt, pepper, and 1 tablespoon of the oil in a small bowl. Rub all over the fish. Place the tomatoes and onion in a 5- to 6-quart slow cooker lightly greased with cooking spray; drizzle with the remaining 1 tablespoon oil, and top with the fish. Cover and cook on LOW until the fish flakes easily with a fork, about 1 hour and 30 minutes.

2 Flake the fish into large chunks. Spoon the fish evenly into the tortillas, and top evenly with the cooked tomatoes and onions, sour cream, cabbage, and cilantro leaves. Serve with the lime wedges, if desired.

(SERVING SIZE: 2 tacos): CALORIES 389; FAT 15g (sat 4g, unsat 9g); PROTEIN 27g; CARB 41g; FIBER 6g; SUGARS 5g (added sugars 0g); SODIUM 525mg; CALC 15% DV; POTASSIUM 23% DV

TIP

To toast corn tortillas, heat a nonstick skillet over high. Dip a tortilla in cold water and place it directly in the hot skillet. After about 30 seconds (or longer for more toasting), flip it. Remove from the skillet and cover with a kitchen towel. Repeat the procedure with the remaining tortillas. Let the covered tortillas steam about 5 minutes. The finished tortillas should be soft and moist with flaky brown spots.

TUNA WITH ESCAROLE-CHICKPEA SALAD

HANDS-ON: 10 MINUTES **TOTAL:** 1 HOUR, 50 MINUTES **SERVES** 4

This fish salad is a unique twist on traditional slow-cooker fare. The tuna carries the bright lemon and rosemary flavors well, which results in an aromatic and fresh fish that perfectly complements the lettuce and chickpeas. Chill it for an easy work lunch the next day. Garnish with fresh rosemary leaves, if desired.

1 cup extra-virgin olive oil
½ cup thinly sliced shallots (about 1½ ounces)
1 tablespoon thinly sliced garlic (from 4 small garlic cloves)
3 fresh rosemary sprigs
1 bay leaf
1 pound albacore, yellowfin, or ahi tuna fillets
1½ tablespoons fresh lemon juice (from 1 lemon)

¾ teaspoon kosher salt
½ teaspoon black pepper
1 (10-ounce) head escarole, trimmed and coarsely chopped
1 (15-ounce) can no-salt-added chickpeas (garbanzo beans), drained and rinsed
1 ounce Parmigiano-Reggiano cheese, shaved (about ½ cup)

1 Stir together the oil, shallots, garlic, rosemary, and bay leaf in a 4-quart slow cooker. Cover and cook on LOW until fragrant, about 1 hour. Add the tuna to the slow cooker, turning to coat in the oil mixture. Cover and cook on LOW until the fish is opaque and firm, about 40 minutes. Remove the tuna from the slow cooker, reserving the oil mixture in the slow cooker. Flake the tuna into large pieces.

2 Whisk together the lemon juice, ½ teaspoon of the salt, ¼ teaspoon of the pepper, and 3 tablespoons of the reserved oil mixture from the slow cooker in a small bowl until blended and smooth.

3 Combine the escarole and chickpeas in a large bowl. Top with the tuna, and sprinkle with the remaining ¼ teaspoon each salt and pepper. Drizzle evenly with the dressing, and sprinkle each serving with the Parmigiano-Reggiano.

(SERVING SIZE: 4 ounces tuna, 1¼ cups escarole-chickpea salad): CALORIES 411; FAT 19g (sat 4g, unsat 14g); PROTEIN 36g; CARB 20g; FIBER 6g; SUGARS 1g (added sugars 0g); SODIUM 552mg; CALC 16% DV; POTASSIUM 25% DV

MULTICOOKER DIRECTIONS

IN STEP 1, stir together the oil, shallots, garlic, rosemary, and bay leaf in the inner pot of a 6-quart multicooker. Lock the lid; turn Pressure Valve to "Venting." Cook on SLOW COOK [Normal] until fragrant, about 1 hour. Add the tuna to the pot, turning to coat in the oil mixture. Lock the lid; turn Pressure Valve to "Venting." Cook on SLOW COOK [Normal] until the fish is opaque and firm, about 40 minutes. Turn off the cooker. Remove the tuna from the pot, reserving the oil mixture in the pot. Flake the tuna into large pieces. **COMPLETE STEPS 2 AND 3.**

MISO–BLACK PEPPER SALMON

HANDS-ON: 10 MINUTES **TOTAL:** 2 HOURS, 10 MINUTES **SERVES** 4

As a true dump-it-and-leave-it dish, this salmon is a weeknight-dinner go-to. The lime and scallion flavors will soak into the salmon, leaving it with a light Asian flavor. Be sure to spray the foil with cooking spray before adding food to the slow cooker to ensure that nothing sticks to it.

Cooking spray
1 lime, cut into ¼-inch-thick slices
1 bunch scallions, cut into 6-inch pieces
1 (24-ounce) skin-on center-cut salmon fillet
2 tablespoons honey
2 tablespoons water

1½ tablespoons red miso
1½ tablespoons lower-sodium soy sauce
¾ teaspoon black pepper
2 tablespoons minced fresh chives
4 teaspoons toasted sesame seeds

1 Line a 5- to 6-quart slow cooker with aluminum foil, allowing 2 to 3 inches to extend over 2 opposite sides; coat the foil with cooking spray.

2 Layer the lime slices and scallions in the slow cooker; top with the salmon, skin side down. Stir together the honey, water, miso, soy sauce, and black pepper in a small bowl; spread ¼ cup of the miso mixture over the salmon. Cover and cook on HIGH until the fish flakes easily with a fork, about 2 hours. Using the foil as handles, transfer the salmon to a serving plate. Discard the foil. Drizzle the remaining miso mixture over the salmon, and sprinkle with the chives and sesame seeds.

(**SERVING SIZE:** 6 ounces salmon): **CALORIES** 319; **FAT** 13g (sat 2g, unsat 10g); **PROTEIN** 36g; **CARB** 15g; **FIBER** 2g; **SUGARS** 10g (added sugars 9g); **SODIUM** 573mg; **CALC** 7% DV; **POTASSIUM** 27% DV

NOTE

Miso is a Japanese seasoning paste made with fermented soybeans. There are different types of miso—white, yellow, and red—primarily differentiated based on how long the soybeans are fermented. White miso is fermented for the shortest time, red for the longest time, and yellow somewhere in between. Red miso has an intense umami flavor—use it in moderation.

CITRUS SALMON WITH MELTED LEEKS

HANDS-ON: 10 MINUTES **TOTAL:** 3 HOURS, 40 MINUTES **SERVES** 4

We've discovered the perfect pairing for this moist, lemony salmon—slightly chewy leeks. Like other alliums, leeks become sweet and rich when roasted slowly for a long time. When cooked in the slow cooker they "melt," becoming jam-like but still retaining pleasant chewiness. Garnish with fresh sage leaves and thyme sprigs, if desired.

Cooking spray
3 cups sliced leeks (from 2 leeks)
1 tablespoon finely chopped fresh thyme
1 teaspoon chopped fresh sage
1 teaspoon kosher salt
½ teaspoon black pepper

¼ cup dry white wine
2 tablespoons unsalted butter, cut into 8 pieces
4 (6-ounce) skinless salmon fillets
1 lemon, thinly sliced
1 tablespoon olive oil

1 Coat a 5- to 6-quart slow cooker with cooking spray. Place the leeks in the slow cooker; toss with the thyme, sage, and ½ teaspoon of the salt and ¼ teaspoon of the pepper, and spread in an even layer. Drizzle the leeks with the wine, and dot with the butter. Cover and cook on LOW until the leeks are tender, about 2 hours and 30 minutes.

2 Place the salmon on top of the leeks in the slow cooker. Sprinkle the salmon with the remaining ½ teaspoon salt and ¼ teaspoon pepper; top with the lemon slices, and drizzle with the oil. Cover and cook on LOW until a thermometer inserted in thickest portion of the salmon registers 140°F, about 1 hour. Transfer the salmon to a platter, and serve with the leeks.

(SERVING SIZE: 1 fillet, ½ cup leeks): CALORIES 369; FAT 20g (sat 6g, unsat 13g); PROTEIN 35g; CARB 10g; FIBER 1g; SUGARS 3g (added sugars 0g); SODIUM 569mg; CALC 7% DV; POTASSIUM 28% DV

RED WINE–BRAISED OCTOPUS OVER LINGUINE

HANDS-ON: 20 MINUTES **TOTAL:** 5 HOURS, 35 MINUTES **SERVES** 6

Don't be afraid to slow-cook octopus! Expand your palate and enjoy this tender, light meat that tastes similar to chicken. This sauce is very rich, briny, and deeply flavored, so much so that you only need to serve half of it with the octopus.

2 tablespoons olive oil

1 cup chopped carrots (from 2 carrots)

1 cup chopped celery (from 3 celery stalks)

½ cup chopped shallots (from 3 to 4 shallots)

1 tablespoon minced garlic (from 3 garlic cloves)

1 (26.46-ounce) package chopped tomatoes (such as Pomi)

1 cup dry red wine

2 tablespoons no-salt-added tomato paste

¾ teaspoon kosher salt

4 fresh thyme sprigs

1 bay leaf

2 pounds cleaned octopus (tubes and tentacles), rinsed

12 ounces uncooked whole-grain linguine

1 teaspoon black pepper

½ cup chopped fresh flat-leaf parsley

1 Heat the oil in a large skillet over medium-high. Add the chopped carrots, celery, and shallots, and cook, stirring occasionally, until softened and beginning to brown, about 5 minutes. Add the garlic, and cook, stirring constantly, until fragrant, about 1 minute. Add the tomatoes, red wine, tomato paste, salt, thyme, and bay leaf; bring to a boil. Transfer to a 6-quart slow cooker. Nestle the octopus into the sauce. Cover and cook on LOW until the octopus is tender, 5 hours to 5 hours and 30 minutes.

2 Meanwhile, cook the linguine according to the package directions, omitting the salt and fat, and transfer to a serving platter or bowl, and keep warm.

3 Remove the octopus, reserving the sauce in the slow cooker. Cut the octopus into 1-inch pieces, and add to the pasta; cover with aluminum foil to keep warm. Pour the reserved sauce through a wire-mesh strainer into a medium saucepan to equal 5 cups, discarding the solids. Bring to a boil over high, and boil until reduced to 4 cups, 15 to 20 minutes. Stir in the pepper. Spoon about 2 cups of the sauce over the octopus and pasta; sprinkle with the parsley.

(SERVING SIZE: 1⅓ cups pasta, ⅓ cup sauce, about ½ cup octopus pieces): CALORIES 406; FAT 8g (sat 1g, unsat 6g); PROTEIN 34g; CARB 55g; FIBER 9g; SUGARS 9g (added sugars 0g); SODIUM 629mg; CALC 13% DV; POTASSIUM 22% DV

MULTICOOKER DIRECTIONS

IN STEP 1, remove the lid of a 6-quart multicooker. Place the oil in the inner pot. Press SAUTÉ [Normal], and heat, swirling to coat the bottom of the pot. Add the chopped carrots, celery, and shallots, and cook uncovered, stirring occasionally, until softened and beginning to brown. Add the garlic; cook, stirring constantly, until fragrant, about 1 minute. Add the tomatoes and the next 5 ingredients; bring to a boil. Turn off the cooker. Nestle the octopus into the sauce. Lock the lid; turn Pressure Valve to "Venting." Cook on SLOW COOK [Normal] until the octopus is tender, about 5 hours and 30 minutes. **COMPLETE STEP 2. IN STEP 3,** remove the octopus, reserving the sauce in the pot. Pour the reserved sauce through a wire-mesh strainer into a medium saucepan to equal 5 cups, discarding the solids. **FINISH STEP 3.**

EASY SHRIMP BOIL

HANDS-ON: 10 MINUTES **TOTAL:** 3 HOURS, 25 MINUTES **SERVES** 6

Tender red potatoes, corn, and shrimp; smoky sausage; and flavorful Old Bay seasoning give this dish classic shrimp-boil flavor. Because it's all made in the slow cooker, pulling this meal together is a breeze. It's perfect for a party—just serve with lemon wedges, cocktail sauce, bay leaves, and ice-cold beer. If you can't find turkey andouille, use chicken andouille instead.

2½ cups water

1 (12-ounce) bottle or can light beer

3 tablespoons lower-sodium Old Bay seasoning

1½ pounds small red potatoes, halved

1 medium-sized yellow onion, cut into ½-inch wedges

1 small lemon, sliced

2 bay leaves

8 ounces turkey andouille sausage, cut into 1-inch pieces

4 ears fresh corn, husks removed, cut crosswise into thirds

2 pounds large unpeeled raw shrimp

1 Stir together the water, beer, and Old Bay seasoning in a 5- to 7-quart slow cooker; add the potatoes, onion, lemon, and bay leaves. Cover and cook on HIGH until the potatoes are tender-crisp, about 2 hours.

2 Add the sausage and corn; cover and cook on HIGH until the potatoes and corn are tender, about 1 hour. Stir in the shrimp; cover and cook on HIGH until the shrimp turn pink, 12 to 14 minutes. Drain well; discard the bay leaves and lemon slices.

(SERVING SIZE: 2 cups): CALORIES 294; FAT 5g (sat 2g, unsat 2g); PROTEIN 31g; CARB 35g; FIBER 4g; SUGARS 7g (added sugars 0g); SODIUM 508mg; CALC 10% DV; POTASSIUM 26% DV

SHRIMP-AND-CHORIZO PAELLA

HANDS-ON: 20 MINUTES **TOTAL:** 3 HOURS, 30 MINUTES **SERVES** 6

Paella is an iconic Spanish dish made with rice, seasonings, and various meats or seafood, depending on the paella type. Our recipe features shrimp, brown rice, turmeric, a host of vegetables, and Spanish chorizo—not to be confused with Mexican chorizo, which isn't dried or cured like the Spanish variety.

6 ounces dry-cured Spanish chorizo, chopped (about 1 cup)
1½ cups chopped yellow onion (from 1 onion)
1 cup chopped red bell pepper (from 1 bell pepper)
1½ cups uncooked medium-grain brown rice
3 garlic cloves, minced (about 1 tablespoon)
½ cup dry white wine
2 cups unsalted chicken stock
1 (14.5-ounce) can no-salt-added fire-roasted diced tomatoes, undrained

1¼ teaspoons kosher salt
½ teaspoon ground turmeric
1½ pounds medium-sized raw shrimp, peeled and deveined
1½ cups frozen sweet peas, thawed (from 1 [10-ounce] package)
2 tablespoons chopped fresh flat-leaf parsley
1 lemon, cut into 6 wedges

1 Heat a large nonstick skillet over medium; add the chorizo, and cook, stirring occasionally, until the sausage is browned, about 5 minutes. Remove the chorizo from the skillet with a slotted spoon, reserving the drippings in the skillet; drain the chorizo on paper towels. Add the onion and bell pepper to the reserved drippings in the skillet; cook, stirring occasionally, until slightly softened, about 5 minutes. Add the rice and garlic; cook, stirring often, until the rice is lightly toasted, about 1 minute. Add the wine, and remove from the heat. Pour into a 6-quart slow cooker; stir in the stock, tomatoes, salt, turmeric, and chorizo. Cover and cook on HIGH until the rice is tender and the liquid is almost absorbed, about 3 hours.

2 Stir in the shrimp and peas; cover and cook on HIGH until the shrimp turn pink, 10 to 15 minutes. Divide the mixture among 6 plates; sprinkle evenly with the parsley, and serve with the lemon wedges.

(SERVING SIZE: 1⅓ cups): CALORIES 425; FAT 10g (sat 3g, unsat 6g); PROTEIN 30g; CARB 52g; FIBER 6g; SUGARS 7g (added sugars 0g); SODIUM 670mg; CALC 12% DV; POTASSIUM 14% DV

NOTE
Adding the wine to the hot, rice-filled skillet heats up the wine and quick-starts its evaporation process. The rice, too, gets a head start in absorbing the wine, which gives it a tasty risotto-like flavor without overly alcoholic notes.

SHRIMP VINDALOO

HANDS-ON: 20 MINUTES **TOTAL:** 5 HOURS, 30 MINUTES **SERVES** 4

This delicious dump-and-go, Indian-inspired curry comes together in a snap. The rich tomato sauce nicely coats the vegetables and shrimp, and the garam masala (Indian curry seasoning) and paprika amp up the spice. Serve this one-dish meal with naan, crushed red pepper flakes, and thinly slice the lemon wedges, if desired.

2 cups lower-sodium marinara sauce (such as Amy's Light in Sodium Organic Family Marinara Pasta Sauce)
½ cup unsalted chicken stock
1 tablespoon olive oil
1 tablespoon light brown sugar
2 teaspoons garam masala
1 teaspoon hot paprika
8 ounces small red potatoes, quartered
8 ounces cauliflower florets

1 cup diagonally sliced carrots (from 3 carrots)
1½ pounds large raw shrimp, peeled and deveined
⅜ teaspoon kosher salt
2 (8.5-ounce) packages precooked microwavable brown basmati rice (such as Uncle Ben's Ready Rice)
4 lemon wedges
Fresh cilantro leaves (optional)

1 Stir together the marinara sauce, chicken stock, oil, brown sugar, garam masala, and hot paprika in a 5- to 6-quart slow cooker. Stir in the potatoes, cauliflower, and carrots. Cover and cook on LOW until the vegetables are tender, about 5 hours. Stir in the shrimp; cover and cook on LOW until the shrimp turn pink, 10 to 15 minutes. Stir in the salt.

2 Meanwhile, prepare the rice according to the package directions. Divide the rice evenly among 4 plates, and top evenly with the shrimp mixture. Serve with the lemon wedges; garnish with the cilantro leaves, if desired.

(SERVING SIZE: 1½ cups): **CALORIES** 520; **FAT** 12g (sat 1g, unsat 9g); **PROTEIN** 32g; **CARB** 63g; **FIBER** 7g; **SUGARS** 12g (added sugars 3g); **SODIUM** 801mg; **CALC** 14% DV; **POTASSIUM** 23% DV

MULTICOOKER DIRECTIONS

IN STEP 1, stir together the marinara sauce, chicken stock, oil, brown sugar, garam masala, and hot paprika in the inner pot of a 6-quart multicooker. Stir in the potatoes, cauliflower, and carrots. Lock the lid; turn Pressure Valve to "Venting." Cook on SLOW COOK [Normal] until the vegetables are tender, about 5 hours. Stir in the shrimp. Lock the lid; turn Pressure Valve to "Venting." Cook on SLOW COOK [Normal] just until the shrimp turn pink, about 15 minutes. Stir in the salt. **COMPLETE STEP 2.**

LEMON-CORIANDER SHRIMP AND GRITS

HANDS-ON: 30 MINUTES   **TOTAL:** 3 HOURS, 40 MINUTES   **SERVES** 6

Creamy shrimp and grits is a comfort food classic, and everyone at your table will love this version with coriander-accented shrimp. Turn on the slow cooker before picking up the kids from school, and add the shrimp and make the grits right before dinnertime. Serve with Brussels Sprouts with Lemon (page 259) or Braised Collard Greens with Pepperoncini (page 260).

3 center-cut bacon slices

1 tablespoon olive oil

1 (8-ounce) container refrigerated prechopped onion, bell pepper, and celery mix

2 garlic cloves, sliced (about 2 teaspoons)

2 teaspoons chopped fresh thyme

1 teaspoon ground coriander

¼ teaspoon cayenne pepper

1 (14.5-ounce) can no-salt-added diced tomatoes, undrained

1 lemon, cut into quarters

2¼ cups unsalted chicken stock

2 pounds large raw shrimp, peeled and deveined

1 teaspoon kosher salt

2 cups water

¼ teaspoon black pepper

1 cup uncooked quick-cooking grits

¼ cup unsalted butter

Fresh thyme leaves (optional)

Hot sauce (optional)

1 Cook the bacon in a large nonstick skillet over medium-high until crisp, about 5 minutes. Remove the bacon, and drain on paper towels, reserving the drippings in the skillet. Crumble the bacon. Add the oil, onion mix, and garlic to the reserved drippings in the skillet; cook, stirring occasionally, until slightly softened, about 5 minutes. Add the thyme, coriander, and cayenne; cook, stirring often, 1 minute. Transfer to a 5- to 6-quart slow cooker; stir in the tomatoes, lemon, and ¼ cup of the stock. Cover and cook on LOW until the flavors blend, about 3 hours. Stir in the shrimp and ½ teaspoon of the salt; cover and cook on LOW until the shrimp turn pink, 10 to 12 minutes. Discard the lemon quarters.

2 Bring the water, black pepper, and remaining 2 cups stock and ½ teaspoon salt to a boil in a medium saucepan over medium-high. Gradually whisk in the grits; reduce the heat to medium-low, and cook, whisking often, until the grits are tender and thickened, about 5 minutes. Remove from the heat, and whisk in the butter. Divide the grits among 6 shallow bowls; top with the shrimp mixture. Sprinkle evenly with the crumbled bacon, and, if desired, thyme leaves. Serve with the hot sauce, if desired.

(SERVING SIZE: 1 cup grits, 1 cup shrimp mixture): **CALORIES** 342; **FAT** 13g (sat 6g, unsat 5g); **PROTEIN** 27g; **CARB** 28g; **FIBER** 3g; **SUGARS** 3g (added sugars 0g); **SODIUM** 667mg; **CALC** 12% DV; **POTASSIUM** 12% DV

SHRIMP NOODLE BOWLS

HANDS-ON: 20 MINUTES   **TOTAL:** 3 HOURS, 30 MINUTES   **SERVES** 6

The aromatic vegetables in the broth create a light yet distinct flavor of classic noodle bowls. Adding the lime juice, fish sauce, and shrimp at the end keeps them from overcooking and their flavors from becoming diluted. If you have it, drizzle toasted sesame oil on top of this one-dish meal for nutty flair. For the prettiest appearance, use whole basil and cilantro leaves, instead of chopping them.

6 cups unsalted chicken stock

4 scallions, cut into 2-inch lengths

2 tablespoons sliced garlic (from 6 garlic cloves)

1½ tablespoons finely chopped fresh ginger

1 (2-inch) piece lemongrass

1 cup matchstick carrots

1 (8-ounce) package fresh white mushrooms, thinly sliced

¼ cup fresh lime juice (from 2 limes)

4 teaspoons fish sauce

2 pounds medium-sized raw shrimp, peeled and deveined

8 ounces uncooked rice vermicelli

1½ cups bean sprouts (about 4 ounces)

1 red Fresno chile, thinly sliced

6 tablespoons chopped fresh basil

6 tablespoons chopped fresh cilantro

1 Stir together the stock, scallions, garlic, ginger, lemongrass, carrots, and mushrooms in a 5- to 6-quart slow cooker. Cover and cook on LOW until the vegetables are tender and the broth is aromatic, 3 to 4 hours. Remove and discard the lemongrass. Stir in the lime juice, fish sauce, and shrimp; cover and cook on LOW until the shrimp turn pink, about 10 minutes.

2 Meanwhile, soak the rice vermicelli according to the package directions; divide among 6 bowls. Ladle the broth over the noodles. Top with the shrimp mixture. Top evenly with the bean sprouts, chile slices, basil, and cilantro.

(SERVING SIZE: ⅙ of the vermicelli, 1 cup broth, 1½ cups shrimp mixture): **CALORIES** 307; **FAT** 2g (sat 0g, unsat 1g); **PROTEIN** 30g; **CARB** 39g; **FIBER** 2g; **SUGARS** 5g (added sugars 0g); **SODIUM** 676mg; **CALC** 11% DV; **POTASSIUM** 15% DV

TIP

Lemongrass is just what it sounds like: grass with a light citrus flavor. Look for packaged lemongrass stalks near the plastic clamshells of herbs in the produce section of your supermarket. Use the leftover lemongrass in stir-fries and sauces, and steeped in hot tea.

SHRIMP POSOLE TACOS

HANDS-ON: 20 MINUTES   **TOTAL:** 4 HOURS, 30 MINUTES   **SERVES** 4

Literally translated, "posole" means "hominy." Traditional posole dishes are soups or stews made with hominy along with pork, chicken, or seafood. Here, the hominy, cumin, oregano, and shrimp render classic posole flavors that are amplified by the addition of typical posole toppings: cabbage, radishes, cilantro, and lime. Toast the corn tortillas for extra crunch, if desired (see the tip on page 129 for directions).

1 cup unsalted chicken stock

1 cup drained and rinsed white hominy (from 1 [15-ounce] can)

1 cup chopped yellow onion (from 1 onion)

1 cup chopped poblano chiles (from 2 chiles)

1½ tablespoons ground cumin

1 tablespoon minced garlic (about 3 garlic cloves)

2 teaspoons dried oregano

1½ pounds medium-sized raw shrimp, peeled and deveined

⅜ teaspoon kosher salt

2 cups angel hair cabbage (from 1 [10-ounce] package)

¾ cup thinly sliced radishes (from 4 radishes)

½ cup roughly chopped fresh cilantro leaves

2 limes

1 tablespoon olive oil

8 (6-inch) corn tortillas

1 Stir together the chicken stock, hominy, onion, chiles, cumin, garlic, and oregano in a 5- to 6-quart slow cooker. Cover and cook on LOW until the vegetables are very tender, about 4 hours. Add the shrimp to the slow cooker; cover and cook until the shrimp turn pink, about 10 to 15 minutes. Using a slotted spoon, transfer the shrimp mixture to a bowl; season with ¼ teaspoon of the salt.

2 Combine the cabbage, radishes, and cilantro in a medium bowl. Squeeze 1 lime to equal 2 tablespoons juice. Drizzle the cabbage mixture with the lime juice and olive oil; sprinkle with the remaining ⅛ teaspoon salt. Toss gently to coat.

3 Divide the shrimp mixture and slaw mixture evenly among the tortillas. Cut the remaining lime into wedges, and serve with the tacos.

(**SERVING SIZE:** 2 tacos): **CALORIES** 369; **FAT** 8g (sat 1g, unsat 5g); **PROTEIN** 30g; **CARB** 48g; **FIBER** 8g; **SUGARS** 6g (added sugars 0g); **SODIUM** 645mg; **CALC** 19% DV; **POTASSIUM** 11% DV

TIP

Peeled and deveined shrimp is readily available in the seafood section of supermarkets; however, if you can only find the peel-on variety, ask your fishmonger to peel and devein the shrimp for you. It will save you time and hassle.

GREEN CURRY SCALLOPS AND VEGETABLES

HANDS-ON: 25 MINUTES **TOTAL:** 4 HOURS, 3 MINUTES **SERVES** 4

Cooking the spicy coconut milk mixture for longer and at a lower temperature, and then adding the crunchy bok choy and scallops for a short time at high temperature crafts complex flavor. To make this recipe gluten free, use a gluten-free green curry paste such as the one from Thai Kitchen.

2½ tablespoons green curry paste

2 teaspoons minced fresh ginger

2 teaspoons finely chopped garlic (from 2 garlic cloves)

1 (13.5-ounce) can light coconut milk

1 cup diagonally sliced carrots (from 2 carrots)

2 cups chopped bok choy (about 10 ounces)

1 pound sea scallops

3 tablespoons fresh cilantro leaves

1½ tablespoons fresh basil leaves

2 tablespoons fresh lime juice (from 1 lime)

8 ounces uncooked wide rice noodles

Finely chopped red jalapeño chile (optional)

1 Stir together the curry paste, ginger, garlic, and coconut milk in a 5- to 6-quart slow cooker. Add the carrots; cover and cook on LOW until mostly tender, about 3 hours and 30 minutes. Increase the heat to HIGH, and add the chopped bok choy and scallops. Cover and cook until the scallops reach the desired degree of doneness, about 8 minutes for medium. Stir in the cilantro, basil, and lime juice.

2 Meanwhile, prepare the noodles according to the package directions, omitting the salt and fat. Divide the noodles among 4 bowls; top with the scallops and curry mixture. Garnish with the chopped jalapeño, if desired. Serve immediately.

(SERVING SIZE: 1 cup rice noodles, 4 to 5 scallops, ½ cup curry mixture): CALORIES 372; FAT 7g (sat 4g, unsat 2g); PROTEIN 18g; CARB 60g; FIBER 5g; SUGARS 4g (added sugars 0g); SODIUM 739mg; CALC 6% DV; POTASSIUM 14% DV

MULTICOOKER DIRECTIONS

IN STEP 1, stir together the curry paste, ginger, garlic, and coconut milk in the inner pot of a 6-quart multicooker. Add the sliced carrots. Lock the lid; turn Pressure Valve to "Venting." Cook on SLOW COOK [Normal] until mostly tender, about 3 hours and 30 minutes. Turn off the cooker. With the lid off, press SAUTÉ [Normal]; gently stir in the bok choy and scallops. Cook, uncovered, until the scallops reach the desired degree of doneness, gently stirring occasionally. Stir in the cilantro, basil, and lime juice. **COMPLETE STEP 2.**

SWEET-AND-SOUR SCALLOPS

HANDS-ON: 20 MINUTES **TOTAL:** 4 HOURS, 28 MINUTES **SERVES** 4

This recipe is sure to become a tried-and-true favorite for any seafood lover. Tender scallops quickly poach in a sweet and spicy sauce that has been cooking for hours. Brown rice completes the meal.

⅓ cup no-salt-added ketchup
¼ cup fresh orange juice (from 1 orange)
3 tablespoons rice vinegar
2 tablespoons cornstarch
1 tablespoon lower-sodium soy sauce
¾ teaspoon kosher salt
1½ cups 1-inch-cubed fresh pineapple (about 1 pound)
1 medium-sized red bell pepper, cut into 1-inch pieces (about 1 cup)

1 medium-sized yellow onion, cut into 1-inch pieces (about 1½ cups)
1 small jalapeño chile, seeded and sliced (about ¼ cup)
1 pound sea scallops
2 cups hot cooked brown rice
Thinly sliced scallions (optional)

Whisk together the ketchup, orange juice, vinegar, cornstarch, soy sauce, and salt in a small bowl; pour into a 5- to 6-quart slow cooker. Add the pineapple, bell pepper, onion, and jalapeño to the slow cooker. Cover and cook on LOW until the vegetables are mostly tender, about 4 hours. Add the scallops, and stir to combine; cover and cook until the scallops reach the desired degree of doneness, about 8 minutes for medium. Divide the brown rice among 4 bowls. Serve the scallops and sauce over the brown rice; garnish with the scallions, if desired.

(SERVING SIZE: ½ cup rice, 4 to 5 scallops, about ½ cup sauce): CALORIES 304; FAT 2g (sat 0g, unsat 1g); PROTEIN 18g; CARB 55g; FIBER 4g; SUGARS 16g (added sugars 1g); SODIUM 701mg; CALC 3% DV; POTASSIUM 22% DV

MULTICOOKER DIRECTIONS

Whisk together the ketchup, orange juice, vinegar, cornstarch, soy sauce, and salt in the inner pot of a 6-quart multicooker. Add the pineapple, bell pepper, onion, and jalapeño to the pot. Lock the lid; turn Pressure Valve to "Venting." Cook on SLOW COOK [Normal] until the vegetables are mostly tender, about 4 hours. Turn off the cooker. Gently stir in the scallops. With the lid off, press SAUTÉ [Normal]; cook uncovered until the scallops reach the desired degree of doneness. **FINISH THE RECIPE.**

CLAMS WITH BACON, LEEKS, AND WHITE WINE

HANDS-ON: 20 MINUTES **TOTAL:** 4 HOURS, 35 MINUTES **SERVES** 4

Savory bacon enriches this broth while white wine permeates the entire dish. Serve the remaining wine to guests with dinner. Don't skip out on the bread! There's much satisfaction to be had in sopping up the broth with a toasted baguette.

4 center-cut bacon slices, chopped
2 cups chopped leeks (from 1 leek)
⅓ cup chopped shallots (from 1 shallot)
3 fresh thyme sprigs
1 (8-ounce) bottle clam juice
½ cup dry white wine

1 tablespoon fresh lemon juice (from 1 lemon)
2½ pounds littleneck clams, scrubbed
8 (½-ounce) whole-grain baguette slices
1 tablespoon olive oil
¼ cup chopped fresh flat-leaf parsley

1 Cook the bacon in a medium-sized nonstick skillet over medium-high, stirring occasionally, until crisp, 5 to 6 minutes. Transfer the bacon to a plate lined with paper towels to drain, reserving the drippings in the skillet. Add the leeks and shallots to the reserved drippings in the skillet, and cook, stirring often, until the vegetables are softened and slightly browned, about 5 minutes. Transfer the leek mixture to a 6-quart slow cooker; stir in the thyme, clam juice, wine, and bacon. Cover and cook on LOW until the leeks are tender and the broth is very aromatic, about 3 hours. Stir in the lemon juice. Increase the heat to HIGH, and add the clams to the slow cooker. Cover and cook until all the clams have opened, about 1 hour and 15 minutes. (Discard any clams that do not open.) Remove and discard the thyme sprigs.

2 Meanwhile, preheat the broiler with the oven rack about 8 inches from the heat. Place the bread slices on a baking sheet, and brush with half of the olive oil. Broil until golden brown, about 1 minute. Turn the slices over, and repeat the procedure on the other side with the remaining olive oil.

3 Divide the clams and broth among 4 bowls; sprinkle evenly with the parsley, and serve with the bread slices.

(SERVING SIZE: about 1 dozen clams, 10 tablespoons broth, 2 bread slices): CALORIES 408; FAT 8g (sat 2g, unsat 4g); PROTEIN 48g; CARB 32g; FIBER 2g; SUGARS 3g (added sugars 0g); SODIUM 511mg; CALC 16% DV; POTASSIUM 11% DV

TIP

Scrubbing clams prior to cooking is an important step in making sure they are in safe and prime condition to be eaten. The simplest way to clean them is to submerge the clams in fresh, cool tap water for 20 minutes to an hour. This will allow sand or dirt to escape. Then remove the clams from the water and scrub them using a brush. If the clams open at any point prior to cooking, or if they float when soaked, throw them out, as they have gone bad.

SPICY MUSSELS IN TOMATO-FENNEL RAGU

HANDS-ON: 30 MINUTES **TOTAL:** 4 HOURS **SERVES** 4

Cooking mussels in a slow cooker? You bet! It's the right tool for building the rich and spicy broth in which these shellfish cook to perfection. Use the freshest mussels you can find, and have the fishmonger clean them for you.

1 tablespoon olive oil
1 fennel bulb (about 3 ounces), thinly sliced, fronds reserved for garnish
1 yellow onion (about 4½ ounces), chopped
1 carrot (about 6 ounces), chopped
1 celery stalk (about 1½ ounces), chopped
3 garlic cloves, smashed
¾ cup dry white wine

2 tomatoes, roughly chopped (about 2 cups)
2 bay leaves
1 lemon, halved
¾ teaspoon kosher salt
½ teaspoon crushed red pepper
2 pounds small mussels, scrubbed and debearded
8 ounces uncooked whole-wheat linguine

1 Heat the olive oil in a large nonstick skillet over medium-high. Add the sliced fennel, onion, carrot, and celery, and cook, stirring occasionally, until starting to brown, about 8 minutes. Add the garlic, and cook, stirring occasionally, until fragrant, about 2 minutes. Add the white wine; reduce the heat to medium, and cook until the wine is mostly reduced, 4 to 5 minutes. Transfer the mixture to a 6-quart slow cooker; stir in the tomatoes, bay leaves, lemon halves, salt, and red pepper. Cover and cook on HIGH until the vegetables are very tender, about 3 hours.

2 Add the mussels to the slow cooker; cover and cook on HIGH until the mussels open, 30 to 40 minutes. Discard the bay leaves, lemon halves, and any mussels that do not open.

3 Meanwhile, cook the linguine according to the package directions, omitting the salt and fat. Divide the pasta, mussels, and sauce among 4 shallow bowls. Garnish with the fennel fronds, if desired.

(SERVING SIZE: ¾ cup pasta, 8 ounces mussels, ¼ cup sauce): **CALORIES** 453; **FAT** 7g (sat 1g, unsat 5g); **PROTEIN** 44g; **CARB** 57g; **FIBER** 8g; **SUGARS** 7g (added sugars 0g); **SODIUM** 521mg; **CALC** 15% DV; **POTASSIUM** 15% DV

5 MEATLESS MAINS

CAPRESE–WHITE BEAN SPAGHETTI SQUASH

HANDS-ON: 15 MINUTES **TOTAL:** 6 HOURS, 15 MINUTES **SERVES** 2

This recipe feels and looks indulgent without being high in calories. The "caprese" components—fresh mozzarella, basil leaves, and tomatoes—beautifully shine through, while the white beans add protein and a creamy texture. If you can't find fresh small mozzarella balls, tear a large ball of fresh mozzarella into small pieces.

1 spaghetti squash (about 2½ pounds)
2 cups water
1 tablespoon olive oil
2 garlic cloves, minced (about 2 teaspoons)
2 cups cherry tomatoes, quartered
1 cup drained and rinsed no-salt-added
   cannellini beans

⅓ cup chopped fresh basil
½ teaspoon kosher salt
3 ounces fresh small mozzarella balls,
   quartered
Fresh sliced basil leaves (optional)

1 Pierce the squash several times with a fork or knife. Place the squash and water in a 6-quart slow cooker. Cover and cook on LOW until the squash is tender, 5 to 6 hours.

2 Remove the squash, and let cool slightly. Cut the squash in half lengthwise. Scoop out and discard the seeds. Using a fork, scrape the insides of the squash shells to remove the spaghetti-like strands to yield 3 to 4 cups. Return the spaghetti squash shells to the slow cooker, cut-sides up. Set the squash strands aside.

3 Heat the oil in a large skillet over medium-high. Add the garlic and tomatoes; cook, stirring often, until the tomatoes begin to soften, about 3 minutes. Remove from the heat. Add the squash strands, beans, basil, and salt to the tomato mixture, stirring to combine. Gently fold in the mozzarella.

4 Spoon the squash mixture evenly into each squash half in the slow cooker. Cover and cook on LOW until the cheese is melted and the mixture is heated throughout, about 1 hour. Garnish with the basil leaves, if desired.

(SERVING SIZE: 1 stuffed squash half): CALORIES 375; FAT 19g (sat 7g, unsat 11g); PROTEIN 17g; CARB 39g; FIBER 10g; SUGARS 11g (added sugars 0g); SODIUM 593mg; CALC 27% DV; POTASSIUM 26% DV

TIP

For an oven option in Step 4, bake the filled squash halves in a preheated 425°F oven until the tops are lightly browned and the mixture is heated through, about 10 minutes.

MEATLESS MAINS

RATATOUILLE AND GOAT CHEESE TOASTS

HANDS-ON: 15 MINUTES   **TOTAL:** 4 HOURS, 15 MINUTES   **SERVES** 6

Ratatouille is a classic French dish made with a sundry of fresh vegetables including onion, bell pepper, garlic, eggplant, zucchini, and tomatoes. Our take on it includes these classic flavors and makes use of the slow cooker for a hands-free version.

3 tablespoons olive oil

1 large yellow onion, chopped (about 1½ cups)

1 red bell pepper, chopped (about 1 cup)

4 garlic cloves, minced (about 4 teaspoons)

5 cups ¾-inch-cubed peeled eggplant (about 11 ounces)

2 medium zucchini, halved lengthwise and cut into half-moon slices

1 (14.5-ounce) can diced fire-roasted tomatoes, undrained

1 cup no-salt-added tomato sauce (such as Pomi)

½ teaspoon kosher salt

½ teaspoon black pepper

6 (2-ounce) whole-grain rustic country-style bread slices

⅓ cup chopped fresh basil

3 ounces goat cheese, crumbled (about ¾ cup)

1 Heat 1½ tablespoons of the oil in a large skillet over medium. Add the onion and bell pepper, and cook, stirring often, 5 minutes. Add the garlic; cook, stirring occasionally, 2 minutes. Place the vegetable mixture in a 5- to 6-quart slow cooker. Add the eggplant, zucchini, tomatoes, tomato sauce, salt, and pepper, and stir gently to combine. Cover and cook on LOW until the eggplant is tender, about 4 hours.

2 Preheat the oven to 450°F. Brush the bread slices with the remaining 1½ tablespoons oil; place on a baking sheet. Bake in the preheated oven until lightly toasted, about 5 minutes.

3 Cut each bread slice in half diagonally; divide the pieces among 6 plates. Top with the ratatouille mixture. Sprinkle evenly with the basil and goat cheese.

(SERVING SIZE: 2 toast pieces, 1 cup ratatouille): CALORIES 343; FAT 14g (sat 4g, unsat 8g); PROTEIN 12g; CARB 43g; FIBER 7g; SUGARS 14g (added sugars 0g); SODIUM 583mg; CALC 17% DV; POTASSIUM 16% DV

MULTICOOKER DIRECTIONS

IN STEP 1, remove the lid of a 6-quart multicooker. Press SAUTÉ [Normal]. Add 1½ tablespoons of the oil to the inner pot; heat until the oil is hot, swirling to coat the bottom of the pot. Add the onion and bell pepper, and cook, stirring often, 5 minutes. Add the garlic; cook, stirring occasionally, about 2 minutes. Turn off the cooker. Add the eggplant, zucchini, tomatoes, tomato sauce, salt, and pepper, and stir gently to combine. Lock the lid; turn Pressure Valve to "Venting." Cook on SLOW COOK [Normal] until the eggplant is tender, about 4 hours. **COMPLETE STEPS 2 AND 3.**

EGGPLANT-AND-WHITE BEAN RAGOUT

HANDS-ON: 25 MINUTES **TOTAL:** 5 HOURS, 35 MINUTES **SERVES** 4

Hearty and filling, this is vegetarian comfort food. Tossing the eggplant with salt draws out excess moisture from the vegetable, making it less bitter and more firm upon cooking. To make this recipe gluten free, sub rice or gluten-free pasta for the couscous. Garnish with additional chopped flat-leaf parsley or basil, if desired.

1 (1½-pound) eggplant, peeled and cut into
  ¾-inch cubes
1¼ teaspoons kosher salt
1 (8.5-ounce) jar sun-dried tomatoes in olive oil
3 garlic cloves, minced (about 1 tablespoon)
1 medium-sized yellow onion, minced (about
  1 cup)
1 medium-sized green bell pepper, chopped
  (about 1 cup)
2 (15.5-ounce) cans unsalted cannellini
  beans, drained and rinsed

½ cup unsalted vegetable stock
1 tablespoon unsalted tomato paste
2 teaspoons chopped fresh thyme
¼ teaspoon black pepper
2 tablespoons chopped fresh flat-leaf parsley
  or basil
1 tablespoon balsamic or red wine vinegar
3 cups hot cooked whole-wheat couscous
Crushed red pepper (optional)

1 Toss together the eggplant and ½ teaspoon of the salt, and let drain in a colander 10 minutes. Rinse; pat dry.

2 Drain the tomatoes, reserving the oil. Chop the tomatoes to equal ½ cup; reserve the remaining tomatoes for another use. Place 2 tablespoons of the oil from the tomatoes in a large nonstick skillet, and heat over medium-high. Add the eggplant, and cook, stirring often, until browned on all sides, about 5 minutes. Add the garlic, onion, and bell pepper, and cook, stirring often, 2 minutes.

3 Place the eggplant mixture in a 5- to 6-quart slow cooker. Add the ½ cup chopped tomatoes, beans, stock, tomato paste, thyme, black pepper, and remaining ¾ teaspoon salt, and stir to combine. Cover and cook on LOW until the eggplant is very tender, about 5 hours. Turn off the slow cooker, and stir in the parsley and vinegar. Divide the couscous among 4 plates. Serve the ragout over the couscous. Sprinkle with the crushed red pepper, if desired.

(SERVING SIZE: ¾ cup couscous, 1¼ cups ragout): CALORIES 498; FAT 11g (sat 1g, unsat 9g); PROTEIN 20g; CARB 85g; FIBER 20g; SUGARS 11g (added sugars 0g); SODIUM 524mg; CALC 12% DV; POTASSIUM 32% DV

MULTICOOKER DIRECTIONS

COMPLETE STEPS 1 AND 2. IN STEP 3, place the eggplant mixture in the inner pot of a 6-quart multicooker. Stir in the ½ cup chopped tomatoes, beans, stock, tomato paste, thyme, black pepper, and remaining ¾ teaspoon salt. Lock the lid; turn Pressure Valve to "Venting." Cook on SLOW COOK [Normal] until the eggplant is very tender, about 5 hours. Turn off the cooker. Stir in the parsley and vinegar. **FINISH STEP 3.**

TORTELLINI WITH CREAMY BUTTERNUT SAUCE

HANDS-ON: 15 MINUTES   **TOTAL:** 4 HOURS, 40 MINUTES   **SERVES** 4

Butternut sauce is an innovative alternative to traditional tomato sauce for pasta-based recipes. This sauce is smooth and rich with complex flavors from the squash, onion, garlic, tomatoes, and wine. The half-and-half makes it extra creamy.

1 tablespoon olive oil

1 yellow onion (about 8 ounces), chopped

3 garlic cloves, minced (about 1 tablespoon)

3 cups peeled, cubed butternut squash (about 14 ounces)

1 cup San Marzano chopped tomatoes (from carton) (such as Pomi)

1½ cups unsalted vegetable stock

½ cup dry white wine

2 teaspoons chopped fresh rosemary

¼ teaspoon kosher salt

¼ teaspoon black pepper

¼ teaspoon crushed red pepper

1 fresh basil sprig, plus torn leaves for garnish

¼ cup half-and-half

1 (9-ounce) package refrigerated whole-wheat cheese tortellini

1 ounce Parmesan cheese, shaved (about ¼ cup)

1 Heat the oil in a skillet over medium-high. Add the onion, and cook, stirring often, until just beginning to soften, about 3 minutes. Add the garlic; cook, stirring occasionally, 2 minutes.

2 Stir together the onion mixture, squash, tomatoes, stock, wine, rosemary, salt, black pepper, red pepper, and basil sprig in a 5- to 6-quart slow cooker. Cover and cook on LOW until the squash is tender, 4 to 5 hours.

3 Add the half-and-half to the slow cooker, stirring to combine. Using an immersion blender (or food processor in batches), process the squash mixture until smooth. Add the tortellini to the slow cooker; cover and cook until the tortellini is tender, about 25 minutes. Sprinkle the servings evenly with the shaved Parmesan, and garnish with the torn basil.

(SERVING SIZE: about 1½ cups): CALORIES 364; FAT 12g (sat 4g, unsat 7g); PROTEIN 15g; CARB 50g; FIBER 6g; SUGARS 10g (added sugars 0g); SODIUM 591mg; CALC 25% DV; POTASSIUM 13% DV

MULTICOOKER DIRECTIONS

IN STEP 1, remove the lid of a 6-quart multicooker. Place the oil in the inner pot. Press SAUTÉ [Normal], and heat, swirling to coat the bottom of the pot. Add the onion, and cook uncovered, stirring often, until just beginning to soften, about 3 minutes. Add the garlic; cook, stirring occasionally, about 2 minutes. Turn off the cooker. **IN STEP 2,** stir in the squash, tomatoes, stock, wine, rosemary, salt, black pepper, red pepper, and basil sprig. Lock the lid; turn Pressure Valve to "Venting." Cook on SLOW COOK [Normal] until the squash is tender, about 5 hours. **IN STEP 3,** add the tortellini to the puréed squash mixture in the pot. Lock the lid; turn Pressure Valve to "Venting." Cook on SLOW COOK [Normal] until the tortellini is tender. **FINISH STEP 3.**

SUMMER MARINARA OVER LINGUINE

HANDS-ON: 10 MINUTES **TOTAL:** 5 HOURS, 40 MINUTES **SERVES** 6

This marinara is a fantastic way to incorporate vegetables into a meal. Not only will adults love it but kids will, too! You can easily make it on a weekend, and reheat for a quick Monday night meal.

1 tablespoon olive oil

1½ cups chopped yellow onions (from 1 large onion)

½ cup diced celery (from 1 celery stalk)

1 (26.46-ounce) carton San Marzano chopped tomatoes (such as Pomi)

1 (8-ounce) container sliced fresh cremini mushrooms

1 (6-ounce) can no-salt-added tomato paste

1 cup strained San Marzano tomatoes or tomato sauce (such as Pomi)

½ cup dry red wine

1 large zucchini (about 10½ ounces), halved lengthwise and cut into half-moon slices

4 garlic cloves, minced (about 4 teaspoons)

1 tablespoon chopped fresh oregano

1 teaspoon kosher salt

1 (12-ounce) package whole-wheat linguine, cooked according to package directions and kept hot

3 ounces Parmesan cheese, grated (about ¾ cup)

½ cup fresh basil leaves

1 Heat the oil in a large nonstick skillet over medium-high. Add the onions and celery, and cook, stirring often, until the vegetables are just tender, about 6 minutes. Transfer the vegetable mixture to a 5- to 6-quart slow cooker.

2 Add the chopped tomatoes, mushrooms, tomato paste, strained tomatoes, wine, zucchini, garlic, oregano, and salt to the slow cooker; stir well. Cover and cook on LOW until the mixture has thickened, about 5 hours and 30 minutes. Divide the cooked linguine evenly among 6 plates; top evenly with the marinara sauce, cheese, and basil.

(SERVING SIZE: about 1⅓ cups): CALORIES 360; FAT 7g (sat 2g, unsat 4g); PROTEIN 16g; CARB 64g; FIBER 11g; SUGARS 14g (added sugars 0g); SODIUM 543mg; CALC 15% DV; POTASSIUM 28% DV

MULTICOOKER DIRECTIONS

IN STEP 1, remove the lid of a 6-quart multicooker. Place the oil in the inner pot. Press SAUTÉ [Normal], and heat, swirling to coat the bottom of the pot. Add the onions and celery, and cook uncovered, stirring often, until the vegetables are just tender, about 6 minutes. Turn off the cooker. **IN STEP 2,** add the chopped tomatoes, mushrooms, tomato paste, strained tomatoes, wine, zucchini, garlic, oregano, and salt to the pot; stir well. Lock the lid; turn Pressure Valve to "Venting." Cook on SLOW COOK [Normal] until the mixture has thickened, about 5 hours and 30 minutes. **FINISH STEP 2.**

MUSHROOM SAUCE OVER EGG NOODLES

HANDS-ON: 30 MINUTES **TOTAL:** 6 HOURS, 30 MINUTES **SERVES** 6

You won't miss the meat in this dish. The mushrooms make the sauce filling enough to satisfy even the hungriest at your table. Serve with red wine and a hunk of crusty bread or a simple green salad, and an easy meal is at your fingertips.

3 tablespoons olive oil

1 large yellow onion, chopped (about 1½ cups)

½ cup chopped celery (from 1 celery stalk)

½ cup chopped carrots (from 2 carrots)

1 pound sliced cremini mushrooms

12 ounces portobello mushrooms, sliced

1 (14.5-ounce) can diced fire-roasted tomatoes, drained

¾ cup tomato sauce (such as Pomi)

2 teaspoons chopped fresh rosemary or thyme

½ teaspoon kosher salt

½ teaspoon black pepper

¼ cup dry red wine

1 tablespoon lower-sodium soy sauce

1 (8-ounce) package whole-grain extra-broad egg noodles

1 ounce Parmesan cheese, grated (about ¼ cup)

Chopped fresh flat-leaf parsley (optional)

1 Heat 2 tablespoons of the oil in a large skillet over medium-high. Add the onion, celery, and carrots to the skillet; cook, stirring constantly, until the mixture begins to brown, about 5 minutes. Place the onion mixture in a 5- to 6-quart slow cooker.

2 Heat the remaining 1 tablespoon oil in the skillet over medium-high. Add the mushrooms; cook, stirring constantly, until tender, about 8 minutes.

3 Transfer the mushroom mixture to a food processor, and pulse until coarsely chopped, about 5 times. Add the mushrooms, tomatoes, tomato sauce, rosemary, salt, and pepper to the slow cooker. Stir in the wine and soy sauce. Cover and cook on LOW until the mixture has slightly thickened, about 6 hours.

4 Meanwhile, cook the egg noodles according to the package directions. Serve the mushroom sauce over the hot noodles. Sprinkle each serving with the cheese. Garnish with the parsley, if desired.

(SERVING SIZE: about 1½ cups mushroom sauce, 1 cup noodles, 2 teaspoons cheese): **CALORIES** 282; **FAT** 9g (sat 2g, unsat 6g); **PROTEIN** 11g; **CARB** 43g; **FIBER** 7g; **SUGARS** 9g (added sugars 0g); **SODIUM** 675mg; **CALC** 9% DV; **POTASSIUM** 22% DV

MULTICOOKER DIRECTIONS

PREPARE STEP 1, placing the cooked onion mixture in the inner pot of a 6-quart multicooker. **COMPLETE STEP 2. IN STEP 3,** add the coarsely chopped mushroom mixture, tomatoes, tomato sauce, rosemary, salt, and pepper to the pot. Stir in the wine and soy sauce. Lock the lid; turn Pressure Valve to "Venting." Cook on SLOW COOK [Normal] until the mixture has slightly thickened, about 6 hours. **COMPLETE STEP 4.**

SPINACH-MUSHROOM LASAGNA

HANDS-ON: 20 MINUTES **TOTAL:** 4 HOURS, 20 MINUTES **SERVES** 8

Cooking lasagna in your slow cooker rather than in the oven keeps it super moist and cheesy—just like lasagna should be. You can easily assemble this dish in the slow cooker ahead of time and refrigerate it. Just be sure to let the slow cooker come to room temperature before starting it so that the cook time is accurate. Serve with a green salad, if desired.

2 teaspoons olive oil
1 yellow onion, chopped (about 1 cup)
1 (8-ounce) package sliced fresh mushrooms
2 garlic cloves, minced (about 2 teaspoons)
4 cups torn baby spinach (about 4 ounces)
¼ teaspoon fine sea salt
¼ teaspoon black pepper
3 cups cabernet marinara or tomato-and-basil marinara (such as Muir Glen)
1 cup no-salt-added tomato sauce (such as Pomi)
4 ounces part-skim ricotta cheese (about ¼ cup)

¼ cup chopped fresh basil
1 large egg, beaten
8 ounces preshredded Italian cheese blend (about 2 cups)
2 ounces Parmesan cheese, grated (about ½ cup)
Cooking spray
1 (8-ounce) package whole-wheat wavy lasagna noodles (about 9 noodles depending on brand)

1 Heat the oil in a large nonstick skillet over medium-high. Add the onion, and cook, stirring often, until just tender, about 5 minutes. Add the mushrooms and garlic; cook, stirring often, 2 minutes. Add the spinach; cook until the spinach just begins to wilt, about 1 minute. Remove from the heat. Sprinkle the vegetables with ⅛ teaspoon each of the salt and pepper. Add the marinara and tomato sauce, stirring to combine.

2 Stir together the ricotta, basil, egg, 1¼ cups of the Italian cheese blend, ¼ cup of the Parmesan, and the remaining ⅛ teaspoon each salt and pepper in a bowl.

3 Coat the inside of a 6-quart slow cooker with cooking spray. Spread 1 cup of the marinara mixture into the bottom of the slow cooker. Arrange 3 noodles over the marinara, breaking the noodles to fit the slow cooker as necessary. Top with half of the cheese mixture and 1 cup of the marinara mixture. Repeat the layers once, beginning with the noodles and ending with the marinara mixture. Place the remaining 3 noodles over the marinara. Spread the remaining marinara mixture over the noodles. Sprinkle with the remaining ¾ cup Italian cheese blend and ¼ cup Parmesan. Cover and cook on LOW until the noodles are tender, 4 to 5 hours.

(SERVING SIZE: 1½ cups): CALORIES 321; FAT 13g (sat 6g, unsat 6g); PROTEIN 18g; CARB 39g; FIBER 6g; SUGARS 7g (added sugars 0g); SODIUM 607mg; CALC 36% DV; POTASSIUM 9% DV

SPRING VEGGIE POT PIE

HANDS-ON: 20 MINUTES   **TOTAL:** 4 HOURS, 25 MINUTES   **SERVES** 6

You'll reach for this recipe on early spring days for warmth and satisfaction.

2 tablespoons, plus 2 teaspoons olive oil

2 (8-ounce) packages sliced cremini mushrooms

8 ounces red potatoes, cut into 1- to 1½-inch cubes

1 cup sliced leek (from 1 leek)

1 cup diagonally-sliced carrots (from 2 carrots)

3 garlic cloves, minced (about 1 tablespoon)

1⅜ teaspoons kosher salt

Cooking spray

½ cup (about 2⅛ ounces), plus 3 tablespoons all-purpose flour

1½ cups unsalted vegetable stock

2 teaspoons chopped fresh thyme

¼ teaspoon black pepper

½ cup (about 1¾ ounces) whole-wheat pastry flour

1½ teaspoons baking powder

3 tablespoons chilled unsalted butter, cut into small pieces

1½ ounces sharp Cheddar cheese, shredded (about ⅓ cup)

2 tablespoons chopped fresh chives, plus more for garnish (optional)

¼ cup 1% low-fat milk

1 cup fresh or frozen (thawed) green peas

2 tablespoons half-and-half

1 Heat 2 teaspoons of the oil in a large nonstick skillet over medium-high. Add the mushrooms, potatoes, leek, and carrots; cook, stirring often, 5 minutes. Add the garlic; cook, stirring often, 1 minute. Sprinkle the vegetables with ¼ teaspoon of the salt. Coat a 6-quart slow cooker with cooking spray. Transfer the vegetable mixture to the slow cooker.

2 Heat the remaining 2 tablespoons oil in the skillet over medium-high; whisk in 3 tablespoons of the all-purpose flour. Cook 1 minute, whisking constantly. Reduce the heat to medium, and gradually whisk in the stock. Cook, whisking constantly, until thickened and bubbly, about 3 minutes. Stir in the thyme, pepper, and ⅞ teaspoon of the salt. Pour the sauce into the slow cooker; stir gently to combine. Cover; cook on LOW until the vegetables are tender, 3 to 4 hours.

3 Whisk together the pastry flour, baking powder, and remaining ½ cup all-purpose flour and ¼ teaspoon salt. Cut in the chilled butter with a pastry blender or 2 knives until the mixture resembles a coarse meal. Stir in the cheese and chives. Add the milk, stirring just until moistened.

4 Add the peas and half-and-half to the slow cooker; stir to combine. Increase the slow cooker heat to HIGH. Drop the biscuits onto the filling in 6 equal mounds. Cover and cook on HIGH until the biscuits are cooked through, about 1 hour. Uncover; let stand 5 minutes before serving. Garnish with the additional chopped chives, if desired.

(**SERVING SIZE:** 1 biscuit, ¾ cup filling): **CALORIES** 340; **FAT** 15g (sat 6g, unsat 8g); **PROTEIN** 10g; **CARB** 43g; **FIBER** 6g; **SUGARS** 7g (added sugars 0g); **SODIUM** 646mg; **CALC** 20% DV; **POTASSIUM** 22% DV

TIP

You can bake the biscuits in a 450°F oven instead. Place the biscuits on a baking sheet in a preheated oven, and bake until golden, 9 to 11 minutes. Serve the pot pie filling topped with the baked biscuits.

KALE-AND-GRUYÈRE STRATA WITH TOMATOES

HANDS-ON: 15 MINUTES **TOTAL:** 4 HOURS **SERVES** 8

For a lazy-morning breakfast or when hosting a brunch, make this easy recipe your game plan. Be sure to use crusty, freshly baked bread from the bakery section of your supermarket instead of a premade loaf from the bread aisle. Serve with seasonal fruit and juice to balance the richness of the egg and cheese.

½ tablespoon olive oil

1 medium-sized yellow onion, chopped (about 1 cup)

6 garlic cloves, minced (about 2 tablespoons)

Cooking spray

1 (1-pound) multigrain bread loaf, crusts removed, cut into 1-inch cubes

4 ounces chopped Tuscan kale (about 4 cups)

½ cup chopped, drained sun-dried tomatoes in olive oil

3 cups 2% reduced-fat milk

1 tablespoon Dijon mustard

½ teaspoon kosher salt

½ teaspoon black pepper

10 large eggs, well beaten

3 ounces Gruyère cheese, shredded (about ¾ cup)

1 Heat the oil in a medium skillet over medium. Add the onions, and cook, stirring often, until softened, about 6 minutes. Add the garlic; cook, stirring often, until fragrant, about 1 minute.

2 Lightly coat a 5- to-6-quart slow cooker with cooking spray. Toss together the onion mixture, bread, kale, and tomatoes in the slow cooker.

3 Whisk together the milk, Dijon, salt, pepper, and eggs in a large bowl. Pour into the slow cooker; press the bread mixture, submerging into the milk mixture. Top with the Gruyère. Place a clean, dry towel over the top of the slow cooker; cover with the lid. Cook on LOW until the strata reaches an internal temperature of 165°F, about 3 hours and 45 minutes.

(**SERVING SIZE:** about 1½ cups): **CALORIES** 316; **FAT** 14g (sat 5g, unsat 7g); **PROTEIN** 22g; **CARB** 29g; **FIBER** 6g; **SUGARS** 8g (added sugars 0g); **SODIUM** 565mg; **CALC** 37% DV; **POTASSIUM** 12% DV

NOTE

Gruyère cheese is a firm cheese with a pale yellow coloring. It's a type of Swiss cheese and has a rich, nutty flavor. It melts extremely well, making it perfect for soups, fondues, and baked goods.

SOUTH-OF-THE-BORDER SHAKSHUKA

HANDS-ON: 20 MINUTES **TOTAL:** 3 HOURS, 40 MINUTES **SERVES** 4

Start your day with hearty, slightly spicy shakshuka full of Southwestern flavor. To avoid one large egg blob on top, be sure to make wells in the sauce using a spoon. It's important to use corn tortillas and not flour tortillas if you're going gluten free. Lightly toast the tortillas, if desired (see the tip on page 129 for directions).

1 tablespoon olive oil
1 medium-sized yellow onion, chopped (about 1 cup)
1 large poblano chile, chopped (about 1 cup)
3 garlic cloves, minced (about 1 tablespoon)
1 (26.46-ounce) carton San Marzano chopped tomatoes (such as Pomi)
¼ cup water
1 teaspoon ground cumin

¼ teaspoon cayenne pepper
¾ teaspoon kosher salt
½ teaspoon black pepper
8 large eggs
1 ounce queso fresco (fresh Mexican cheese), crumbled (about ¼ cup)
2 tablespoons chopped fresh cilantro
4 (6-inch) corn tortillas, toasted

1 Heat the oil in a large skillet over medium. Add the onion and poblano; cook, stirring often, 5 minutes. Add the garlic; cook, stirring occasionally, 1 minute.

2 Place the onion mixture in a 6-quart slow cooker. Add the tomatoes, water, cumin, cayenne, ½ teaspoon of the salt, and ¼ teaspoon of the black pepper; stir well. Cover and cook on LOW until heated through, 3 to 4 hours.

3 Increase the heat to HIGH. Make 8 indentations in the sauce with the back of a spoon. Crack 1 egg into each indentation. Sprinkle the eggs with the remaining ¼ teaspoon each salt and pepper. Cover and cook on HIGH until the whites are set and the yolks are to the desired degree of doneness, about 20 minutes for slightly runny yolks. Divide the eggs and sauce among 4 plates. Sprinkle with the cheese and cilantro, and serve with the tortillas.

(SERVING SIZE: 2 eggs, ¾ cup sauce mixture, 1 tablespoon cheese, ½ tablespoon cilantro, 1 tortilla): **CALORIES** 317; **FAT** 16g (sat 5g, unsat 9g); **PROTEIN** 17g; **CARB** 27g; **FIBER** 6g; **SUGARS** 9g (added sugars 0g); **SODIUM** 571mg; **CALC** 11% DV; **POTASSIUM** 6% DV

NOTE

Many recipes in this book call specifically for San Marzano tomatoes. Here's why: These plum tomatoes are from the San Marzano region in Italy, where they're canned at their peak ripeness, giving them superior quality to typical canned tomatoes. We recommend the Pomi brand of San Marzano tomatoes because Pomi sells them in a carton, rather than a can, so the tomatoes don't taste metallic.

TOFU LO MEIN

HANDS-ON: 30 MINUTES **TOTAL:** 2 HOURS, 30 MINUTES **SERVES** 5

Crisp-tender veggies cooked in a sweet Asian sauce and served with noodles and tofu is a refreshingly different slow cooker dinner. Removing the excess moisture from the tofu helps it soak up the sauce, giving the unassuming ingredient full flavor.

1 yellow onion (about 8 ounces), thinly sliced
2 cups fresh broccoli florets (from 1 head broccoli)
1 cup diagonally sliced carrots (about 4½ ounces)
1 cup trimmed fresh snow peas (from 1 [8-ounce] package)
⅔ cup unsalted vegetable stock
¼ cup sliced scallions (from 2 scallions)

3 tablespoons lower-sodium soy sauce
3 tablespoons oyster sauce
2 tablespoons rice vinegar
1 tablespoon minced fresh ginger
1 tablespoon sesame oil
2 teaspoons honey
3 garlic cloves, minced (about 1 tablespoon)
8 ounces uncooked whole-wheat linguine
1 (14-ounce) package extra-firm tofu, drained

1 Place the onions, broccoli, carrots, and snow peas in a 4- to 5-quart slow cooker. Whisk together the stock, scallions, soy sauce, oyster sauce, vinegar, ginger, oil, honey, and garlic; pour over the vegetables in the slow cooker. Cover and cook on LOW until the vegetables are tender, 2 to 3 hours.

2 Meanwhile, cook the pasta to al dente according to the package directions. Drain well.

3 Place the tofu on several layers of paper towels; cover with additional paper towels. Press to absorb the excess moisture; cut into ½-inch cubes.

4 Add the tofu and the hot cooked linguine to the slow cooker, stirring to combine.

(SERVING SIZE: about 1¾ cups): **CALORIES** 306; **FAT** 8g (sat 1g, unsat 7g); **PROTEIN** 18g; **CARB** 46g; **FIBER** 7g; **SUGARS** 8g (added sugars 2g); **SODIUM** 698mg; **CALC** 12% DV; **POTASSIUM** 7% DV

NOTE

Tofu is soybean curds that have been compressed into blocks, making them easier to grill, fry, and bake. That may not sound impressive, but tofu's health benefits certainly are—the food is rich in protein and low in saturated fat. Moreover, tofu has a neutral flavor and easily absorbs the flavors of other foods, which makes it a versatile meat substitute in vegetarian dishes.

ASIAN TEMPEH WITH SPINACH AND MANGO

HANDS-ON: 10 MINUTES   **TOTAL:** 4 HOURS, 10 MINUTES   **SERVES** 4

Making a flavorful, well-balanced meatless dish doesn't get simpler than this. Sweet mango is the right complement to the earthy tempeh. A drizzle of the sweet and salty cooking liquid is the perfect addition of moisture and brightness.

⅓ cup water

¼ cup mirin

¼ cup fresh lime juice (from 3 limes)

2 tablespoons unseasoned rice vinegar

2 tablespoons honey

2 teaspoons Sriracha chili sauce

¾ teaspoon kosher salt

4 garlic cloves, smashed

1 (8-ounce) package tempeh

2 cups hot cooked brown rice

1 (5-ounce) package baby spinach

1½ tablespoons toasted sesame oil

1 medium-sized ripe mango, peeled and thinly sliced

1 Stir together the water, mirin, lime juice, vinegar, honey, Sriracha, salt, and garlic in a 5- to 6-quart slow cooker. Nestle the tempeh into the liquid; cover and cook on LOW until heated through, 4 hours.

2 Remove the tempeh with a slotted spoon, reserving ¼ cup of the cooking liquid. Cut the tempeh into 12 slices.

3 Divide the rice among 4 plates. Toss the spinach with the sesame oil, and place over the rice. Top with the tempeh slices and mango slices. Drizzle the reserved cooking liquid evenly over each serving.

(SERVING SIZE: ½ cup rice, 1½ cups spinach, 3 slices tempeh, about 6 slices mango, about 1 tablespoon cooking liquid): **CALORIES** 393; **FAT** 10g (sat 2g, unsat 7g); **PROTEIN** 16g; **CARB** 60g; **FIBER** 10g; **SUGARS** 22g (added sugars 9g); **SODIUM** 467mg; **CALC** 13% DV; **POTASSIUM** 13% DV

NOTE

Tempeh, like tofu, is made from soybeans and is a fantastic meat substitution, but that's where the two foods' similarities end. Tempeh is fermented soybeans that have been shaped into a thick rectangle. It doesn't crumble easily, like tofu does, and it has a nutty flavor.

EDAMAME SUCCOTASH

HANDS-ON: 20 MINUTES **TOTAL:** 4 HOURS, 25 MINUTES **SERVES** 4

Vegetables and edamame (soybeans) crown a bed of whole-wheat couscous for a hearty, healthy meal. You can use fresh-shelled edamame and fresh corn, but using the frozen varieties saves time and produces the same delicious results.

1 tablespoon olive oil
1 yellow onion (about 8 ounces), chopped
1 red bell pepper (about 8 ounces), chopped
1 (8-ounce) package frozen shelled edamame
1½ cups fresh or frozen yellow corn kernels (from 2 ears)
1 cup unsalted vegetable stock
¼ teaspoon black pepper

1 cup chopped ripe tomato (from 1 tomato)
2 tablespoons chopped fresh dill, plus more for garnish
1 tablespoon red wine vinegar
2 cups water
1 teaspoon kosher salt
1 cup uncooked whole-wheat couscous

1 Heat the oil in a large skillet over medium-high. Add the onion and bell pepper; cook, stirring often, 4 minutes. Combine the onion mixture, edamame, corn, stock, and pepper in a 5- to 6-quart slow cooker. Cover and cook on LOW until the vegetables are tender and the flavors blend, 4 to 5 hours.

2 Add the tomato, dill, and vinegar to the slow cooker, stirring gently.

3 Bring the water and ¼ teaspoon of the salt to a boil in a small saucepan; stir in the couscous. Remove from the heat; cover and let stand 5 minutes. Fluff with a fork. Sprinkle the edamame mixture with the remaining ¾ teaspoon salt. Divide the couscous among 4 plates. Using a slotted spoon, serve the edamame mixture over the couscous. Garnish with the additional dill, if desired.

(SERVING SIZE: 1 cup couscous, about ¾ cup edamame mixture): **CALORIES** 351; **FAT** 8g (sat 1g, unsat 6g); **PROTEIN** 16g; **CARB** 61g; **FIBER** 12g; **SUGARS** 9g (added sugars 0g); **SODIUM** 549mg; **CALC** 7% DV; **POTASSIUM** 10% DV

MULTICOOKER DIRECTIONS

IN STEP 1, remove the lid of a 6-quart multicooker. Place the oil in the inner pot. Press SAUTÉ [Normal], and heat, swirling to coat the bottom of the pot. Add the onion and bell pepper; cook uncovered, stirring often, 4 minutes. Turn off the cooker. Stir in the edamame, corn, stock, and pepper. Lock the lid; turn Pressure Valve to "Venting." Cook on SLOW COOK [Normal] until the vegetables are tender and the flavors blend, about 5 hours. **COMPLETE STEPS 2 AND 3.**

EDAMAME-RICE BOWL WITH CHERRIES AND PECANS

HANDS-ON: 10 MINUTES **TOTAL:** 3 HOURS, 55 MINUTES **SERVES** 6

With wild and brown rice, edamame, dried cherries, and pecans, this dish boasts varied textures as well as an abundance of nutrients. Wild rice is rich in fiber and protein while brown rice is high in manganese, which helps the body digest fats. Cherries are packed with antioxidants, while pecans are loaded with healthy unsaturated fat.

1 cup uncooked wild rice
¾ cup uncooked brown rice
1 tablespoon unsalted butter, melted
Cooking spray
3¾ cups unsalted vegetable stock
1 cup chopped yellow onions (from 1 onion)
1 (8-ounce) package frozen shelled edamame

1 teaspoon kosher salt
½ cup dried cherries (about 2½ ounces), chopped
½ cup chopped pecans, toasted
1 tablespoon red wine vinegar
Fresh flat-leaf parsley leaves (optional)

1 Stir together the rice and butter in a 5- to 6-quart slow cooker coated with cooking spray, stirring until the rice is evenly coated. Stir in the stock, onions, edamame, and ¾ teaspoon of the salt.

2 Cover and cook on HIGH until the rice is tender, 3 hours and 30 minutes to 4 hours. Stir in the cherries; turn off the heat, cover, and let stand 15 minutes.

3 Stir the pecans, vinegar, and remaining ¼ teaspoon salt into the rice just before serving. Garnish with the parsley, if desired.

(SERVING SIZE: 1⅛ cups): CALORIES 381; FAT 12g (sat 2g, unsat 8g); PROTEIN 12g; CARB 61g; FIBER 7g; SUGARS 13g (added sugars 0g); SODIUM 459mg; CALC 5% DV; POTASSIUM 7% DV

MULTICOOKER DIRECTIONS

IN STEP 1, stir together the rice and butter in the inner pot of a 6-quart multicooker coated with cooking spray, stirring until the rice is evenly coated. Stir in the stock, onion, edamame, and ¾ teaspoon of the salt. **IN STEP 2,** lock the lid; turn Pressure Valve to "Venting." Cook on SLOW COOK [More] until the rice is tender, about 4 hours. Stir in the cherries; turn off the cooker. Cover with the lid, and let stand 15 minutes. **COMPLETE STEP 3.**

COCONUT-CHICKPEA CURRY

HANDS-ON: 15 MINUTES   **TOTAL:** 6 HOURS, 15 MINUTES   **SERVES** 6

Make this healthy dish for a sick friend or a family after the birth of their child. If the recipients are vegetarian or avoid gluten, you'll be set—and even if they don't have food restrictions, they'll love this dish for its satisfying flavor.

2 teaspoons canola oil

1½ cups chopped yellow onions (from 1 large onion)

2 garlic cloves, minced (about 2 teaspoons)

2 (15.5-ounce) cans no-salt-added chickpeas (garbanzo beans), drained and rinsed

2 (14.5-ounce) cans no-salt-added fire-roasted diced tomatoes, undrained

1 (13.5-ounce) can light coconut milk, well shaken and stirred

2 tablespoons red curry paste

¾ teaspoon kosher salt

½ cup chopped fresh cilantro

3 cups hot cooked brown basmati rice

Fresh cilantro leaves (optional)

1 Heat the oil in a large nonstick skillet over medium. Add the onions and garlic; cook, stirring often, until the onions are tender, about 5 minutes.

2 Stir together the onion mixture, chickpeas, tomatoes, coconut milk, curry paste, and salt in a 3½-quart slow cooker; stir well. Cover and cook on LOW until the flavors blend, about 6 hours. Stir in the cilantro, and serve over the rice. Garnish with the cilantro leaves, if desired.

(SERVING SIZE: ½ cup rice, 1 cup curry mixture): **CALORIES** 350; **FAT** 6g (sat 2g, unsat 3g); **PROTEIN** 12g; **CARB** 58g; **FIBER** 10g; **SUGARS** 7g (added sugars 0g); **SODIUM** 649mg; **CALC** 13% DV; **POTASSIUM** 11% DV

MULTICOOKER DIRECTIONS

IN STEP 1, remove the lid of a 6-quart multicooker. Place the oil in the inner pot. Press SAUTÉ [Normal], and heat the oil, swirling to coat the bottom of the pot. Add the onions and garlic; cook uncovered, stirring often, until the onions are tender, about 5 minutes. Turn off the cooker. **IN STEP 2,** stir in the chickpeas, tomatoes, coconut milk, curry paste, and salt. Lock the lid; turn Pressure Valve to "Venting." Cook on SLOW COOK [Normal] until the flavors blend, about 6 hours. **FINISH STEP 2.**

MEDITERRANEAN QUINOA WITH ARUGULA

HANDS-ON: 15 MINUTES **TOTAL:** 3 HOURS, 25 MINUTES **SERVES** 6

Chock-full of quinoa, chickpeas, and vegetables, this salad is a meal in itself. The roasted red peppers, lemon, olives, and feta add familiar Mediterranean flavor. If you want to provide a meat option, serve with grilled chicken.

2¼ cups unsalted vegetable stock

1½ cups uncooked quinoa, rinsed

1 cup sliced red onions (from 1 onion)

2 garlic cloves, minced (about 2 teaspoons)

1 (15.5-ounce) can no-salt-added chickpeas (garbanzo beans), drained and rinsed

2½ tablespoons olive oil

¾ teaspoon kosher salt

2 teaspoons fresh lemon juice (from 1 lemon)

½ cup drained, chopped roasted red bell peppers (from jar)

4 cups baby arugula (about 4 ounces)

2 ounces feta cheese, crumbled (about ½ cup)

12 pitted kalamata olives, halved lengthwise

2 tablespoons coarsely chopped fresh oregano

1 Stir together the stock, quinoa, onions, garlic, chickpeas, 1½ teaspoons of the olive oil, and ½ teaspoon of the salt in a 5- to 6-quart slow cooker. Cover and cook on LOW until the quinoa is tender and the stock is absorbed, 3 to 4 hours.

2 Turn off the slow cooker. Fluff the quinoa mixture with a fork. Whisk together the lemon juice and remaining 2 tablespoons olive oil and ¼ teaspoon salt. Add the olive oil mixture and red bell peppers to the slow cooker; toss gently to combine. Gently fold in the arugula. Cover and let stand until the arugula is slightly wilted, about 10 minutes. Sprinkle each serving evenly with the feta cheese, olives, and oregano.

(SERVING SIZE: about 1½ cups): **CALORIES** 352; **FAT** 13g (sat 3g, unsat 9g); **PROTEIN** 12g; **CARB** 46g; **FIBER** 7g; **SUGARS** 5g (added sugars 0g); **SODIUM** 575mg; **CALC** 14% DV; **POTASSIUM** 13% DV

MULTICOOKER DIRECTIONS

IN STEP 1, stir together the stock, quinoa, onions, garlic, chickpeas, 1½ teaspoons of the olive oil, and ½ teaspoon of the salt in the inner pot of a 6-quart multicooker. Lock the lid; turn Pressure Valve to "Venting." Cook on SLOW COOK [Normal] until the quinoa is tender and the stock is absorbed, about 4 hours. **IN STEP 2,** turn off the cooker. **FINISH STEP 2.**

SOUTHWEST QUINOA BOWLS

HANDS-ON: 20 MINUTES   **TOTAL:** 4 HOURS, 30 MINUTES   **SERVES** 6

This taco-bowl–style recipe will be a hit with both adults and children. The 10-minute sit time allows the cheese to melt into the quinoa, making this dish super decadent. If you cannot find Cheddar-Jack cheese, use Monterey Jack or sharp Cheddar. Garnish with fresh cilantro leaves, lime wedges, and additional cheese, if desired.

1 tablespoon olive oil
1 yellow onion (about 8 ounces), chopped
1 red bell pepper (about 8 ounces), chopped
3 garlic cloves, minced (about 1 tablespoon)
1 teaspoon ground cumin
1 teaspoon ancho chile powder
1 (15-ounce) can no-salt-added black beans, drained and rinsed
1 (14.5-ounce) can fire-roasted diced tomatoes

2 cups water
1 cup fresh or frozen corn kernels (from 1 ear)
1 cup uncooked quinoa, rinsed
¾ teaspoon kosher salt
¼ cup chopped fresh cilantro
4 ounces Cheddar-Jack cheese blend, shredded (about 1 cup)
1 ripe avocado, cubed

1 Heat the oil in a large skillet over medium-high. Add the onions and bell pepper; cook, stirring often, until just tender, 4 to 5 minutes. Add the garlic, cumin, and chile powder; cook, stirring often, 1 minute. Stir together the onion mixture, black beans, tomatoes, water, corn, quinoa, and salt in a 6-quart slow cooker. Cover and cook on LOW until the quinoa is tender and the liquid is almost absorbed, 4 to 5 hours.

2 Add the cilantro to the slow cooker, stirring gently to combine. Sprinkle the cheese over the quinoa mixture; cover and let stand until the cheese is melted, about 10 minutes. Divide the mixture among 6 bowls; top evenly with the avocado.

(**SERVING SIZE:** about 1 cup): **CALORIES** 364; **FAT** 16g (sat 5g, unsat 9g); **PROTEIN** 15g; **CARB** 44g; **FIBER** 10g; **SUGARS** 7g (added sugars 0g); **SODIUM** 536mg; **CALC** 21% DV; **POTASSIUM** 18% DV

MULTICOOKER DIRECTIONS

IN STEP 1, remove the lid of a 6-quart multicooker. Place the oil in the inner pot. Press SAUTÉ [Normal], and heat, swirling to coat the bottom of the pot. Add the onions, bell pepper, garlic, cumin, and chile powder; cook uncovered, stirring often, 1 minute. Stir in the black beans, tomatoes, water, corn, quinoa, and salt. Lock the lid; turn Pressure Valve to "Venting." Cook on SLOW COOK [Normal] until the quinoa is tender and the liquid is almost absorbed, about 5 hours. **IN STEP 2,** gently stir in the cilantro. Turn off the cooker. Sprinkle the cheese over the quinoa mixture; replace the lid, and let stand until the cheese melts, about 10 minutes. **FINISH STEP 2.**

MEATLESS MAINS

TANDOORI RICE BOWL

HANDS-ON: 15 MINUTES **TOTAL:** 4 HOURS, 15 MINUTES **SERVES** 4

Using the chickpeas both in and on top of this rice bowl is a great way to stretch the ingredient; they cook and become soft in the slow cooker and also act as a toothsome topping. Don't skip the yogurt sauce—it adds the perfect cooling finish for the hot spices. Garnish with additional chopped fresh cilantro, if desired. To make this recipe gluten free, use gluten-free garam masala.

1 (14.5-ounce) can fire-roasted diced
   tomatoes
1¾ cups unsalted vegetable stock
1 cup uncooked brown rice
1 tablespoon olive oil
1 tablespoon garam masala
2 teaspoons grated fresh ginger
2 garlic cloves, minced (about 2 teaspoons)
1 (15-ounce) can no-salt-added chickpeas
   (garbanzo beans), drained and rinsed

¾ teaspoon kosher salt
⅓ cup chopped fresh cilantro
½ cup plain whole-milk Greek yogurt
1 tablespoon water
2 teaspoons fresh lime juice (from 1 lime)
½ teaspoon ground cumin
1 cup sliced cucumber (from 1 medium
   cucumber)

1 Stir together the tomatoes, stock, rice, olive oil, garam masala, ginger, garlic, half of the chickpeas, and ⅝ teaspoon of the salt in a 5- to 6-quart slow cooker. Cover and cook on LOW until the rice is tender and most of the liquid is absorbed, 4 to 5 hours.

2 Stir in the cilantro. Stir together the yogurt, water, lime juice, cumin, and remaining ⅛ teaspoon salt in a bowl. Divide the rice mixture evenly among 4 bowls. Top each serving evenly with the cucumber, remaining half of the chickpeas, and the yogurt sauce.

(SERVING SIZE: 1¼ cups): CALORIES 389; FAT 7g (sat 2g, unsat 5g); PROTEIN 13g; CARB 65g; FIBER 8g; SUGARS 8g (added sugars 0g); SODIUM 721mg; CALC 12% DV; POTASSIUM 12% DV

MULTICOOKER DIRECTIONS

IN STEP 1, stir together the tomatoes, stock, rice, olive oil, garam masala, ginger, garlic, half of the chickpeas, and ⅝ teaspoon of the salt in the inner pot of a 6-quart multicooker. Lock the lid; turn Pressure Valve to "Venting." Cook on SLOW COOK [Normal] until the rice is tender and most of the liquid is absorbed, about 5 hours. **COMPLETE STEP 2.**

CHEESY RICE WITH BROCCOLI

HANDS-ON: 20 MINUTES **TOTAL:** 4 HOURS, 40 MINUTES **SERVES** 6

This dish is sure to be a kid favorite that adults will crave, too. Broccoli and cheese is a classic pairing for a reason, and when served with rice and umami-rich mushrooms, the combo is even more comforting. Garnish with shaved Parmesan and additional kosher salt and black pepper, if desired.

1 tablespoon unsalted butter

1 (8-ounce) package sliced white mushrooms

1 cup chopped yellow onions (from 1 onion)

1½ cups uncooked brown rice

2 garlic cloves, minced (about 2 teaspoons)

3½ cups unsalted vegetable stock

¾ teaspoon kosher salt

¼ teaspoon black pepper

3 cups fresh broccoli florets (about 8 ounces), cut into smaller pieces

¼ cup whole milk

4 ounces sharp white Cheddar cheese, shredded (about 1 cup)

1½ ounces Parmesan cheese, grated (about ⅓ cup)

Chopped fresh flat-leaf parsley (optional)

1 Heat the butter in a large nonstick skillet over medium-high. Add the mushrooms and onions, and cook, stirring often, until softened and lightly browned, about 5 minutes. Add the rice and garlic; cook, stirring often, until toasted and fragrant, about 2 minutes. Transfer the vegetable mixture to a 5- to 6-quart slow cooker. Add the stock, salt, and pepper, stirring to combine. Cover and cook on LOW until the rice is almost tender, 3 hours and 30 minutes to 4 hours. Stir in the broccoli and milk; cover and cook until the broccoli and rice are tender, about 40 more minutes.

2 Turn off the slow cooker; add the cheeses, stirring to combine. Cover and let stand until the cheese is melted, about 10 minutes. Garnish with the parsley, if desired.

(SERVING SIZE: about 1¼ cups): CALORIES 437; FAT 11g (sat 6g, unsat 4g); PROTEIN 12g; CARB 49g; FIBER 5g; SUGARS 5g (added sugars 0g); SODIUM 584mg; CALC 23% DV; POTASSIUM 13% DV

MULTICOOKER DIRECTIONS

IN STEP 1, remove the lid of a 6-quart multicooker. Place the butter in the inner pot. Press SAUTÉ [Normal], and heat until melted, swirling to coat the bottom of the pot. Add the mushrooms and onions; cook uncovered, stirring often, until softened and lightly browned, about 5 minutes. Add the rice and garlic; cook uncovered, stirring often, until toasted and fragrant, about 2 minutes. Stir in the stock, salt, and pepper. Turn off the cooker. Lock the lid; turn Pressure Valve to "Venting." Cook on SLOW COOK [Normal] until the rice is almost tender, about 4 hours. Stir in the broccoli and milk. Lock the lid, ensuring that the Pressure Valve is turned to "Venting." Cook on SLOW COOK [Normal] until the broccoli and rice are tender, about 40 more minutes. **COMPLETE STEP 2.**

BARLEY RISOTTO WITH BUTTERNUT SQUASH

HANDS-ON: 30 MINUTES **TOTAL:** 4 HOURS, 30 MINUTES **SERVES** 6

It's hard to believe this filling dish that's full of rich flavor is also good for you! This recipe creatively combines "melted" butternut squash with tender cooked barley for an ultra-creamy, ultra-comforting risotto.

1 teaspoon olive oil

1 yellow onion (about 8 ounces), chopped

2 (8-ounce) packages sliced fresh cremini mushrooms

1½ cups uncooked whole-grain hulled barley (not pearled; about 10½ ounces)

1 fresh sage sprig, plus 3 tablespoons fresh leaves

Cooking spray

4 cups unsalted vegetable stock

⅞ teaspoon kosher salt

½ teaspoon black pepper

½ teaspoon granulated sugar

4 cups peeled and chopped butternut squash (about 20 ounces)

⅓ cup heavy cream

1½ teaspoons sherry vinegar

1½ ounces Parmesan cheese, grated (about ⅓ cup)

1 Heat the oil in a large skillet over medium-high. Add the onions, and cook, stirring often, until the onions just begin to soften, about 5 minutes. Add the mushrooms to the skillet; cook, stirring often, until the liquid evaporates, about 8 minutes. Add the barley and sage sprig to the skillet; cook, stirring often, 1 minute.

2 Coat a 5- to 6-quart slow cooker with cooking spray. Stir together the barley mixture, stock, salt, pepper, and sugar in the slow cooker; stir to combine. Sprinkle the squash over the top. Cover and cook on HIGH until the barley and squash are tender, about 4 to 5 hours. Remove the sage sprig.

3 Using the back of a spoon, mash the butternut squash cubes into the risotto until smooth. Stir in the heavy cream and vinegar until incorporated. Sprinkle the servings evenly with the cheese and sage leaves.

(SERVING SIZE: 1⅓ cups): CALORIES 335; FAT 9g (sat 4g, unsat 4g); PROTEIN 13g; CARB 54g; FIBER 11g; SUGARS 5g (added sugars 0g); SODIUM 555mg; CALC 18% DV; POTASSIUM 21% DV

MULTICOOKER DIRECTIONS

COMPLETE STEP 1. IN STEP 2, coat the inner pot of a 6-quart multicooker with cooking spray. Stir together the barley mixture, stock, salt, pepper, and sugar in the pot. Sprinkle the squash over the top. Lock the lid; turn Pressure Valve to "Venting." Cook on SLOW COOK [More] until the barley and squash are tender, about 5 hours. Turn off the cooker. Remove the sage sprig. **COMPLETE STEP 3.**

PARMESAN-PEA FARRO WITH FENNEL SALAD

HANDS-ON: 25 MINUTES **TOTAL:** 3 HOURS, 5 MINUTES **SERVES** 5

This is reminiscent of a farroto, where risotto-like textures and Parmesan-rich flavor reign supreme. The yogurt adds lusciousness and tang that balances the overall savoriness of the dish. The fennel salad is bright and crisp.

1 tablespoon unsalted butter
1½ cups sliced leek (from 1 leek)
1½ cups uncooked farro
⅓ cup dry white wine
2 garlic cloves, minced (about 2 teaspoons)
4 cups unsalted vegetable stock
1 (2- to 3-inch) Parmesan cheese rind
1 fresh thyme sprig
¾ teaspoon kosher salt

1½ cups fresh or frozen, thawed green peas
⅓ cup 2% reduced-fat plain Greek yogurt
1 ounce grated Parmesan cheese (about ¼ cup)
¼ teaspoon black pepper
1 fennel bulb
½ teaspoon lemon zest plus 1 tablespoon fresh juice (from 1 lemon)
1 tablespoon olive oil

1 Heat the butter in a large nonstick skillet over medium-high. Add the leek, farro, wine, and garlic, and cook, stirring often, 2 to 3 minutes. Transfer the farro mixture to a 5- to 6-quart slow cooker. Stir in the stock, cheese rind, thyme sprig, and ½ teaspoon of the salt.

2 Cover and cook on LOW until the farro is tender and the liquid is almost absorbed, about 2 hours and 30 minutes.

3 Turn off the slow cooker; remove the cheese rind and thyme sprig. Gently stir in the peas, yogurt, grated Parmesan, and pepper. Cover and let stand until the cheese is melted, about 10 minutes.

4 Meanwhile, trim the fennel bulb, reserving the fronds. Using a mandoline, thinly slice the fennel to measure about 4 cups. Coarsely chop the fronds to measure about ¼ loosely packed cup. Combine the sliced fennel, fronds, lemon zest, lemon juice, olive oil, and remaining ¼ teaspoon salt in a medium bowl. Serve the cooked farro mixture topped with the fennel salad.

(SERVING SIZE: 1 cup farro mixture, about ¾ cup fennel mixture): **CALORIES** 330; **FAT** 7g (sat 3g, unsat 4g); **PROTEIN** 13g; **CARB** 56g; **FIBER** 8g; **SUGARS** 9g (added sugars 0g); **SODIUM** 595mg; **CALC** 15% DV; **POTASSIUM** 11% DV

MULTICOOKER DIRECTIONS

IN STEP 1, remove the lid of a 6-quart multicooker. Place the butter in the inner pot. Press SAUTÉ [Normal]; heat until melted, swirling to coat the bottom of the pot. Add the leek, farro, wine, and garlic, and cook uncovered, stirring often, 2 to 3 minutes. Stir in the stock, cheese rind, thyme sprig, and ½ teaspoon of the salt. Turn off the cooker. **IN STEP 2,** lock the lid; turn Pressure Valve to "Venting." Cook on SLOW COOK [Normal] until the farro is tender and the liquid is almost absorbed, about 2 hours and 30 minutes. **COMPLETE STEPS 3 AND 4.**

POLENTA WITH ROASTED TOMATOES AND PARMESAN

HANDS-ON: 25 MINUTES **TOTAL:** 3 HOURS, 35 MINUTES **SERVES** 4

Searching for an easy yet elegant dinner-party dish? This recipe is for you. The lightly charred cherry tomatoes (you can also use grape tomatoes) are not only a vivid topping but also add sweet smokiness that complements the polenta.

2 cups unsalted vegetable stock

2 cups 1% low-fat milk

1 cup water

1 cup uncooked stone-ground polenta or cornmeal

½ teaspoon kosher salt

½ teaspoon black pepper

1½ ounces Parmesan cheese, grated (about ⅓ cup)

1½ tablespoons unsalted butter

3 cups cherry tomatoes (about 15 ounces)

1 tablespoon olive oil

2 tablespoons chopped fresh basil

1 teaspoon balsamic or red wine vinegar

1 ounce watercress or mesclun greens

½ ounce Parmesan cheese, shaved (about 2 tablespoons)

1 Stir together the stock, milk, water, polenta, and ¼ teaspoon each of the salt and pepper in a 5- to 6-quart slow cooker. Cover and cook on LOW until the liquid is absorbed and the polenta is soft, 3 to 4 hours, stirring every hour. Add the grated Parmesan and butter, stirring to combine. Cover and let stand until serving.

2 Preheat the oven to 450°F. Stir together the tomatoes, olive oil, and remaining ¼ teaspoon each salt and pepper. Place the tomatoes on an aluminum foil-lined baking sheet. Bake in the preheated oven until the tomatoes are soft and lightly charred, 10 to 12 minutes.

3 Place the charred tomatoes and juices in a bowl; add the basil and vinegar, stirring gently to combine. Divide the polenta among 4 bowls; top with the tomato mixture, watercress, and shaved Parmesan.

(SERVING SIZE: 1 cup polenta, ⅓ cup tomato mixture, ¼ cup watercress, ⅛ ounce shaved Parmesan): **CALORIES** 326; **FAT** 12g (sat 6g, unsat 6g); **PROTEIN** 11g; **CARB** 42g; **FIBER** 3g; **SUGARS** 11g (added sugars 0g); **SODIUM** 579mg; **CALC** 27% DV; **POTASSIUM** 14% DV

NOTE

You may have wondered what the difference is between polenta and grits. Both are made from stone-ground cornmeal, which is dried, ground corn; however the differences lie in the type of corn and how many times the corn is ground. Need to tell them apart in a pinch? Grits are finely ground while polenta has a grittier texture.

TEX-MEX TORTILLA STACK

HANDS-ON: 20 MINUTES **TOTAL:** 3 HOURS, 20 MINUTES **SERVES** 6

You won't believe this enchilada-like casserole isn't made with meat! The smoky chili powder and cumin give it a satisfying meat-like flavor. Look for meatless crumbles in the produce section of the supermarket near the other vegetarian and vegan products. For a twist, swap the meatless crumbles for black beans or ground beef.

4 teaspoons olive oil

1 yellow onion, chopped (about 1 cup)

3 garlic cloves, minced (about 1 tablespoon)

½ (12-ounce) package meatless burger crumbles (about 1 cup)

2 teaspoons chili powder

1 teaspoon ground cumin

¼ teaspoon kosher salt

1 cup chopped plum tomatoes (from 3 tomatoes)

1½ cups fresh corn kernels (from 2 ears)

¼ cup chopped fresh cilantro

2 teaspoons fresh lime juice (from 1 lime)

Cooking spray

2 cups refrigerated fresh pico de gallo or salsa

9 (6-inch) corn tortillas

6 ounces preshredded Mexican cheese blend (about 1½ cups)

Fresh cilantro leaves (optional)

1 Heat 2 teaspoons of the oil in a large nonstick skillet over medium. Add the onions to the skillet; cook, stirring often, until tender, about 3 minutes. Add the garlic and meatless crumbles; cook, stirring occasionally, until the crumbles are lightly browned, about 4 minutes. Stir in the chili powder, cumin, salt, and ½ cup of the tomatoes.

2 Stir together the corn, cilantro, juice, and remaining 2 teaspoons oil in a bowl.

3 Coat the bottom and sides of a 5- to 6-quart slow cooker with cooking spray. Spread ½ cup of the pico de gallo in the bottom of the slow cooker. Top with a layer of 3 tortillas, tearing as needed to evenly cover. Layer with half of the meatless crumble mixture, ½ cup of the pico de gallo, half of the corn mixture, and ½ cup of the cheese. Add another layer of 3 torn tortillas. Repeat the layers once starting with the remaining meatless crumble mixture and ending with the remaining 3 tortillas. Top the casserole with the remaining ½ cup pico de gallo and remaining ½ cup cheese. Cover and cook on LOW until the mixture is heated through and the cheese is melted, 3 to 4 hours. Top with the remaining ½ cup tomatoes; garnish with the cilantro leaves, if desired. Cut into 6 stacks.

(SERVING SIZE: 1 stack): **CALORIES** 293; **FAT** 13g (sat 5g, unsat 6g); **PROTEIN** 17g; **CARB** 35g; **FIBER** 6g; **SUGARS** 8g (added sugars 0g); **SODIUM** 567mg; **CALC** 26% DV; **POTASSIUM** 8% DV

MEATLESS MAINS

6

SOUPS & STEWS

CARROT-LEEK BISQUE

HANDS-ON: 20 MINUTES   **TOTAL:** 6 HOURS, 30 MINUTES   **SERVES** 12

Creamy and delicate carrot soup is a welcome appetizer. The addition of millet—a whole grain similar to quinoa—adds body to the soup as well as protein and fiber. Garnish with additional black pepper, if desired.

1 tablespoon canola oil
1 tablespoon dry mustard
2 leeks (white and light green parts only), cut into ¼-inch-thick slices (about 4 cups)
1 teaspoon kosher salt
½ teaspoon black pepper
7 cups unsalted chicken stock

2 pounds carrots, peeled and cut into 2-inch pieces (about 5 cups)
½ cup uncooked millet
⅓ cup whole milk
1 teaspoon lemon zest plus 2 tablespoons fresh juice (from 1 lemon)
2 tablespoons chopped fresh chives

1 Heat the oil in a large nonstick skillet over medium-high. Add the mustard to the skillet; cook, stirring constantly, 15 seconds. Add the leeks, salt, and ¼ teaspoon of the pepper; cook, stirring often, until the leek has softened slightly, 3 to 4 minutes. Transfer the leek mixture to a 5- to 6-quart slow cooker. Add the stock, carrots, and millet to the slow cooker. Cover and cook on HIGH until the carrots are very tender, about 6 hours. Cool the soup 10 minutes.

2 Transfer one-third of the soup to a blender. Remove the center piece of the blender lid (to allow steam to escape); secure the blender lid on the blender. Place a clean towel over the opening in the blender lid (to avoid splatters). Blend until smooth. Pour into a large bowl. Repeat the procedure with the remaining soup. Stir in the milk, lemon zest, lemon juice, and remaining ¼ teaspoon pepper. Ladle the bisque into bowls; sprinkle evenly with the chives before serving.

(SERVING SIZE: about ¾ cup): CALORIES 110; FAT 2g (sat 0g, unsat 2g); PROTEIN 5g; CARB 18g; FIBER 4g; SUGARS 6g (added sugars 0g); SODIUM 304mg; CALC 6% DV; POTASSIUM 8% DV

MULTICOOKER DIRECTIONS

IN STEP 1, remove the lid of a 6-quart multicooker; press SAUTÉ [Normal]. When the display reads "Hot", swirl in the oil. Add the leeks, salt, and ¼ teaspoon of the pepper; cook uncovered, stirring often, until the leek has softened slightly. Stir in the mustard; cook 15 seconds. Add the stock, carrots, and millet. Cook until thoroughly heated; turn off the cooker. Lock the lid; turn Pressure Valve to "Venting." Cook on SLOW COOK [More] until the carrots are very tender, about 6 hours. Turn off the cooker. Remove the inner pot from the cooker, and place on a wire rack; cool the soup 10 minutes. **COMPLETE STEP 2.**

SHERRIED MUSHROOM SOUP

HANDS-ON: 20 MINUTES   **TOTAL:** 5 HOURS   **SERVES** 12

Treat dinner guests to this premeal soup loaded with earthy, umami flavor from the mushrooms and soy sauce. Puréeing only some of the soup, and then mixing it with the remaining soup gives the dish complex texture and eye appeal. Garnish with additional black pepper and chopped fresh thyme, if desired.

4 cups boiling water
2 cups dried porcini mushrooms (about
   1½ ounces)
1 tablespoon cornstarch
1 tablespoon lower-sodium soy sauce
⅝ teaspoon kosher salt
½ teaspoon black pepper
2 tablespoons olive oil

2 cups sliced shallots (about 8 ounces)
1 garlic clove, minced (about 1 teaspoon)
1 cup dry sherry
3 pounds assorted fresh mushrooms
   (such as cremini, portobello, shiitake,
   and button), sliced
1½ tablespoons chopped fresh thyme
⅓ cup heavy cream

1 Pour 2 cups of the boiling water over the porcini mushrooms. Let stand 20 minutes. Drain the porcini mushrooms in a colander over a bowl, reserving the mushroom broth; set the mushrooms aside. Strain the mushroom broth through a cheesecloth-lined colander into a bowl; discard the solids. Stir in the cornstarch, soy sauce, salt, pepper, and remaining 2 cups boiling water into the mushroom broth; set aside.

2 Heat the oil in a medium-sized nonstick skillet over medium-high. Add the shallots and garlic; cook, stirring occasionally, until the shallots are soft, 4 to 5 minutes. Add the sherry; bring to a boil, and cook 30 seconds. Remove from the heat.

3 Stir together the porcini mushrooms, broth mixture, shallot mixture, fresh mushrooms, and thyme in a 5-quart slow cooker. Cover and cook on HIGH until the vegetables are very tender and the flavors blend, about 4 hours. Uncover and cook until slightly thickened, about 20 minutes. Transfer 2 cups of the soup to a blender. Remove the center piece of the blender lid (to allow steam to escape); secure the lid on the blender. Place a clean towel over the opening in the blender lid (to avoid splatters). Blend until smooth, about 10 seconds. Return the puréed soup to the slow cooker; gently stir in the cream. Ladle the soup into bowls, and serve hot.

(SERVING SIZE: about ¾ cup): CALORIES 101; FAT 5g (sat 2g, unsat 3g); PROTEIN 5g; CARB 11g; FIBER 2g; SUGARS 4g (added sugars 0g); SODIUM 173mg; CALC 3% DV; POTASSIUM 17% DV

MULTICOOKER DIRECTIONS

COMPLETE STEP 1. IN STEP 2, add the oil to the inner pot of a 6-quart multicooker. With the lid off, press SAUTÉ [Normal]. When the oil is hot, add the shallots and garlic; cook uncovered, stirring often, until the shallots are soft. Carefully stir in the sherry; turn off the cooker. **IN STEP 3,** stir in the porcini mushrooms, broth mixture, fresh mushrooms, and thyme. Lock the lid; turn Pressure Valve to "Venting." Cook on SLOW COOK [More] until the vegetables are very tender and the flavors blend, about 4 hours. Turn off the cooker. Remove the lid; press SAUTÉ [Normal], and cook uncovered, stirring often, until slightly thickened. Turn off the cooker. Transfer 2 cups of the soup to a blender, and blend until smooth as in Step 3. Return the puréed soup to the pot; gently stir in the cream. **FINISH STEP 3.**

CREAMY BUTTERNUT SQUASH–APPLE SOUP

HANDS-ON: 25 MINUTES **TOTAL:** 6 HOURS, 25 MINUTES **SERVES** 12

The sweetness of the Granny Smith apple shines through the creaminess of the blended butternut squash, a combination that is sure to whet appetites. Don't be afraid to keep blending the soup—more air yields tastier, frothier soup. Garnish with additional fresh rosemary sprigs, if desired.

8 cups chopped peeled butternut squash (about 2 pounds)

3 cups water

2 cups chopped Vidalia or other sweet onions (from 1 onion)

2 cups chopped peeled parsnips (from 2 parsnips)

2 cups unsalted vegetable stock

1½ cups chopped peeled Granny Smith apple (from 1 apple)

1 fresh rosemary sprig

1½ teaspoons kosher salt

½ teaspoon black pepper

¼ cup heavy cream

1 Stir together the butternut squash, water, onions, parsnips, stock, apple, rosemary sprig, salt, and pepper in a 5-quart slow cooker. Cover and cook on LOW until the vegetables are tender, about 6 hours. Remove and discard the rosemary sprig.

2 Transfer half of the squash mixture to a blender. Remove the center piece of the blender lid (to allow steam to escape); secure the blender lid on the blender. Place a clean towel over the opening in the blender lid (to avoid splatters). Blend until smooth. Pour into a large bowl. Repeat the procedure with the remaining squash mixture. Stir in the heavy cream. Ladle the soup into bowls, and serve hot.

(SERVING SIZE: about ¾ cup): CALORIES 88; FAT 2g (sat 1g, unsat 1g); PROTEIN 2g; CARB 18g; FIBER 3g; SUGARS 6g (added sugars 0g); SODIUM 289mg; CALC 5% DV; POTASSIUM 12% DV

MULTICOOKER DIRECTIONS

IN STEP 1, stir together the butternut squash, water, onions, parsnips, stock, apple, rosemary sprig, salt, and pepper in the inner pot of a 6-quart multicooker. Lock the lid; turn Pressure Valve to "Venting." Cook on SLOW COOK [Normal] until the vegetables are tender, about 7 hours. Turn off the cooker. Remove and discard the rosemary sprig. **COMPLETE STEP 2.**

SOUPS & STEWS

BEEF-BARLEY SOUP WITH RED WINE AND PESTO

HANDS-ON: 20 MINUTES **TOTAL:** 4 HOURS, 20 MINUTES **SERVES** 6

Hearty, thick, rich—this is just how a winter soup should be. The meat and carrots become tender yet retain their texture, and the kale offers freshness. Garnish each serving with additional pesto and fresh basil and oregano sprigs, if desired.

1 pound boneless beef chuck roast, cut into bite-sized pieces
½ teaspoon black pepper
2 tablespoons olive oil
1½ cups ½-inch-thick diagonally sliced carrots (from 3 carrots)
1 cup chopped yellow onion (from 1 onion)
½ cup dry red wine

3 cups unsalted beef stock
1 (14.5-ounce) can diced tomatoes with basil, garlic, and oregano
¼ cup jarred pesto
½ cup uncooked whole-grain hulled barley (not pearled; about 4 ounces)
1 (5-ounce) package baby kale leaves
½ teaspoon kosher salt

1 Pat the beef dry with a paper towel; sprinkle with the pepper. Heat 1 tablespoon of the oil in a large nonstick skillet over medium-high. Add the beef to the skillet; cook, stirring occasionally, until lightly browned on all sides, about 4 minutes. Transfer the beef to a 5- to 6-quart slow cooker. Add the carrots, onions, and remaining 1 tablespoon oil to the skillet; cook, stirring occasionally, until the vegetables are softened, 3 to 4 minutes. Transfer to the slow cooker.

2 Add the wine to the skillet; cook over medium-high 1 minute, stirring and scraping to loosen the browned bits from the bottom of the skillet. Pour over the beef mixture in the slow cooker.

3 Stir the stock, tomatoes, and pesto into the slow cooker. Cover; cook on HIGH 2 hours. Stir in the barley; cover and cook on HIGH until the beef and barley are tender, about 2 hours. Stir in the kale and salt. Ladle the soup into bowls, and serve hot.

(SERVING SIZE: 1½ cups): CALORIES 301; FAT 12g (sat 2g, unsat 9g); PROTEIN 22g; CARB 25g; FIBER 6g; SUGARS 6g (added sugars 0g); SODIUM 630mg; CALC 15% DV; POTASSIUM 19% DV

MULTICOOKER DIRECTIONS

IN STEP 1, transfer the browned beef and softened vegetables to the inner pot of a 6-quart multicooker. **IN STEP 2,** pour the hot wine mixture over the beef mixture in the pot. **IN STEP 3,** stir the stock, tomatoes, and pesto into the pot. Lock the lid; turn Pressure Valve to "Venting." Cook on SLOW COOK [More] 2 hours. Stir in the barley. Lock the lid; turn Pressure Valve to "Venting." Cook on SLOW COOK [More] until the beef and barley are tender, about 2 hours. **FINISH STEP 3.**

KOREAN BEEF AND CABBAGE STEW

HANDS-ON: 25 MINUTES **TOTAL:** 7 HOURS, 35 MINUTES **SERVES** 8

Brown sugar makes this stew a tad sweet, which beautifully complements the spicy kimchi. You can make this soup ahead and refrigerate it until ready to eat. If you opt to make it ahead, wait until you reheat the soup to add the cabbage.

1 tablespoon canola oil

1 (2-pound) boneless beef chuck roast, trimmed

¼ cup dry white wine

3 tablespoons light brown sugar

3 tablespoons lower-sodium soy sauce

4 cups unsalted chicken stock

1 yellow onion, halved

2 tablespoons minced garlic (from 6 garlic cloves)

1 jalapeño chile, seeded and chopped (about 2 tablespoons)

4 cups chopped napa cabbage (about 14 ounces)

¾ teaspoon kosher salt

½ teaspoon black pepper

¾ cup kimchi

⅓ cup thinly sliced scallions (from 2 scallions)

1 Heat the oil in a large nonstick skillet over medium-high. Add the beef to the skillet; cook, turning once, until well browned, about 10 minutes. Transfer the beef to a 5- to 6-quart slow cooker.

2 Add the wine, brown sugar, and soy sauce to the skillet; bring to a boil over medium-high. Pour the wine mixture over the beef in the slow cooker. Stir the stock, onion halves, garlic, and jalapeño into the slow cooker; cover and cook on LOW until the beef is very tender, 7 to 8 hours.

3 Using a slotted spoon, remove the onions from the slow cooker and discard; transfer the beef to a large bowl. Coarsely shred the beef using 2 forks; return the beef to the slow cooker. Stir in the cabbage, salt, and pepper. Cover and cook on LOW until the cabbage is wilted, about 10 minutes. Ladle the stew into bowls; top evenly with the kimchi and scallions.

(SERVING SIZE: about 1 cup): CALORIES 225; FAT 7g (sat 2g, unsat 4g); PROTEIN 28g; CARB 11g; FIBER 1g; SUGARS 7g (added sugars 5g); SODIUM 634mg; CALC 6% DV; POTASSIUM 14% DV

MULTICOOKER DIRECTIONS

IN STEP 1, transfer the browned beef to the inner pot of a 6-quart multicooker. **IN STEP 2,** pour the boiling wine mixture over the beef in the pot. Stir the stock, onion halves, garlic, and jalapeño into the pot. Lock the lid; turn Pressure Valve to "Venting." Cook on SLOW COOK [Normal] until the beef is very tender, about 8 hours. Turn off the cooker. **IN STEP 3,** remove and discard the onions; transfer the beef to a large bowl. Shred the beef as in Step 3; return to the pot. Stir in the cabbage, salt, and pepper. With the lid off, press SAUTÉ [Normal]; cook, uncovered, just until the cabbage wilts. **FINISH STEP 3.**

BORSCHT

HANDS-ON: 20 MINUTES **TOTAL:** 8 HOURS, 5 MINUTES **SERVES** 12

Borscht is an Eastern European soup that typically features beets as a prominent ingredient, thus the resulting dish has a purple-red color. Our rendition is literally beefed up with brisket and showcases whole-grain rye berries, a source of fiber.

2 tablespoons canola oil

1 (1½-pound) beef brisket, trimmed and cut in half

2 cups chopped yellow onions (from 2 onions)

2 tablespoons chopped fresh thyme

8 garlic cloves, chopped (about 2½ tablespoons)

1 tablespoon caraway seeds

½ teaspoon crushed red pepper

1 tablespoon unsalted tomato paste

6 cups unsalted beef stock

2 pounds beets, peeled and cubed

1 pound parsnips, peeled and cubed

1 cup rye berries

2 teaspoons kosher salt

4 cups very thinly sliced red cabbage (from 1 [32-ounce] cabbage head)

2 tablespoons red wine vinegar

1 teaspoon black pepper

½ cup reduced-fat sour cream

¼ cup fresh dill fronds

1 Heat the oil in a large skillet over medium-high. Add the brisket pieces, and cook, turning to brown on all sides, about 8 minutes. Place the brisket pieces in a 4- to 6-quart slow cooker. Add the onions, thyme, and garlic to the skillet, and cook, stirring often and scraping to loosen the browned bits from the bottom of the skillet, about 4 minutes. Add the caraway seeds and crushed red pepper; cook 30 seconds. Add the tomato paste and 2 cups of the stock to the skillet; stir to combine, and bring to a boil. Add the onion mixture to the slow cooker. Stir the beets, parsnips, rye berries, salt, and remaining 4 cups stock into the slow cooker. Cover and cook on LOW until the brisket is tender, 7 hours and 30 minutes.

2 Remove the brisket pieces, and set aside. Add the cabbage and red wine vinegar to the slow cooker; increase the heat to HIGH, and cook, uncovered, just until the cabbage is wilted, about 15 to 20 minutes.

3 Meanwhile, shred the brisket using 2 forks. Add the shredded brisket and black pepper to the slow cooker, and stir to combine. Ladle the soup into bowls. Top evenly with the sour cream and dill.

(SERVING SIZE: about 1 cup): CALORIES 257; FAT 7g (sat 2g, unsat 4g); PROTEIN 19g; CARB 32g; FIBER 8g; SUGARS 10g (added sugars 0g); SODIUM 514mg; CALC 8% DV; POTASSIUM 22% DV

MULTICOOKER DIRECTIONS

IN STEP 1, place the browned brisket pieces in the inner pot of a 6-quart multicooker. Continue with Step 1, adding the cooked onion mixture to the pot; stir in the beets, parsnips, rye berries, salt, and remaining 4 cups stock. Lock the lid; turn Pressure Valve to "Venting." Cook on SLOW COOK [Normal] until the brisket is very tender, about 8 hours. Turn off the cooker. **IN STEP 2,** remove the brisket pieces; set aside. Add the cabbage and vinegar to the pot. With the lid off, press SAUTÉ [Normal]; cook, uncovered, just until the cabbage is wilted, stirring occasionally. **MEANWHILE, COMPLETE STEP 3.**

SPLIT PEA SOUP WITH GARLICKY CROUTONS

HANDS-ON: 15 MINUTES **TOTAL:** 8 HOURS, 15 MINUTES **SERVES** 8

Fans of split pea soup will go crazy for bowls of this version that requires almost no hands-on time. If you sop up every last drop of this soup, fantastic; if you have leftovers, even better—it might just be tastier the next day once the flavors have melded. Garnish with fresh thyme sprigs, if desired.

2 tablespoons olive oil

6 ounces diced ham

1½ cups chopped yellow onions (from 1 onion)

1 cup chopped carrots (from 1 carrot)

½ cup chopped celery (from 1 celery stalk)

2 tablespoons minced garlic (about 6 garlic cloves)

½ teaspoon black pepper

6 cups unsalted chicken stock

1 pound dried split peas

1 cup chopped peeled russet potato (from 1 potato)

1 teaspoon kosher salt

1½ teaspoons fresh thyme leaves

4 ounces French bread, cut into ½-inch cubes

1 Heat 1 tablespoon of the oil in a large nonstick skillet over medium-high. Add the ham, onions, carrots, celery, 1 tablespoon of the garlic, and ¼ teaspoon of the pepper; cook, stirring often, until the mixture is lightly browned and the vegetables are slightly softened, about 10 minutes. Transfer the mixture to a 5- to 6-quart slow cooker.

2 Stir the stock, split peas, potato, salt, and ¾ teaspoon of the thyme into the slow cooker. Cover and cook on LOW until the peas are tender, about 8 hours.

3 Meanwhile, preheat the oven to 350°F. Toss the bread cubes with the remaining 1 tablespoon oil, 1 tablespoon garlic, ¼ teaspoon pepper, and ¾ teaspoon thyme. Spread the bread cubes on a baking sheet, and bake in the preheated oven until browned and crisp, about 10 minutes, stirring after 5 minutes.

4 Remove 2 cups of the soup mixture from the slow cooker, and place in a blender. Remove the center piece of the blender lid (to allow steam to escape); secure the lid on the blender. Place a clean towel over the opening in the blender lid (to avoid splatters). Blend until smooth. Stir the puréed mixture into the soup in the slow cooker. Ladle the soup into bowls. Top evenly with the croutons.

(SERVING SIZE: 1¼ cups soup, ½ cup croutons): **CALORIES** 346; **FAT** 5g (sat 1g, unsat 4g); **PROTEIN** 23g; **CARB** 54g; **FIBER** 16g; **SUGARS** 8g (added sugars 0g); **SODIUM** 620mg; **CALC** 5% DV; **POTASSIUM** 21% DV

MULTICOOKER DIRECTIONS

IN STEP 1, transfer the cooked ham and vegetables to the inner pot of a 6-quart multicooker. **IN STEP 2,** stir in the stock, split peas, potato, salt, and ¾ teaspoon of the thyme. Lock the lid; turn Pressure Valve to "Venting." Cook on SLOW COOK [Normal] until the peas are tender, about 8 hours. Turn off the cooker. **MEANWHILE, COMPLETE STEP 3. IN STEP 4,** purée 2 cups of the soup as in Step 4. Stir the puréed mixture into the soup in the pot. **FINISH STEP 4.**

PORK POSOLE

HANDS-ON: 20 MINUTES **TOTAL:** 7 HOURS, 20 MINUTES **SERVES** 10

Mexican pork posole is the perfect dish to serve to a crowd. It's hearty, comforting, and full of well-loved ingredients. Mashing some of the beans and hominy thickens the soup and releases more of their earthy flavor. For a twist, substitute thinly sliced jalapeño chiles, finely shredded green cabbage, and fresh thyme or cilantro leaves for the radishes, scallions, and oregano.

1 (3-pound) lean boneless pork shoulder, trimmed and cut into 1½-inch pieces
1 tablespoon ground cumin
1 teaspoon kosher salt
1 teaspoon black pepper
1 tablespoon canola oil
1½ cups chopped poblano chiles (from 2 chiles)
1½ cups chopped yellow onions (from 1 onion)

4 cups unsalted chicken stock
1 (15-ounce) can white hominy, drained and rinsed
1 (15-ounce) can no-salt-added pinto beans, drained and rinsed
1 cup salsa verde
Thinly sliced radishes (optional)
Thinly sliced scallions (optional)
Fresh oregano leaves (optional)

1 Sprinkle the pork evenly with the cumin, salt, and black pepper. Heat the oil in a large skillet over medium-high. Add half of the pork to the skillet; cook, stirring occasionally, until golden brown, about 4 minutes. Transfer to a 5- to 6-quart slow cooker. Repeat the procedure with the remaining pork.

2 Add the poblano chiles and onions to the skillet. Cook, stirring often, until the vegetables are almost tender and lightly caramelized, about 5 minutes. Add ½ cup of the stock to the skillet. Cook 1 minute, stirring and scraping to loosen the browned bits from the bottom of the skillet; transfer to the slow cooker. Stir in the hominy, pinto beans, salsa verde, and remaining 3½ cups stock. Cover and cook on LOW until the pork is tender, 7 to 8 hours. Skim the fat from the surface of the soup. Mash some of the beans and hominy with a potato masher. Ladle the soup into bowls. Serve with the sliced radishes, scallions, and oregano leaves, if desired.

(SERVING SIZE: 1¼ cups): CALORIES 311; FAT 12g (sat 4g, unsat 7g); PROTEIN 32g; CARB 18g; FIBER 4g; SUGARS 3g (added sugars 0g); SODIUM 645mg; CALC 6% DV; POTASSIUM 20% DV

MULTICOOKER DIRECTIONS

IN STEP 1, transfer both halves of the browned pork pieces to the inner pot of a 6-quart multicooker. **IN STEP 2,** transfer the cooked onion mixture to the pot. Stir in the hominy, pinto beans, salsa verde, and remaining 3½ cups stock. Lock the lid; turn Pressure Valve to "Venting." Cook on SLOW COOK [Normal] until the pork is tender, about 8 hours. Turn off the cooker. Remove the lid; skim the fat from the surface of the soup. **FINISH STEP 2.**

SPICY BARBECUE PORK STEW

HANDS-ON: 35 MINUTES **TOTAL:** 8 HOURS, 45 MINUTES **SERVES** 10

Eat this dish along with cornbread on a cold day. It's filling, and the heat from the spicy barbecue sauce and vinegar from the hot peppers will warm you. Reduce the amount of barbecue sauce or use a sweet variety if you can't handle the heat.

1 tablespoon canola oil

1 (3-pound) boneless pork shoulder, trimmed and cut into 3-inch pieces

1 teaspoon smoked paprika

1 teaspoon black pepper

1¼ teaspoons kosher salt

1 cup chopped yellow onions (from 1 onion)

1 cup chopped poblano chile (from 1 chile)

4 cups unsalted chicken stock

1 (15-ounce) can no-salt-added pinto beans, drained and rinsed

1 (14.5-ounce) can no-salt-added fire-roasted diced tomatoes, undrained

1 cup fresh yellow corn kernels (from 1 ear)

1 cup bottled spicy barbecue sauce (such as Stubb's)

¼ cup julienned smoked sun-dried tomatoes, chopped (about ⅞ ounce)

1 tablespoon liquid from hot peppers in vinegar

1 Heat the oil in a large nonstick skillet over medium-high. Sprinkle the pork with the paprika, black pepper, and ¾ teaspoon of the salt. Add the pork to the skillet; cook, turning once, until browned, 8 to 10 minutes. Transfer the pork to a 5- to 6-quart slow cooker. Add the onions and poblano to the skillet; cook, stirring often, until slightly softened and lightly browned, 3 to 4 minutes. Add the onion mixture to the slow cooker.

2 Stir the stock, beans, diced tomatoes, corn, barbecue sauce, and sun-dried tomatoes into the slow cooker. Cover and cook on LOW until the pork is tender, about 8 hours. Remove the pork from the slow cooker, and let cool 10 minutes. Skim any visible fat from the surface of the stew. Tear or break the pork into large pieces, and return the pork to the stew; stir in the liquid from the hot peppers and remaining ½ teaspoon salt. Ladle the stew into bowls, and serve hot.

(SERVING SIZE: about 1 cup): CALORIES 303; FAT 12g (sat 4g, unsat 7g); PROTEIN 32g; CARB 18g; FIBER 3g; SUGARS 7g (added sugars 2g); SODIUM 615mg; CALC 5% DV; POTASSIUM 20% DV

MULTICOOKER DIRECTIONS

IN STEP 1, transfer the browned pork to the inner pot of a 6-quart multicooker. Add the cooked onion mixture to the pot. **IN STEP 2,** stir the stock, beans, diced tomatoes, corn, barbecue sauce, and sun-dried tomatoes into the pot. Lock the lid; turn Pressure Valve to "Venting." Cook on SLOW COOK [Normal] until the pork is tender, about 8 hours. **FINISH STEP 2.**

INDIAN LAMB AND BUTTERNUT SQUASH STEW

HANDS-ON: 35 MINUTES   **TOTAL:** 7 HOURS, 35 MINUTES   **SERVES** 8

We call for lamb shoulder because it's tougher than other cuts and holds up well throughout the long cook time. If you can't find shoulder, use boneless leg of lamb.

1 tablespoon canola oil

2 pounds boneless lamb shoulder, trimmed and cut into 1-inch cubes

3 cups prechopped butternut squash (about 12 ounces)

2 cups chopped red onions (from 1 onion)

1 (15-ounce) can no-salt-added chickpeas (garbanzo beans), drained and rinsed

1 cup unsalted chicken stock

1 tablespoon Madras curry powder

1 tablespoon minced garlic (from 3 garlic cloves)

2 teaspoons kosher salt

2 teaspoons grated fresh ginger

1 (13.5-ounce) can light coconut milk

¼ cup fresh mint leaves

4 cups hot cooked brown basmati rice (optional)

1 Heat the oil a large nonstick skillet over medium-high. Add half of the lamb to the skillet; cook, stirring once, until browned, 5 to 6 minutes. Using a slotted spoon, transfer the lamb to a 5- to 6-quart slow cooker. Repeat the procedure with the remaining lamb. Discard the drippings in the skillet.

2 Stir the squash, onions, chickpeas, stock, curry powder, garlic, salt, and ginger into the lamb mixture in the slow cooker. Cover and cook on LOW until the lamb is tender, about 6 hours and 30 minutes. Skim the fat from the surface of the cooking liquid. Stir in the coconut milk. Cook, uncovered, on HIGH, stirring occasionally, 30 minutes. Sprinkle with the mint, and, if desired, serve over the rice.

(SERVING SIZE: 1½ cups): CALORIES 297; FAT 11g (sat 5g, unsat 5g); PROTEIN 28g; CARB 21g; FIBER 4g; SUGARS 4g (added sugars 0g); SODIUM 601mg; CALC 8% DV; POTASSIUM 19% DV

MULTICOOKER DIRECTIONS

IN STEP 1, transfer all of the browned lamb to the inner pot of a 6-quart multicooker, discarding the drippings in the skillet. **IN STEP 2,** stir the squash, onions, chickpeas, stock, curry powder, garlic, salt, and ginger into the lamb mixture in the pot. Lock the lid; turn Pressure Valve to "Venting." Cook on SLOW COOK [Normal] until the lamb is tender, about 7 hours. Turn off the cooker. Skim the fat from the surface of the cooking liquid. Stir in the coconut milk. With the lid off, press SAUTÉ [Normal]; cook uncovered, stirring often, until slightly reduced, about 30 minutes. **FINISH STEP 2.**

CHICKEN SOUP WITH ZUCCHINI AND HOMINY

HANDS-ON: 20 MINUTES **TOTAL:** 3 HOURS, 40 MINUTES **SERVES** 8

This excellent chicken soup—packed with hearty, nutritious ingredients—is easy to make and may become your new standby. It makes enough to freeze a portion for easy lunches or when you need to deliver food to someone in a pinch.

2½ pounds bone-in, skinless chicken breasts
½ teaspoon black pepper
1 teaspoon kosher salt
2 tablespoons olive oil
2 (15-ounce) cans white hominy, drained and rinsed
1½ cups chopped yellow onions (from 1 onion)
4 garlic cloves, chopped (about 4 teaspoons)

2 teaspoons ground coriander
3¼ cups unsalted chicken stock
1½ cups chopped zucchini (from 1 zucchini)
2 (15-ounce) cans no-salt-added fire-roasted diced tomatoes, undrained
½ cup julienned sun-dried tomatoes
Fresh cilantro sprigs
Lime wedges (optional)

1 Trim the excess fat from the chicken breasts; sprinkle the chicken with the pepper and ½ teaspoon of the salt. Heat 1 tablespoon of the oil in a large nonstick skillet over medium-high. Add the chicken to the skillet, and cook until golden brown, 1 to 2 minutes per side. Transfer the chicken to a 5- to 6-quart slow cooker.

2 Heat the remaining 1 tablespoon oil in the skillet over medium-high; add the hominy, onions, garlic, and coriander. Cook, stirring occasionally, until the onions begin to brown, about 4 minutes. Add ¼ cup of the stock to the skillet, and cook 1 minute, stirring and scraping to loosen the browned bits from the bottom of the skillet. Transfer the mixture to the slow cooker.

3 Stir the zucchini, diced tomatoes, sun-dried tomatoes, and remaining 3 cups stock into the slow cooker. Cover and cook on LOW until the chicken is done and the vegetables are tender, about 3 hours.

4 Remove the chicken from the slow cooker, and let cool. When the chicken is cool enough to handle (about 20 minutes), remove and discard the bones. Cut or shred the chicken into bite-sized pieces; stir the chicken and remaining ½ teaspoon salt into the soup. Ladle the soup into bowls. Garnish with the cilantro, and serve with the lime wedges, if desired.

(SERVING SIZE: 1½ cups): **CALORIES** 304; **FAT** 8g (sat 1g, unsat 5g); **PROTEIN** 31g; **CARB** 26g; **FIBER** 5g; **SUGARS** 8g (added sugars 0g); **SODIUM** 738mg; **CALC** 7% DV; **POTASSIUM** 18% DV

TIP

Hominy is dried corn kernels that have been soaked in alkaline liquid to soften their kernels and loosen their hulls. You can use dry hominy, but the canned variety is easy to find at the supermarket.

UMAMI CHICKEN AND VEGETABLE RAMEN BOWL

HANDS-ON: 20 MINUTES **TOTAL:** 3 HOURS, 20 MINUTES **SERVES** 6

Not only is this show-stopping dish beautiful, it also contains all the protein, carbs, and vegetables needed for a complete meal. And the fact that it only requires 20 minutes of hands-on time means that you can make it anytime.

1 tablespoon canola oil

2 pounds skinless, bone-in chicken breasts

6 cups unsalted chicken stock

3 tablespoons white miso

2 cups packed finely shredded cabbage (from 1 cabbage head)

1½ cups matchstick carrots

1 (8-ounce) package presliced fresh shiitake mushrooms

1 (8-ounce) package vermicelli rice noodles

½ teaspoon kosher salt

¼ cup thinly sliced scallions (green parts only)

½ cup chopped fresh mint

½ cup chopped fresh cilantro

1 red Fresno chile, thinly sliced

2 teaspoons toasted sesame oil

1 Heat the canola oil in a large nonstick skillet over medium-high. Add the chicken to the skillet, and cook until lightly browned, 2 to 3 minutes per side. Transfer the chicken to a 5- to 6-quart slow cooker.

2 Stir the stock and miso into the slow cooker. Stir in the cabbage, carrots, and mushrooms. Cover and cook on LOW until the chicken is done, about 3 hours. Remove the chicken from the slow cooker, and let cool.

3 While the chicken cools, cook the noodles according to the package directions; set aside, and cover to keep warm.

4 When the chicken is cool enough to handle, remove and discard the bones. Shred the chicken into bite-sized pieces; stir the chicken and salt into the broth mixture in the slow cooker.

5 Divide the noodles among 6 bowls. Spoon the chicken and broth mixture over the noodles. Top evenly with the scallions, mint, cilantro, and chile slices. Drizzle each serving evenly with the sesame oil.

(SERVING SIZE: 1 cup noodles, 1½ cups soup): CALORIES 391; FAT 8g (sat 1g, unsat 5g); PROTEIN 40g; CARB 41g; FIBER 5g; SUGARS 8g (added sugars 0g); SODIUM 649mg; CALC 5% DV; POTASSIUM 23% DV

MULTICOOKER DIRECTIONS

IN STEP 1, transfer the browned chicken to the inner pot of a 6-quart multicooker. **IN STEP 2,** stir the stock and miso into the pot. Stir in the cabbage, carrots, and mushrooms. Lock the lid; turn Pressure Valve to "Venting." Cook on SLOW COOK [Normal] until the chicken is done and vegetables are tender, about 3 hours. Remove the chicken from the pot, and let cool. **COMPLETE STEP 3. IN STEP 4,** stir the shredded chicken and salt into the broth mixture in the pot. **COMPLETE STEP 5.**

LEMONY CHICKEN NOODLE SOUP

HANDS-ON: 25 MINUTES **TOTAL:** 4 HOURS, 25 MINUTES **SERVES** 8

This is a classic chicken noodle soup with bright lemony flavor. Because the noodles are whole-wheat, they have added pleasant chewiness—not to mention more fiber and nutrients—than the regular variety. Pair with crusty bread and red wine.

2 tablespoons olive oil

2 pounds bone-in, skinless chicken breasts

½ teaspoon black pepper

1¾ teaspoons kosher salt

8 cups unsalted chicken stock

1½ cups chopped yellow onions (from 1 onion)

1 cup diagonally sliced carrots (from 1 to 2 carrots)

1 cup diagonally sliced celery (from 2 celery stalks)

1½ teaspoons minced garlic (from 2 garlic cloves)

3 fresh thyme sprigs

8 ounces uncooked whole-wheat egg noodles

½ teaspoon lemon zest plus ⅓ cup fresh juice (from 2 lemons)

2 tablespoons chopped fresh flat-leaf parsley

1 Heat the oil in a large nonstick skillet over medium-high. Sprinkle the chicken with the pepper and ½ teaspoon of the salt. Add the chicken to the skillet; cook until golden brown, about 3 minutes per side. Transfer the chicken to a 6-quart slow cooker. Stir the stock, onions, carrots, celery, garlic, thyme sprigs, and remaining 1¼ teaspoons salt into the slow cooker. Cover and cook on LOW until the vegetables are tender, about 3 hours and 30 minutes. Add the noodles; cover and cook on LOW until the noodles are al dente and the chicken is done, 30 minutes to 1 hour. Discard the thyme sprigs.

2 Remove the chicken from the slow cooker; cool slightly. Remove and discard the bones from the chicken. Shred the chicken using 2 forks. Return the shredded chicken to the slow cooker; stir in the lemon zest, juice, and parsley. Ladle the soup into bowls, and serve hot.

(SERVING SIZE: 1½ cups): **CALORIES** 274; **FAT** 6g (sat 1g, unsat 4g); **PROTEIN** 29g; **CARB** 28g; **FIBER** 4g; **SUGARS** 4g (added sugars 0g); **SODIUM** 619mg; **CALC** 3% DV; **POTASSIUM** 13% DV

MULTICOOKER DIRECTIONS

IN STEP 1, transfer the browned chicken to the inner pot of a 6-quart multicooker. Stir the stock, onions, carrots, celery, garlic, thyme sprigs, and remaining 1¼ teaspoons salt into the pot. Lock the lid; turn Pressure Valve to "Venting." Cook on SLOW COOK [Normal] until the vegetables are tender, about 4 hours. Add the noodles to the pot; stir. Re-lock the lid; ensure that the Pressure Valve is turned to "Venting." Cook on SLOW COOK [Normal] until the noodles are al dente and the chicken is done, 30 minutes to 1 hour. Discard the thyme sprigs. **DEBONE AND SHRED THE CHICKEN AS IN STEP 2,** and return to the pot; stir in the lemon zest, juice, and parsley. Ladle the soup into bowls, and serve hot.

MOROCCAN-SPICED CHICKEN STEW

HANDS-ON: 30 MINUTES **TOTAL:** 5 HOURS, 30 MINUTES **SERVES** 8

The chicken, sweet potato, and chickpeas all contribute to the nice textured bite of this stew. And the tomato broth takes it to the next level. When eating, you'll want to have a toasted baguette at the ready to soak it all up.

1 teaspoon ground cumin

½ teaspoon ground cinnamon

½ teaspoon ground coriander

¼ teaspoon cayenne pepper

8 skinless, boneless chicken thighs (about 2¼ pounds), trimmed

2 tablespoons olive oil

1 cup vertically sliced yellow onions (from 1 onion)

2 teaspoons minced fresh ginger

1½ cups unsalted chicken stock

1½ cups chopped peeled sweet potato (from 1 sweet potato)

1 (28-ounce) can no-salt-added whole peeled tomatoes

1 (15-ounce) can no-salt-added chickpeas (garbanzo beans), drained and rinsed

¼ cup golden raisins

1½ teaspoons kosher salt

1 teaspoon lemon zest plus 1½ tablespoons fresh juice (from 1 lemon)

¼ cup fresh cilantro sprigs (optional)

1 Stir together the cumin, cinnamon, coriander, and cayenne pepper in a small bowl. Sprinkle the chicken thighs evenly with the spice mixture. Heat 1 tablespoon of the oil in a large nonstick skillet over medium-high. Add half of the chicken to the skillet; cook until browned on 1 side, about 5 minutes. Turn the chicken over, and cook 1 minute. Transfer the chicken to a 5- to 6-quart slow cooker. Repeat the procedure with the remaining oil and chicken.

2 Add the onions and ginger to the skillet; cook, stirring often, until slightly softened, about 3 minutes. Add the stock to the skillet; cook 1 minute, stirring and scraping to loosen the browned bits from the bottom of the skillet. Transfer the onion mixture to the slow cooker. Stir the sweet potato into the slow cooker.

3 Using kitchen scissors, chop the tomatoes in the can. Stir the chopped tomatoes and tomato liquid, chickpeas, raisins, and salt into the slow cooker. Cover and cook on LOW until the chicken is done and the vegetables are tender, about 5 hours. Remove the chicken to a cutting board; cut or tear into bite-sized pieces. Stir the lemon zest and lemon juice into the mixture in the slow cooker; gently stir in the chicken. Ladle the stew into bowls, and top with the cilantro, if desired.

(SERVING SIZE: about 1⅓ cups): CALORIES 302; FAT 9g (sat 2g, unsat 6g); PROTEIN 31g; CARB 23g; FIBER 4g; SUGARS 8g (added sugars 0g); SODIUM 608mg; CALC 5% DV; POTASSIUM 18% DV

VEGETABLE AND CHICKEN MEATBALL SOUP

HANDS-ON: 25 MINUTES **TOTAL:** 2 HOURS, 55 MINUTES **SERVES** 6

Don't skip cooking the onions for the meatballs. This step softens the onions so they more easily add their sweet flavor to the meatball mixture.

1 tablespoon olive oil
2 cups chopped yellow onions (from 1 onion)
5 garlic cloves, minced (about 5 teaspoons)
1½ teaspoons kosher salt
½ teaspoon black pepper
4 cups unsalted chicken stock
1 cup chopped carrots (from 1 carrot)
1 cup chopped zucchini (from 1 zucchini)
4 ounces green beans, trimmed and cut into 1½-inch pieces (about 1 cup)

½ cup thinly sliced celery (from 1 celery stalk)
1 (14.5-ounce) can no-salt-added diced tomatoes
1 pound ground chicken
⅓ cup whole-wheat panko (Japanese-style breadcrumbs)
2½ tablespoons chopped fresh flat-leaf parsley
2 teaspoons chopped fresh oregano

1 Heat the oil in a large nonstick skillet over medium-high. Add the onions, garlic, salt, and pepper to the skillet; cook, stirring often, until softened, about 6 minutes. Remove ½ cup of the cooked onion mixture, and place in a medium bowl; set aside. Transfer the remaining onion mixture to a 5- to 6-quart slow cooker. Stir the stock, carrots, zucchini, green beans, celery, and tomatoes into the slow cooker.

2 Add the chicken, panko, ½ tablespoon of the parsley, and 1 teaspoon of the oregano to the reserved ½ cup onion mixture in the bowl; stir gently with a fork to combine. Shape the chicken mixture into 18 (1¼-inch) meatballs. Carefully submerge the meatballs into the chicken stock mixture in the slow cooker without stirring. Cover and cook on HIGH until the meatballs are done and the vegetables are tender, about 2 hours and 30 minutes. Stir in the remaining 2 tablespoons parsley and 1 teaspoon oregano. Ladle the soup into bowls, and serve hot.

(SERVING SIZE: 1⅔ cups): CALORIES 210; FAT 9g (sat 2g, unsat 6g); PROTEIN 18g; CARB 16g; FIBER 3g; SUGARS 7g (added sugars 0g); SODIUM 647mg; CALC 6% DV; POTASSIUM 22% DV

MULTICOOKER DIRECTIONS

IN STEP 1, transfer the remaining onion mixture to the inner pot of a 6-quart multicooker. Stir the stock, carrots, zucchini, green beans, celery, and tomatoes into the pot. **IN STEP 2,** carefully submerge the meatballs in the chicken stock mixture in the pot without stirring. Lock the lid; turn Pressure Valve to "Venting." Cook on SLOW COOK [More] until the meatballs are done and the vegetables are tender, about 3 hours. **FINISH STEP 2.**

WHITE BEAN, SPINACH, AND SAUSAGE STEW

HANDS-ON: 30 MINUTES   **TOTAL:** 15 HOURS, 50 MINUTES, INCLUDING 8 HOURS SOAKING   **SERVES** 6

Reach for this recipe on a chilly morning when you know you'll want a steaming bowl of stew for supper. To make this recipe gluten free, use gluten-free sausage.

2 cups dried cannellini beans

5 cups unsalted chicken stock

1 plum tomato, stem end trimmed (about 5 ounces)

1 teaspoon kosher salt

½ teaspoon black pepper

4 garlic cloves, lightly crushed

2 fresh rosemary sprigs

6 ounces spinach-and-feta chicken-and-turkey sausage (such as Applegate Organics), cut diagonally into ½-inch-thick slices

5 ounces baby spinach, roughly chopped

¼ cup chopped fresh flat-leaf parsley

2 tablespoons extra-virgin olive oil

1 Sort and wash the beans; place in a large Dutch oven. Cover with water to 2 inches above the beans; cover and let stand 8 hours. Drain the beans. Place the beans in a 5- to 6-quart slow cooker. Add the stock, tomato, salt, pepper, garlic, and rosemary sprigs. Cover and cook on LOW until the beans are tender, about 7 hours.

2 Lightly mash the bean mixture with a potato masher, breaking up the tomato and garlic. Add the sausage to the slow cooker; cover and cook on LOW until thoroughly heated, about 20 minutes. Add the spinach and parsley, stirring just until the spinach begins to wilt. Discard the rosemary sprigs. Ladle the stew into bowls; drizzle evenly with the oil before serving.

(SERVING SIZE: 1⅓ cups): CALORIES 314; FAT 9g (sat 2g, unsat 5g); PROTEIN 21g; CARB 39g; FIBER 22g; SUGARS 2g (added sugars 0g); SODIUM 642mg; CALC 11% DV; POTASSIUM 25% DV

MULTICOOKER DIRECTIONS

IN STEP 1, place the drained soaked beans in the inner pot of a 6-quart multicooker. Add the stock, tomato, salt, pepper, garlic, and rosemary sprigs. Lock the lid; turn Pressure Valve to "Venting." Cook on SLOW COOK [Normal] until the beans are tender, about 7 hours. Turn off the cooker. **IN STEP 2,** add the sausage to the mashed bean mixture in the pot. With the lid off, press SAUTÉ [Normal], and cook uncovered, stirring often, until thoroughly heated. **FINISH STEP 2.**

TURKEY-AND-KALE MINESTRONE SOUP

HANDS-ON: 20 MINUTES   **TOTAL:** 3 HOURS, 50 MINUTES   **SERVES** 10

Adjust the heat level in the dish by choosing either hot or mild Italian sausage. You can add red pepper, too, to make it extra hot. Serve with crusty bread, if desired.

10 ounces spicy turkey Italian sausage, casings removed

2 cups chopped yellow onions (from 1 onion)

1 cup chopped carrots (from 1 carrot)

¾ cup chopped celery (from 2 celery stalks)

6 cups unsalted chicken stock

2 (14.5-ounce) cans no-salt-added fire-roasted diced tomatoes, undrained

1 (15-ounce) can no-salt-added kidney beans, drained and rinsed

1 teaspoon kosher salt

½ teaspoon black pepper

1 cup uncooked ditalini pasta

2 cups packed fresh baby kale leaves, roughly chopped

1 Heat a large nonstick skillet over medium-high. Add the sausage to the skillet, and cook, stirring to crumble with a wooden spoon, 4 minutes. Add the onions, carrots, and celery to the skillet; cook, stirring occasionally, until the sausage is browned and the vegetables are lightly caramelized, about 6 minutes. Add 1 cup of the stock; cook 1 minute, stirring and scraping to loosen the browned bits from the bottom of the skillet.

2 Transfer the sausage mixture to a 5- to 6-quart slow cooker. Stir in the tomatoes, beans, salt, ¼ teaspoon of the pepper, and the remaining 5 cups stock. Cover and cook on LOW until the vegetables are tender, about 2 hours and 30 minutes. Stir in the pasta; cover and cook on LOW until the pasta is al dente, about 1 hour. Stir in the kale and remaining ¼ teaspoon pepper. Ladle the soup into bowls, and serve hot.

(SERVING SIZE: about 1¼ cups): CALORIES 169; FAT 3g (sat 1g, unsat 1g); PROTEIN 13g; CARB 24g; FIBER 5g; SUGARS 6g (added sugars 0g); SODIUM 607mg; CALC 6% DV; POTASSIUM 8% DV

MULTICOOKER DIRECTIONS

COMPLETE STEP 1. IN STEP 2, transfer the sausage mixture to the inner pot of a 6-quart multicooker. Stir in the tomatoes, beans, salt, ¼ teaspoon of the pepper, and the remaining 5 cups stock. Lock the lid; turn Pressure Valve to "Venting." Cook on SLOW COOK [Normal] until the vegetables are tender, about 3 hours. Turn off the cooker. Remove the lid; press SAUTÉ [More]. Bring the soup to a boil; stir in the pasta. Cook, uncovered, until the pasta is al dente, stirring often to prevent the pasta from sticking to the bottom of the pot and adjusting the heat to SAUTÉ [Normal], if necessary, to maintain a low boil. Turn off the cooker. **FINISH STEP 2.**

IRISH SAUSAGE, BEAN, AND CABBAGE STEW

HANDS-ON: 20 MINUTES   **TOTAL:** 15 HOURS, 50 MINUTES, INCLUDING 8 HOURS SOAKING   **SERVES** 8

The abundance of springy sausage, soft beans, and tender cabbage packed into this recipe means that each bite is loaded with varied texture. To make this recipe gluten free, use gluten-free sausage. Serve with bread and Guinness, if desired.

1 pound dried navy beans

5 cups unsalted chicken stock

1 cup diced carrots (from 1 carrot)

2 tablespoons minced garlic (from 6 garlic
  cloves)

1 teaspoon caraway seeds

½ teaspoon black pepper

4 cups shredded cabbage (about 10 ounces)

1 (14-ounce) can diced tomatoes

8 ounces fully cooked smoked turkey
  sausage, cut into half moons

2 tablespoons apple cider vinegar

½ teaspoon kosher salt

2 tablespoons olive oil

1 Sort and wash the beans; place in a large Dutch oven. Cover with water to 2 inches above the beans; cover and let stand 8 hours or overnight. Drain the beans. Stir together the beans, stock, carrots, garlic, caraway seeds, and pepper in a 5- to 6-quart slow cooker. Cover and cook on LOW until the beans are just tender, 7 to 8 hours.

2 Mash some of the beans against the side of the slow cooker to thicken and enhance the texture of the soup; stir gently. Add the cabbage, tomatoes, and sausage to the slow cooker; cover and cook on HIGH until the cabbage is tender, about 30 minutes. Stir in the vinegar and salt. Ladle the stew into bowls, and drizzle evenly with the oil.

(SERVING SIZE: 1½ cups): **CALORIES** 314; **FAT** 7g (sat 1g, unsat 5g); **PROTEIN** 21g; **CARB** 43g; **FIBER** 11g; **SUGARS** 7g (added sugars 0g); **SODIUM** 606mg; **CALC** 13% DV; **POTASSIUM** 25% DV

MULTICOOKER DIRECTIONS

IN STEP 1, stir together the drained soaked beans, stock, carrots, garlic, caraway seeds, and pepper in the inner pot of a 6-quart multicooker. Lock the lid; turn Pressure Valve to "Venting." Cook on SLOW COOK [Normal] until the beans are just tender, about 8 hours. Turn off the cooker. **IN STEP 2,** add the cabbage, tomatoes, and sausage to the mashed bean mixture. With the lid off, press SAUTÉ [Normal]. Bring the soup to a boil; cook, uncovered, until the cabbage is tender, stirring occasionally. Turn off the cooker. **FINISH STEP 2.**

SHRIMP-AND-FENNEL CHOWDER

HANDS-ON: 25 MINUTES **TOTAL:** 5 HOURS, 30 MINUTES **SERVES** 6

Look for white, American 22-25 count shrimp—the fresher, the better. They'll poach and become very tender in the hot slow-cooker liquid. Just be sure not to overcook them. Garnish with fennel fronds and serve with bread and olive oil, if desired.

2 tablespoons olive oil

2 cups thinly sliced fennel (from 1 fennel bulb)

1½ cups chopped leek (from 1 leek)

1½ cups chopped celery (from 6 celery stalks)

1 tablespoon minced garlic (from 3 garlic cloves)

1 cup dry white wine

1 (28-ounce) can no-salt-added fire-roasted diced tomatoes

1 russet potato (about 9 ounces), peeled and cut into ½-inch cubes

1 cup water

1 cup clam juice

1 teaspoon kosher salt

⅛ teaspoon saffron threads

1 pound medium-sized raw shrimp, peeled and deveined

1 Heat the oil in a large nonstick skillet over medium-high. Add the fennel, leek, celery, and garlic to the skillet; cook, stirring occasionally, until the vegetables are softened and lightly caramelized, 6 to 8 minutes. Add the wine to the skillet; cook 1 minute, stirring and scraping to loosen the browned the bits from the bottom of the skillet. Transfer the mixture to a 5- to 6-quart slow cooker.

2 Stir the tomatoes, potato, water, clam juice, salt, and saffron threads into the slow cooker. Cover and cook on LOW until the potato is tender, 5 to 6 hours. Increase the slow cooker heat to HIGH; stir in the shrimp. Cover and cook until the shrimp are done, 5 to 7 minutes. Ladle the chowder into bowls, and serve hot.

(SERVING SIZE: 1⅝ cups): CALORIES 190; FAT 5g (sat 1g, unsat 4g); PROTEIN 13g; CARB 20g; FIBER 3g; SUGARS 6g (added sugars 0g); SODIUM 586mg; CALC 13% DV; POTASSIUM 16% DV

MULTICOOKER DIRECTIONS

IN STEP 1, transfer the cooked fennel mixture to the inner pot of a 6-quart multicooker. **IN STEP 2,** stir the tomatoes, potato, water, clam juice, salt, and saffron threads into the pot. Lock the lid; turn Pressure Valve to "Venting." Cook on SLOW COOK [Normal] until the potato is tender, about 6 hours. Turn off the cooker. With the lid off, press SAUTÉ [Normal]. Bring the soup to a boil; stir in the shrimp. Cook, uncovered, until the shrimp are done. **FINISH STEP 2.**

FRENCH ONION SOUP

HANDS-ON: 20 MINUTES **TOTAL:** 12 HOURS, 20 MINUTES **SERVES** 8

Fans of French onion soup who love it for its caramelized onions, beefy broth, and cheesy toast topping won't be disappointed with this recipe, which offers all those elements plus a hands-on time of only 20 minutes.

Cooking spray
10 cups vertically sliced onions (from 5 onions)
2 tablespoons unsalted butter, melted
½ teaspoon black pepper
6 cups unsalted beef stock
¼ cup dry Marsala wine

1 teaspoon chopped fresh thyme, plus more for garnish
¾ teaspoon kosher salt
12 ounces whole-wheat baguette, cut into 16 slices
5 ounces Gruyère cheese, shredded (about 1¼ cups)

1 Coat a 4-quart slow cooker with cooking spray. Stir together the onions, butter, and pepper in the slow cooker; cover and cook on LOW until the onions are very soft and deep golden brown, about 10 hours.

2 Stir in the stock, marsala, thyme, and salt. Cover and cook on HIGH until the flavors are blended, about 2 hours.

3 Preheat the broiler with the oven rack 6 inches from the heat. Place the baguette slices on a baking sheet, and sprinkle evenly with the Gruyère. Broil until the Gruyère melts, 2 to 3 minutes. Ladle the soup into bowls. Top with the cheese toasts. Garnish with the additional thyme, if desired.

(SERVING SIZE: about 1½ cups soup, 2 toasts): CALORIES 259; FAT 10g (sat 5g, unsat 3g); PROTEIN 11g; CARB 32g; FIBER 3g; SUGARS 7g (added sugars 0g); SODIUM 604mg; CALC 21% DV; POTASSIUM 6% DV

TIP

The Gruyère toasts are a smart, tasty application for bread that's beginning to pass its prime. If you have enough day-old bread on hand, don't bother with purchasing a fresh loaf. Toasting it cancels out any differences in flavor that it has from fresh bread.

ITALIAN VEGETABLE AND FARRO SOUP

HANDS-ON: 30 MINUTES **TOTAL:** 4 HOURS, 30 MINUTES **SERVES** 8

The farro—an ancient whole grain rich in iron and fiber—and butternut squash make this soup hearty and filling. If you're looking for an easy way to work whole grains into your diet, this is it.

2 tablespoons olive oil

1 (8-ounce) package presliced fresh cremini mushrooms

½ teaspoon black pepper

2 cups chopped yellow onions (from 1 onion)

1 cup chopped celery (from 3 celery stalks)

4 cups chopped peeled butternut squash (from 1 squash)

4 cups water

4 cups unsalted vegetable stock

1 cup uncooked whole-grain farro

5 cups coarsely chopped baby spinach (about 5 ounces)

¼ cup loosely packed fresh flat-leaf parsley leaves

¼ cup torn fresh basil leaves

3 tablespoons apple cider vinegar

⅞ teaspoon kosher salt

3 ounces Parmigiano-Reggiano cheese, shaved (about 1½ cups)

1 Heat the oil in a large nonstick skillet over medium-high. Add the mushrooms and ¼ teaspoon of the pepper; cook, stirring often, until the mushrooms are browned, 8 to 10 minutes. Add the onions and celery; cook, stirring often, until the onions and celery are slightly softened, about 4 minutes.

2 Transfer the mushroom mixture to a 5- to 6-quart slow cooker. Stir in the squash, water, stock, and farro. Cover and cook on LOW until the farro and vegetables are tender, about 4 hours.

3 Just before serving, add the spinach, parsley, basil, vinegar, salt, and remaining ¼ teaspoon pepper, stirring until the spinach wilts. Ladle the soup into bowls; top evenly with the Parmigiano-Reggiano.

(SERVING SIZE: 1½ cups): CALORIES 212; FAT 7g (sat 2g, unsat 4g); PROTEIN 10g; CARB 31g; FIBER 4g; SUGARS 4g (added sugars 0g); SODIUM 528mg; CALC 21% DV; POTASSIUM 14% DV

MULTICOOKER DIRECTIONS

COMPLETE STEP 1. IN STEP 2, transfer the mushroom mixture to the inner pot of a 6-quart multicooker. Stir in the squash, water, stock, and farro. Lock the lid; turn Pressure Valve to "Venting." Cook on SLOW COOK [Normal] until the farro and vegetables are tender, 4 hours. **COMPLETE STEP 3.**

VEGETABLE-AND-TOFU THAI STEW

HANDS-ON: 20 MINUTES **TOTAL:** 4 HOURS, 35 MINUTES **SERVES** 5

Cauliflower and tofu are ideal ingredients for this soup. The cauliflower soaks up the cooking liquid, and the tofu keeps the dish light, allowing the bold flavors in the liquid—predominantly the curry paste and lemongrass—to take center stage.

1 (13.5-ounce) can light coconut milk

1 cup water

3 tablespoons red curry paste

3 garlic cloves, finely chopped (about 1 tablespoon)

2 teaspoons finely chopped lemongrass

10 ounces small cauliflower florets (about 2½ cups)

3 small carrots, peeled and cut diagonally into ¼-inch-thick slices (about 2 cups)

1 medium-sized red onion, cut into ½-inch wedges and separated (about 1½ cups)

1 medium zucchini, halved lengthwise and cut into ½-inch-thick slices (about 2 cups)

1 (14-ounce) package extra-firm tofu, drained

1 tablespoon canola oil

1 tablespoon light brown sugar

¼ teaspoon kosher salt

¼ cup fresh cilantro leaves

2 tablespoons chopped roasted unsalted peanuts

1 Stir together the coconut milk, water, red curry paste, garlic, and lemongrass in a 5- to 6-quart slow cooker until smooth. Stir in the cauliflower, carrots, and onions. Cover and cook on LOW until the vegetables are tender, about 4 hours. Add the zucchini to the slow cooker; cover and cook until the zucchini is tender, about 15 minutes.

2 Meanwhile, cut the tofu into 1-inch cubes; pat the cubes dry with a paper towel. Heat the oil in a large skillet over medium-high. Add the tofu to the skillet, and cook until deep brown on all sides, 8 to 10 minutes, turning often to brown all sides evenly. Gently stir the tofu, brown sugar, and salt into the slow cooker. Ladle the stew into bowls; top with the cilantro and peanuts.

(**SERVING SIZE:** 1½ cups): **CALORIES** 243; **FAT** 14g (sat 5g, unsat 7g); **PROTEIN** 12g; **CARB** 20g; **FIBER** 4g; **SUGARS** 9g (added sugars 3g); **SODIUM** 325mg; **CALC** 11% DV; **POTASSIUM** 13% DV

SMOKY WHITE BEAN MINESTRONE

HANDS-ON: 30 MINUTES **TOTAL:** 6 HOURS, 45 MINUTES **SERVES** 8

An abundance of vegetables, beans, and pasta makes this soup so hearty you'll hardly notice the lack of meat. The drizzle of olive oil and sprinkle of Parmesan at the end adds a special touch.

3 (14.5-ounce) cans no-salt-added fire-roasted diced tomatoes, undrained

2 (15-ounce) cans no-salt-added Great Northern beans, drained and rinsed

3 cups water

1 cup chopped yellow onions (from 1 onion)

1 cup chopped roasted red bell pepper (about 2 medium peppers)

½ cup chopped celery (from 2 celery stalks)

2 garlic cloves, minced (about 2 teaspoons)

2 teaspoons smoked paprika

¾ teaspoon kosher salt

½ teaspoon black pepper

2 small yellow squash, quartered lengthwise and sliced (about 2 cups)

4 ounces uncooked ditalini pasta (about 1 cup)

1 (6-ounce) package baby spinach

2 tablespoons extra-virgin olive oil

2 ounces Parmesan cheese, shaved (about 1 cup)

Stir together the tomatoes, beans, water, onions, roasted bell pepper, celery, garlic, smoked paprika, salt, and black pepper in a 5- to 6-quart slow cooker. Cover and cook on LOW until the vegetables are tender, about 6 hours. Stir in the squash and pasta; cover and cook on HIGH until the squash and pasta are tender, about 15 minutes. Add the spinach, stirring just until the spinach is wilted. Ladle the soup into bowls. Drizzle each serving evenly with the oil, and top evenly with the Parmesan.

(SERVING SIZE: 1¾ cups): CALORIES 276; FAT 8g (sat 3g, unsat 4g); PROTEIN 12g; CARB 37g; FIBER 7g; SUGARS 7g (added sugars 0g); SODIUM 549mg; CALC 21% DV; POTASSIUM 9% DV

MULTICOOKER DIRECTIONS

Stir together the tomatoes, beans, water, onions, roasted bell pepper, celery, garlic, smoked paprika, salt, and black pepper in the inner pot of a 6-quart multicooker. Lock the lid; turn Pressure Valve to "Venting." Cook on SLOW COOK [Normal] until the vegetables are tender, about 7 hours. Turn off the cooker. With the lid off, press SAUTÉ [Normal]. Bring the soup to a boil. Stir in the squash and pasta. Cook, uncovered, until the squash and pasta are tender, stirring occasionally to prevent the pasta from sticking to the bottom of the pot. Gradually add the spinach, stirring just until it wilts. **FINISH THE RECIPE.**

LENTIL, CARROT, AND POTATO SOUP

HANDS-ON: 30 MINUTES   **TOTAL:** 7 HOURS, 30 MINUTES   **SERVES** 8

Puréeing some of the lentil-vegetable mixture, and then combining it with the remaining vegetables and lentils gives the soup a texture that satisfies those who love a creamy soup and those who prefer it chunky. Serve with crackers.

4 cups unsalted vegetable stock

4 cups water

2 cups chopped peeled sweet potato (from 1 sweet potato)

2 cups sliced carrots (from 3 carrots)

2 cups chopped peeled russet potato (from 1 potato)

1½ cups dried green lentils

1½ cups chopped yellow onions (from 1 onion)

1 cup chopped celery (from 2 celery stalks)

2 tablespoons minced garlic (from 6 garlic cloves)

4 fresh thyme sprigs

1 bay leaf

1⅛ teaspoons kosher salt

1 teaspoon black pepper

6 tablespoons olive oil

3 tablespoons apple cider vinegar

¼ cup chopped fresh flat-leaf parsley

1 Stir together the stock, water, sweet potato, carrots, russet potato, lentils, onions, celery, garlic, thyme sprigs, bay leaf, salt, and pepper in a 5- to 6-quart slow cooker. Cover and cook on LOW until the vegetables and lentils are tender, 7 to 8 hours. Remove and discard the thyme sprigs and bay leaf.

2 Place the oil and 4 cups of the soup in a blender. Remove the center piece of the blender lid (to allow steam to escape); secure the blender lid on the blender. Place a clean towel over the opening in the lid (to avoid splatters). Process until smooth. Return the puréed soup to the slow cooker; stir in the vinegar. Ladle the soup into bowls, and sprinkle evenly with the parsley.

(SERVING SIZE: about 1½ cups): CALORIES 303; FAT 11g (sat 1g, unsat 9g); PROTEIN 11g; CARB 43g; FIBER 9g; SUGARS 5g (added sugars 0g); SODIUM 450mg; CALC 6% DV; POTASSIUM 22% DV

MULTICOOKER DIRECTIONS

IN STEP 1, stir together the stock, water, sweet potato, carrots, russet potato, lentils, onions, celery, garlic, thyme sprigs, bay leaf, salt, and pepper in the inner pot of a 6-quart multicooker. Lock the lid; turn Pressure Valve to "Venting." Cook on SLOW COOK [Normal] until the vegetables and lentils are tender, about 8 hours. Remove and discard the thyme sprigs and bay leaf. Turn off the cooker. **COMPLETE STEP 2.**

7
SIDES

BRUSSELS SPROUTS WITH LEMON

HANDS-ON: 15 MINUTES   **TOTAL:** 1 HOUR, 45 MINUTES   **SERVES** 6

Brussels sprouts are a versatile accompaniment for so many entrées. Here, the burst of lemon juice and the addition of pine nuts and pecorino Romano keep the flavor profile interesting. Furthermore, broiling the sprouts after slow-cooking caramelizes them and gives them crispness.

2 pounds fresh Brussels sprouts, halved
½ cup unsalted chicken stock
½ teaspoon kosher salt
Cooking spray
1 teaspoon lemon zest, plus 3 tablespoons
   fresh juice (from 1 lemon)

¼ teaspoon black pepper
¼ cup pine nuts, toasted
2 tablespoons shaved pecorino Romano
   cheese

1 Stir together the Brussels sprouts, stock, and salt in a 5- to 6-quart slow cooker. Cover and cook on HIGH until the Brussels sprouts are tender, about 1 hour and 30 minutes.

2 Preheat the broiler with the oven rack 6 inches from the heat. Coat an aluminum foil-lined broiler pan or large rimmed baking sheet with cooking spray. Using a slotted spoon, transfer the Brussels sprouts from the slow cooker to the prepared broiler pan. Drizzle with 2 tablespoons of the lemon juice; sprinkle with the pepper. Toss to coat; spread in a single layer.

3 Broil until the Brussels sprouts begin to brown, about 3 minutes. Transfer to a serving platter. Sprinkle the remaining 1 tablespoon lemon juice over the Brussels sprouts. Top evenly with the pine nuts, cheese, and lemon zest.

(SERVING SIZE: about 1 cup): CALORIES 111; FAT 5g (sat 1g, unsat 3g); PROTEIN 7g; CARB 15g; FIBER 6g; SUGARS 4g (added sugars 0g); SODIUM 232mg; CALC 8% DV; POTASSIUM 18% DV

BRAISED COLLARD GREENS WITH PEPPERONCINI

HANDS-ON: 10 MINUTES   **TOTAL:** 8 HOURS, 10 MINUTES   **SERVES** 10

Collard greens have large, dark green leaves that are dense with vitamins, calcium, and fiber. The briny pepperoncini and salty pancetta add enough brightness to this dish to balance the collards' vegetal flavor. This side pairs well with braised meat or barbecue such as Barbecue Brisket Sliders (page 36).

1 (16-ounce) package chopped fresh collard greens

2 cups unsalted chicken stock

1 cup chopped red onions (about 1 small onion)

2 ounces diced pancetta

1 tablespoon minced garlic (about 3 garlic cloves)

1 tablespoon olive oil

4 small fresh thyme sprigs

¼ cup undrained pickled pepperoncini slices

½ teaspoon kosher salt

Stir together the collard greens, chicken stock, onions, pancetta, garlic, oil, and thyme in a 6-quart slow cooker. Cover and cook on LOW until the collards are very tender, about 8 hours. Discard the thyme sprigs. Stir in the pickled pepperoncini and salt. Serve hot.

(SERVING SIZE: ½ cup): CALORIES 62; FAT 3g (sat 1g, unsat 2g); PROTEIN 3g; CARB 5g; FIBER 2g; SUGARS 1g (added sugars 0g); SODIUM 258mg; CALC 11% DV; POTASSIUM 4% DV

MULTICOOKER DIRECTIONS

Stir together the collard greens, chicken stock, onions, pancetta, garlic, oil, and thyme in the inner pot of a 6-quart multicooker. Lock the lid; turn Pressure Valve to "Venting." Cook on SLOW COOK [Normal] until the collards are very tender, about 8 hours. Discard the thyme sprigs. **FINISH THE RECIPE.**

MAPLE-WALNUT CARROTS

HANDS-ON: 10 MINUTES **TOTAL:** 4 HOURS, 10 MINUTES **SERVES** 8

The hint of maple syrup and brandy elevates humble carrots, transforming them into a holiday-worthy side dish. You can easily double this to feed a crowd. We use stem-on rainbow carrots for their beauty, but regular carrots work just as well.

2 pounds carrots, peeled and cut diagonally
   into 3-inch pieces (6 cups)
¼ cup pure maple syrup
¼ cup (2 ounces) brandy
2 tablespoons fresh lemon juice (from
   1 lemon)

1½ tablespoons unsalted butter, cut into
   pieces
½ teaspoon kosher salt
½ cup chopped walnuts, toasted
½ teaspoon chopped fresh rosemary

Stir together the carrots, maple syrup, brandy, and lemon juice in a 6-quart slow cooker. Sprinkle the butter and salt over the carrot mixture. Cover and cook on LOW until the carrots are very tender, about 4 hours. Transfer the carrots to a bowl; top with the walnuts and rosemary.

(SERVING SIZE: about ½ cup): CALORIES 136; FAT 7g (sat 2g, unsat 5g); PROTEIN 2g; CARB 17g; FIBER 3g; SUGARS 11g (added sugars 6g); SODIUM 188mg; CALC 5% DV; POTASSIUM 10% DV

CURRIED CAULIFLOWER AND POTATOES

HANDS-ON: 20 MINUTES **TOTAL:** 4 HOURS, 20 MINUTES **SERVES** 10

The curry mixture coats the potatoes and cauliflower, imparting a bold, hot flavor while the dollop of sour cream on top acts as a cooling agent. Double the serving size, and this dish becomes a hearty meatless main. To make this recipe gluten free, use gluten-free curry powder. Garnish with fresh cilantro leaves, if desired.

1 cup chopped fresh cilantro leaves and stems

1 (15-ounce) can no-salt-added crushed tomatoes

2 cups chopped yellow onions (about 2 medium onions)

1 tablespoon unsalted butter

1½ tablespoons hot Madras curry powder, plus more for garnish

2 pounds baby (2-inch-diameter) red potatoes, halved

4 cups cauliflower florets (about 16 ounces)

Cooking spray

6 ounces baby spinach leaves

1 cup diced plum tomatoes (about 3 to 4 tomatoes)

1¼ teaspoons kosher salt

10 tablespoons reduced-fat sour cream

1 Process the cilantro, crushed tomatoes, and 1 cup of the onions in a blender until smooth.

2 Melt the butter in a medium-sized nonstick skillet over medium. Add the remaining 1 cup onions, and stir to coat. Cover and cook until translucent, about 5 minutes. Add 1½ tablespoons of the curry powder, and cook, stirring constantly, until fragrant, about 1 minute. Add the cilantro mixture to the skillet, and cook, stirring often, until bubbly, about 3 minutes.

3 Place the potatoes and cauliflower in a 5- to 6-quart slow cooker coated with cooking spray. Stir in the curry mixture. Cover and cook on LOW until the vegetables are tender, about 4 hours. Stir in the spinach, plum tomatoes, and salt. Top each serving with the sour cream. Sprinkle evenly with the additional curry powder, if desired.

(SERVING SIZE: about ¾ cup vegetable mixture, 1 tablespoon sour cream): CALORIES 145; FAT 3g (sat 2g, unsat 1g); PROTEIN 5g; CARB 24g; FIBER 4g; SUGARS 6g (added sugars 0g); SODIUM 300mg; CALC 9% DV; POTASSIUM 23% DV

SPICE-DRIZZLED ACORN SQUASH

HANDS-ON: 15 MINUTES **TOTAL:** 2 HOURS, 15 MINUTES **SERVES** 8

With the honey, butter, and cinnamon sauce drizzled on top and the sprinkling of pomegranate arils, this squash side dish is almost like a dessert. You can also drizzle the sauce over oatmeal and baked apples for breakfast.

½ cup water
2 (1¼-pound) acorn squash, seeded and
    quartered
¼ cup honey
2 tablespoons unsalted butter, melted
2 teaspoons ground cinnamon

1 teaspoon ground cumin
1 teaspoon kosher salt
½ teaspoon black pepper
¼ cup pomegranate arils
2 tablespoons chopped fresh cilantro

Pour the water into a 6-quart slow cooker. Place the acorn squash quarters, flesh side up, in the slow cooker. Stir together the honey, butter, cinnamon, cumin, salt, and pepper in a small bowl. Drizzle the honey mixture over the squash. Cover and cook on HIGH until tender, 2 hours to 2 hours and 30 minutes. Sprinkle evenly with the pomegranate arils and cilantro.

(SERVING SIZE: ¼ acorn squash): CALORIES 108; FAT 3g (sat 2g, unsat 1g); PROTEIN 1g; CARB 22g; FIBER 2g; SUGARS 12g (added sugars 9g); SODIUM 245mg; CALC 5% DV; POTASSIUM 11% DV

UMAMI MUSHROOMS

HANDS-ON: 15 MINUTES **TOTAL:** 4 HOURS, 45 MINUTES **SERVES** 6

In addition to being a great stand-alone side, these mushrooms are also excellent tossed in a salad or stir-fry. Be sure to buy whole cremini mushrooms so they will retain their texture and not turn mushy during the long cook time.

2 pounds fresh cremini mushrooms
8 ounces sliced fresh shiitake mushrooms
  (from 3 [3.5-ounce] packages)
2 tablespoons unsalted butter
2 tablespoons lower-sodium soy sauce
1 tablespoon minced garlic (about 3 garlic
  cloves)

⅛ teaspoon kosher salt
¼ teaspoon crushed red pepper
Cooking spray
2 tablespoons rice vinegar
½ cup finely sliced scallions

Stir together the mushrooms, butter, soy sauce, garlic, salt, and red pepper in a 5- to 6-quart slow cooker coated with cooking spray. Cover and cook on HIGH 3 hours. Uncover and cook until the mushrooms are browned and tender, about 1 hour and 30 minutes. Stir in the vinegar, and sprinkle with the scallions.

(SERVING SIZE: ⅔ cup): CALORIES 88; FAT 4g (sat 2g, unsat 1g); PROTEIN 4g; CARB 9g; FIBER 1g; SUGARS 5g (added sugars 0g); SODIUM 249mg; CALC 2% DV; POTASSIUM 22% DV

TIP

If you don't want to wait for the mushroom mixture to concentrate during the 1 hour and 30 minutes of cooking it uncovered, then cook it, uncovered, just long enough for the mushrooms to brown. Then drain the liquid and bring it to a boil in a saucepan. Once the liquid has thickened, stir in the mushrooms and vinegar and sprinkle with the scallions.

CUBAN-STYLE BLACK BEANS

HANDS-ON: 20 MINUTES   **TOTAL:** 8 HOURS, 20 MINUTES   **SERVES** 12

These beans are super flavorful and tender. To save time, process the garlic cloves in a small food processor instead of mincing them by hand. You can also make this a day ahead and refrigerate overnight to give the flavors more time to mingle. Garnish with fresh cilantro leaves, if desired.

1 pound dried black beans (about 2⅓ cups)
3 cups unsalted chicken stock
2 cups water
1 large white onion, quartered through root
1 large green bell pepper, quartered
1 bay leaf
3 tablespoons canola oil

1 large red bell pepper, finely chopped
3 tablespoons minced garlic (about 9 garlic cloves)
1 tablespoon ground cumin
2 tablespoons unsalted tomato paste
½ cup chopped fresh cilantro
2 teaspoons kosher salt

1 Sort and wash the beans according to the package directions. Stir together the beans, chicken stock, water, onion, green bell pepper, and bay leaf in a 6-quart slow cooker. Cover and cook on LOW until the beans are tender, 8 to 10 hours. Discard the onion, bell pepper, and bay leaf.

2 Meanwhile, heat the oil in a medium skillet over medium. Add the red bell pepper and garlic, and cook, stirring often, until very tender, about 8 minutes. Add the cumin, and cook, stirring constantly, until toasted, about 30 seconds. Add the tomato paste, and cook, stirring often, until darkened, about 1 minute. Stir the skillet mixture into the beans. Stir in the cilantro and salt.

(SERVING SIZE: ¾ cup): CALORIES 173; FAT 4g (sat 0g, unsat 3g); PROTEIN 9g; CARB 25g; FIBER 4g; SUGARS 4g (added sugars 0g); SODIUM 356mg; CALC 1% DV; POTASSIUM 2% DV

MULTICOOKER DIRECTIONS

IN STEP 1, stir together the washed beans, chicken stock, water, onion, green bell pepper, and bay leaf in the inner pot of a 6-quart multicooker. Lock the lid; turn Pressure Valve to "Venting." Cook on SLOW COOK [Normal] until the beans are tender, about 10 hours. Discard the onion, bell pepper, and bay leaf. **COMPLETE STEP 2.**

CHERRY BAKED BEANS

HANDS-ON: 15 MINUTES   **TOTAL:** 16 HOURS, 45 MINUTES, INCLUDING 8 HOURS SOAKING   **SERVES** 12

Serve these beans at your next cookout! They pair well with beef or pork barbecue. Cooking them with the sour cherry jam and mustard gives them the unexpected tangy sweetness that makes them unforgettable.

1 pound dried great Northern beans, rinsed, drained, and sorted

1½ cups chopped yellow onions (about 1 onion)

2 cups water

1 (12.5-ounce) jar sour cherry jam (such as Stonewall Kitchen)

1 (8-ounce) smoked ham hock

1 tablespoon smoked paprika

¼ cup whole-grain mustard

¼ cup no-salt-added ketchup

2 tablespoons reduced-sodium Worcestershire sauce

1 Stir together the beans and onions in a large bowl. Add water to cover by about 2 inches. Soak overnight, or a minimum of 8 hours. Drain.

2 Stir together the bean mixture, 2 cups water, jam, ham hock, and paprika in a 5- to 6-quart slow cooker. Cover and cook on LOW until the beans are tender, 8 to 9 hours. Stir in the mustard, ketchup, and Worcestershire sauce; cook, uncovered, 30 minutes. Remove the ham hock; remove the meat from the bone, and stir into the beans. Discard the ham bone, or reserve for another use.

(SERVING SIZE: about ½ cup): CALORIES 255; FAT 2g (sat 1g, unsat 1g); PROTEIN 13g; CARB 46g; FIBER 7g; SUGARS 21g (added sugars 5g); SODIUM 267mg; CALC 9% DV; POTASSIUM 1% DV

MULTICOOKER DIRECTIONS

COMPLETE STEP 1. IN STEP 2, stir together the bean mixture, 2 cups water, jam, ham hock, and paprika in the inner pot of a 6-quart multicooker. Lock the lid; turn Pressure Valve to "Venting." Cook on SLOW COOK [Normal] until the beans are tender, about 9 hours. Stir in the mustard, ketchup, and Worcestershire sauce; continue to cook, uncovered, on SLOW COOK [Normal] until the desired consistency. **FINISH STEP 2.**

BRAISED POTATOES AND GREEN CABBAGE

HANDS-ON: 15 MINUTES   **TOTAL:** 4 HOURS, 15 MINUTES   **SERVES** 8

Everyone will love this new spin on the classic cabbage-and-potatoes combo. The addition of fennel adds earthy and slightly sweet flavor to the dish.

1 head green cabbage (about 2 pounds), thinly sliced

1 pound small red potatoes, cut into 1-inch cubes

1 cup sliced fennel bulb (about 1 bulb)

Cooking spray

½ cup dry white wine

½ cup apple cider vinegar

1 tablespoon granulated sugar

½ teaspoon ground coriander

2 bay leaves

3 tablespoons unsalted butter, melted

⅞ teaspoon kosher salt

½ teaspoon black pepper

1 teaspoon fresh thyme leaves

Stir together the cabbage, potatoes, and fennel in a 5- to 6-quart slow cooker coated with cooking spray. Whisk together the wine, vinegar, sugar, and coriander in a small bowl. Stir the wine mixture into the cabbage mixture. Add the bay leaves to the slow cooker, and submerge in the mixture. Cover and cook on LOW until the cabbage is tender, 4 to 5 hours. Discard the bay leaves. Stir in the butter, salt, and pepper. Sprinkle the top with the thyme leaves.

(SERVING SIZE: about 1½ cups): CALORIES 134; FAT 4g (sat 3g, unsat 1g); PROTEIN 3g; CARB 19g; FIBER 4g; SUGARS 6g (added sugars 2g); SODIUM 248mg; CALC 6% DV; POTASSIUM 9% DV

TIP

To slice a fennel bulb, first trim the stalks and fronds. (Reserve them for other uses, such as soup stocks and garnishes.) Halve the bulb by cutting straight down through the root, and then quarter it by cutting each half in half. Discard any outer wilted layers. Lay each quarter on its largest cut side and slice it into thin strips.

APPLE-RUM SWEET POTATOES

HANDS-ON: 15 MINUTES **TOTAL:** 6 HOURS, 15 MINUTES **SERVES** 6

Dark rum and tart Granny Smith apples bring sweet potatoes to life. This dish makes an exciting side for roasted turkey or pork such as Pork Loin with Port and Rosemary Sauce (page 59). Piercing the potatoes with a fork is essential to keeping them from bursting in the slow cooker.

3 medium-sized sweet potatoes (about 6 ounces each)

2 cups peeled and chopped Granny Smith apples (about 8 ounces)

2 tablespoons (1 ounce) dark rum

1 tablespoon unsalted butter

1 tablespoon apple cider vinegar

½ teaspoon ground cinnamon

½ teaspoon kosher salt

¼ teaspoon black pepper

3 tablespoons chopped pecans, toasted

Small fresh sage leaves (optional)

Scrub the potatoes, and prick with a fork. Stir together the apples, rum, butter, vinegar, and cinnamon in a 6-quart slow cooker; top with the sweet potatoes. Cover and cook on LOW until the potatoes are tender, about 6 hours. Remove the potatoes, and cut in half lengthwise; sprinkle evenly with the salt and pepper. Top the sweet potato halves with the apple mixture and pecans. Sprinkle evenly with the sage leaves, if desired.

(SERVING SIZE: ½ sweet potato, 1 rounded tablespoon apple mixture, ½ tablespoon pecans): CALORIES 117; FAT 4g (sat 1g, unsat 3g); PROTEIN 1g; CARB 19g; FIBER 3g; SUGARS 7g (added sugars 0g); SODIUM 196mg; CALC 3% DV; POTASSIUM 8% DV

BUTTERED MAPLE SWEET POTATO MASH

HANDS-ON: 15 MINUTES **TOTAL:** 3 HOURS, 45 MINUTES **SERVES** 10

You truly can just dump the recipe ingredients and leave it until the cook time is up. The finishing touch of toasted pecans adds the right amount of crunch.

3½ pounds sweet potatoes, peeled and cut into 2-inch chunks
6 tablespoons (3 ounces) unsalted butter, plus more for serving (optional)
¼ cup apple juice

2 tablespoons pure maple syrup
1¼ teaspoons kosher salt
1 teaspoon black pepper
Cooking spray
¼ cup chopped pecans, toasted

Stir together the potatoes, butter, juice, syrup, salt, and pepper in a 5- to 6-quart slow cooker coated with cooking spray. Cover and cook on LOW until the potatoes are tender, about 3 hours and 30 minutes. Coarsely mash the potatoes to the desired consistency. Transfer to a serving platter, and top with the pecans. Serve with additional butter on top, if desired.

(SERVING SIZE: about ½ cup): CALORIES 192; FAT 9g (sat 5g, unsat 4g); PROTEIN 2g; CARB 27g; FIBER 4g; SUGARS 8g (added sugars 2g); SODIUM 305mg; CALC 4% DV; POTASSIUM 12% DV

BROWN RICE PILAF WITH CHERRIES AND HAZELNUTS

HANDS-ON: 15 MINUTES **TOTAL:** 2 HOURS, 30 MINUTES **SERVES** 8

Get creative and try many variations of this recipe. Sub dried cranberries, blueberries, or apricots for the cherries—or use them all. Just be sure to use a dried fruit. You can also swap the hazelnuts for pecans, if desired.

1 tablespoon unsalted butter

½ cup chopped yellow onions (from 1 onion)

1½ cups uncooked long-grain brown rice

3 cups unsalted chicken stock

1 teaspoon kosher salt

¼ teaspoon black pepper

½ cup sweetened dried cherries

1½ tablespoons sliced scallions

1 tablespoon apple cider vinegar

½ cup chopped hazelnuts, toasted

1 Melt the butter in a medium-sized nonstick skillet over medium-high. Add the onions; cook, stirring often, until tender and translucent, 5 minutes. Add the rice, and toss to coat, about 1 minute. Transfer the mixture to a 6-quart slow cooker.

2 Stir in the chicken stock, salt, and pepper. Cover and cook on HIGH until the rice is tender and the liquid is nearly absorbed, 2 to 3 hours. Turn the slow cooker off; stir in the cherries. Cover and let stand 15 minutes. Stir in the scallions and vinegar. Sprinkle with the hazelnuts; toss gently, and serve immediately.

(SERVING SIZE: ¾ cup): CALORIES 232; FAT 7g (sat 1g, unsat 5g); PROTEIN 5g; CARB 37g; FIBER 3g; SUGARS 8g (added sugars 3g); SODIUM 294mg; CALC 2% DV; POTASSIUM 6% DV

MULTICOOKER DIRECTIONS

IN STEP 1, remove the lid from a 6-quart multicooker. Add the butter to the inner pot. Press SAUTÉ [Normal], and melt the butter. Add the onions; cook uncovered, stirring often, until tender and translucent. Turn off the cooker. Add the rice, tossing to coat, about 1 minute. **IN STEP 2,** stir in the chicken stock, salt, and pepper. Lock the lid; turn Pressure Valve to "Venting." Cook on SLOW COOK [More] until the rice is tender and the liquid is nearly absorbed, about 3 hours. Turn off the cooker; stir in the cherries. Replace the lid; let stand 15 minutes. **FINISH STEP 2.**

BACON, LEEK, THYME FARRO

HANDS-ON: 15 MINUTES **TOTAL:** 2 HOURS, 25 MINUTES **SERVES** 8

Al dente farro with earthy leeks, thyme, savory mushrooms, and bacon is a match made in culinary heaven. The result is a hearty and toothsome dish that you'll crave time and again. Garnish with fresh thyme sprigs, if desired.

4 center-cut bacon slices, chopped
2 cups thinly sliced fresh cremini mushrooms (about 4 ounces)
1½ cups thinly sliced leeks (about 1 medium leek)
1 tablespoon chopped fresh thyme
1 tablespoon minced garlic (about 3 garlic cloves)

3 cups unsalted chicken stock
1½ cups uncooked farro
¾ teaspoon kosher salt
½ teaspoon black pepper
1 ounce Gruyère cheese, grated (about ¼ cup)

1 Cook the bacon in a large nonstick skillet over medium-high until crispy, about 5 minutes. Transfer the bacon to a plate lined with paper towels, reserving the drippings in the skillet. Set the bacon aside. Add the mushrooms and leeks to the hot drippings in the skillet, and cook, stirring often, until tender and lightly browned, 6 to 8 minutes. Add the thyme and garlic; cook, stirring often, until fragrant, 1 minute. Transfer the leek mixture to a 5- to 6-quart slow cooker.

2 Stir in the stock, farro, salt, and pepper. Cover and cook on HIGH until the farro is al dente, about 2 hours. Turn the slow cooker off, and let the mixture stand 10 minutes. Sprinkle with the cheese and bacon before serving.

(SERVING SIZE: ¾ cup): CALORIES 158; FAT 2g (sat 1g, unsat 1g); PROTEIN 9g; CARB 26g; FIBER 3g; SUGARS 1g (added sugars 0g); SODIUM 330mg; CALC 8% DV; POTASSIUM 3% DV

MULTICOOKER DIRECTIONS

IN STEP 1, coat the inner pot of a 6-quart multicooker with cooking spray. Place the bacon in the cold pot. With the lid off, press SAUTÉ [Normal]; cook, stirring constantly, until the bacon is crispy. Transfer the bacon to a plate lined with paper towels, reserving the drippings in the pot. Set the bacon aside. Add the mushrooms and leeks to the hot drippings in the pot, and cook uncovered, stirring often, until tender and lightly browned. Turn off the cooker. Add the thyme and garlic; stir until fragrant, 1 minute. Stir in the stock, farro, salt, and pepper. Lock the lid; turn Pressure Valve to "Venting." Cook on SLOW COOK [More] until the farro is al dente, about 2 hours. Turn off the cooker. **COMPLETE STEP 2.**

HERB-INFUSED WHEAT BERRY PILAF

HANDS-ON: 20 MINUTES **TOTAL:** 2 HOURS, 20 MINUTES **SERVES** 6

Olive oil infused with parsley, thyme, and rosemary coats the wheat berries, keeping them moist and chewy and imparting an aromatic flavor. You can make the oil and keep it tightly sealed in the pantry as you would regular olive oil. Drizzle the oil over salads or other grains to amp up their flavor.

¼ cup olive oil
½ cup finely chopped shallots
1 cup uncooked wheat berries (hard winter wheat)
2¼ cups water
1 teaspoon kosher salt

1 very small bunch fresh flat-leaf parsley
4 fresh thyme sprigs
1 fresh rosemary sprig
1 tablespoon white wine vinegar
¼ cup chopped almonds, toasted

1 Heat 1 tablespoon of the oil in a large nonstick skillet over medium. Add the shallots, and cook, stirring often, until translucent, about 3 minutes. Increase the heat to medium-high, and add the wheat berries. Cook, stirring occasionally, until the wheat berries are toasted, 4 to 5 minutes.

2 Stir together the wheat berry mixture, water, and salt in a 5- to 6-quart slow cooker. Cover and cook on LOW until the wheat berries are tender but still slightly chewy, 2 hours to 2 hours and 30 minutes.

3 Meanwhile, heat the remaining 3 tablespoons oil in a small skillet over medium. Finely chop the parsley stems to equal 2 tablespoons. Add the chopped parsley stems, thyme sprigs, and rosemary sprig to the oil; turn off the heat, and let stand at least 2 hours. Pour through a fine wire-mesh strainer into a bowl, discarding the solids.

4 Chop the parsley leaves to equal ⅓ cup. Add the chopped parsley leaves, infused oil, and vinegar to the wheat berries; toss to combine. Sprinkle with the almonds.

(SERVING SIZE: about ⅔ cup): CALORIES 215; FAT 11g (sat 1g, unsat 10g); PROTEIN 5g; CARB 25g; FIBER 5g; SUGARS 1g (added sugars 0g); SODIUM 326mg; CALC 4% DV; POTASSIUM 3% DV

MULTICOOKER DIRECTIONS

IN STEP 1, place 1 tablespoon of the oil in the inner pot of a 6-quart multicooker. With the lid off, press SAUTÉ [Normal] and heat, swirling to coat the bottom of the pot. Add the shallots; cook uncovered, stirring often, until translucent. Add the wheat berries. Cook uncovered, stirring often, until the wheat berries are toasted, about 5 minutes. **IN STEP 2,** stir in the water and salt. Lock the lid; turn Pressure Valve to "Venting." Cook on SLOW COOK [Normal] until the wheat berries are tender, but still slightly chewy, about 2 hours and 30 minutes. Turn off the cooker. **COMPLETE STEPS 3 AND 4.**

SWISS CHARD DRESSING

HANDS-ON: 20 MINUTES **TOTAL:** 2 HOURS, 50 MINUTES **SERVES** 12

Make dressing in the slow cooker? You bet! It comes out tender and full of flavor. The chard tastes very green, like spinach, and is filled with antioxidants and vitamins. For an extra-special touch, serve this dressing with gravy on top.

16 ounces day-old multigrain bread, cut into
   1- to 1½-inch cubes (about 8 cups)
2 tablespoons olive oil
¼ cup chopped shallots (about 2 medium
   shallots)
2 tablespoons minced garlic (about 5 to
   6 garlic cloves)
4 cups coarsely chopped Swiss chard (from
   1 bunch)
10 Castelvetrano olives, pitted and chopped
   (about 3 tablespoons)

¼ cup raisins
2 tablespoons pine nuts, toasted
1 tablespoon chopped fresh flat-leaf parsley
2 teaspoons chopped fresh rosemary
½ teaspoon black pepper
¼ teaspoon kosher salt
1⅔ cups unsalted chicken stock
4 large eggs
Cooking spray

1 Preheat the oven to 375°F. Place the bread cubes in a single layer on a large rimmed baking sheet. Bake in the preheated oven until golden brown and toasted, about 10 minutes, stirring halfway through. Let cool slightly. Transfer to a large bowl.

2 Meanwhile, heat the oil in a large high-sided skillet over medium. Add the shallots and garlic, and cook, stirring often, until softened, about 3 minutes. Add the Swiss chard, and cook, stirring constantly, until wilted, about 2 minutes. Transfer the mixture to the bowl with the bread cubes. Stir in the olives, raisins, pine nuts, parsley, rosemary, pepper, and salt.

3 Whisk together the stock and eggs in a medium bowl; pour over the bread cube mixture. Toss to coat.

4 Transfer the mixture to a 5- to 6-quart slow cooker coated with cooking spray. Cover and cook on LOW until the dressing is tender and moist and the internal temperature is at least 160°F, about 2 hours and 30 minutes.

(SERVING SIZE: about ½ cup): CALORIES 177; FAT 7g (sat 1g, unsat 4g); PROTEIN 8g; CARB 22g; FIBER 4g; SUGARS 3g (added sugars 0g); SODIUM 367mg; CALC 4% DV; POTASSIUM 4% DV

MAPLE, CINNAMON, APPLE, AND PEAR SAUCE

HANDS-ON: 20 MINUTES   **TOTAL:** 6 HOURS, 20 MINUTES   **SERVES** 18

Essentially applesauce with pears added in, this is comforting, cinnamony, and not too sweet. Use it any way you would use applesauce—in cakes, on pork chops, or eaten straight with a spoon. You can leave the apples unblended and use them as an oatmeal topping or a lighter apple pie filling.

Cooking spray

2¼ pounds Golden Delicious apples (about 5 medium apples), peeled and cut into ½-inch-thick slices

2¼ pounds Gala apples (about 4 medium apples), peeled and cut into ½-inch-thick slices

2¼ pounds Bartlett pears (about 5 medium pears), peeled and cut into ½-inch-thick slices

¼ cup water

3 tablespoons pure maple syrup

1 tablespoon ground cinnamon

½ teaspoon ground nutmeg

2 tablespoons fresh lemon juice (from 1 lemon)

Coat a 5- to 6-quart slow cooker with cooking spray. Stir together the apples, pears, water, maple syrup, cinnamon, and nutmeg in the slow cooker. Cover and cook on LOW until the apples and pears are very tender, about 6 hours. Stir in the lemon juice. Process the mixture using an immersion blender until the desired consistency. (Or transfer the mixture to a blender; remove the center piece of the blender lid [to allow steam to escape], and secure the lid on the blender. Place a clean towel over the opening in the lid [to avoid splatters], and process.) Serve warm or chilled.

(SERVING SIZE: about ½ cup): CALORIES 102; FAT 0g; PROTEIN 0g; CARB 25g; FIBER 4g; SUGARS 18g (added sugars 2g); SODIUM 2mg; CALC 2% DV; POTASSIUM 5% DV

MULTICOOKER DIRECTIONS

Coat the inner pot of a 6-quart multicooker evenly with cooking spray. Stir together the apples, pears, water, maple syrup, cinnamon, and nutmeg in the pot. Lock the lid; turn Pressure Valve to "Venting." Cook on SLOW COOK [Normal] until the apples and pears are very tender, about 6 hours. Turn off the cooker, and stir in the lemon juice. **FINISH THE RECIPE.**

SOUTH INDIAN TOMATO CHUTNEY

HANDS-ON: 25 MINUTES **TOTAL:** 8 HOURS, 25 MINUTES **SERVES** 12

Don't expect this chutney to be like the American version, which is jam-like and almost a preserve. This recipe is true to the original Indian style of chutney, which is more of a thick sauce. With spices and tomato, it's both slightly hot and sweet. It's best eaten warm or at room temperature on crackers or grilled meats, and it will keep in the refrigerator for about 5 days.

6 cups chopped, seeded tomatoes (about 6 large tomatoes)
8 garlic cloves, peeled and smashed
2 tablespoons canola oil
1 tablespoon tamarind paste
2 teaspoons brown mustard seeds
2 teaspoons cumin seeds

1 teaspoon fenugreek seeds
1 teaspoon demerara sugar
3 dried red chiles (such as Guntur), seeded and broken into pieces (optional)
Cooking spray
⅞ teaspoon kosher salt

1 Stir together the tomatoes, garlic, oil, tamarind paste, mustard seeds, cumin seeds, fenugreek seeds, sugar, and, if desired, chiles in a 6-quart slow cooker coated with cooking spray; stir gently. Cover and cook on LOW until well incorporated 8 hours.

2 Add the salt, and stir gently; transfer the mixture to a blender. Remove the center piece of the blender lid (to allow steam to escape); secure the lid on the blender, and place a clean towel over the opening in the lid (to avoid splatters). Process until smooth. Serve the chutney warm or at room temperature.

(SERVING SIZE: ¼ cup): CALORIES 52; FAT 3g (sat 0g, unsat 2g); PROTEIN 1g; CARB 6g; FIBER 2g; SUGARS 4g (added sugars 0g); SODIUM 147mg; CALC 2% DV; POTASSIUM 8% DV

MULTICOOKER DIRECTIONS

IN STEP 1, stir together the chopped tomatoes, garlic, oil, tamarind paste, mustard seeds, cumin seeds, fenugreek seeds, sugar, and, if desired, chiles in the inner pot of a 6-quart multicooker coated with cooking spray. Lock the lid; turn Pressure Valve to "Venting." Cook on SLOW COOK [Normal] 8 hours. Turn off the cooker. **COMPLETE STEP 2.**

CARAMELIZED ONIONS AND FENNEL

HANDS-ON: 25 MINUTES   **TOTAL:** 14 HOURS, 25 MINUTES   **SERVES** 24

These onions are an ideal condiment for burgers, steaks, a grilled chicken breast, or sautéed fish. They also make a pleasing addition to a cheese board or topping for Brie. They're best eaten cold or warm, but not hot.

3 pounds yellow onions, vertically sliced (about 10 cups)

5 cups thinly sliced fennel (about 3 bulbs)

3 tablespoons olive oil

1½ teaspoons kosher salt

1 tablespoon, plus 1 teaspoon chopped fresh thyme

2½ teaspoons chopped fresh oregano

1 tablespoon apple cider vinegar

Combine the onions, fennel, oil, salt, 1 tablespoon of the thyme, and 2 teaspoons of the oregano in a 5- to 6-quart slow cooker, tossing to coat. Cover and cook on LOW until the vegetables are golden brown, about 12 hours. Uncover and stir gently. Increase the heat to HIGH, and cook, uncovered, until the mixture thickens, about 2 hours, stirring every 15 minutes. Stir in the vinegar, and the remaining 1 teaspoon thyme and ½ teaspoon oregano.

(SERVING SIZE: ¼ cup): CALORIES 47; FAT 2g (sat 0g, unsat 1g); PROTEIN 1g; CARB 7g; FIBER 2g; SUGARS 4g (added sugars 0g); SODIUM 138mg; CALC 3% DV; POTASSIUM 6% DV

SWEET ONION JAM WITH PANCETTA

HANDS-ON: 25 MINUTES **TOTAL:** 9 HOURS, 25 MINUTES **SERVES** 28

This is a salty, sweet, and smoky onion jam with a noticeable pork and black pepper flavor. It may seem slightly runny when hot, but when cooled it's thick and tender. Eat this on burgers, especially with blue cheese, or serve on a cheese board. It will keep in the refrigerator for about 5 days.

6 cups thinly sliced sweet onions (about 2 large onions)

4 ounces diced pancetta (about ¾ cup)

¾ cup balsamic vinegar

½ cup packed light brown sugar

2 teaspoons chopped fresh thyme

1 teaspoon black pepper

¾ teaspoon kosher salt

Stir together the onions, pancetta, vinegar, brown sugar, thyme, pepper, and salt in a 6-quart slow cooker. Cover and cook on LOW until the onions are very tender, about 7 hours. Uncover and stir well. Increase the heat to HIGH, and cook, uncovered, until the desired consistency, about 1 hour. Skim the fat, and discard. Cool to room temperature, about 1 hour. Serve at room temperature or cold.

(SERVING SIZE: about 2 tablespoons): CALORIES 45; FAT 1g (sat 1g, unsat 0g); PROTEIN 1g; CARB 7g; FIBER 0g; SUGARS 6g (added sugars 4g); SODIUM 121mg; CALC 1% DV; POTASSIUM 1% DV

SEASONAL PRODUCE GUIDE

When you use fresh fruits, vegetables, and herbs, you don't have to do much to make them taste great. Although many fruits, vegetables, and herbs are available year-round, you'll get better flavor and prices when you buy what's in season. This guide helps you choose the best produce so you can create tasty meals all year long.

SPRING

FRUITS
- Bananas
- Blood oranges
- Coconuts
- Grapefruit
- Kiwifruit
- Lemons
- Limes
- Mangoes
- Navel oranges
- Papayas
- Passion fruit
- Pineapples
- Strawberries
- Tangerines
- Valencia oranges

VEGETABLES
- Artichokes
- Arugula
- Asparagus
- Avocados
- Baby leeks
- Beets
- Belgian endive
- Broccoli
- Cauliflower
- Dandelion greens
- Fava beans
- Green onions
- Green peas
- Kale
- Lettuce
- Mushrooms
- Radishes
- Red potatoes
- Rhubarb
- Snap beans
- Snow peas
- Spinach
- Sugar snap peas
- Sweet onions
- Swiss chard

HERBS
- Chives
- Dill
- Garlic chives
- Lemongrass
- Mint
- Parsley
- Thyme

SUMMER

FRUITS
- Apricots
- Blackberries
- Blueberries
- Boysenberries
- Cantaloupes
- Casaba melons
- Cherries
- Crenshaw melons
- Figs
- Grapes
- Guava
- Honeydew melons
- Mangoes
- Nectarines
- Papayas
- Peaches
- Plums
- Raspberries
- Strawberries
- Watermelons

VEGETABLES
- Avocados
- Beans: pole, shell, and snap
- Beets
- Bell peppers
- Cabbage
- Carrots
- Celery
- Chile peppers
- Collards
- Corn
- Cucumbers
- Eggplant
- Green beans
- Jicama
- Lima beans
- Okra
- Pattypan squash
- Peas
- Radicchio
- Radishes
- Summer squash
- Tomatoes

HERBS
- Basil
- Bay leaves
- Borage
- Chives
- Cilantro
- Dill
- Lavender
- Lemon balm
- Marjoram
- Mint
- Oregano
- Rosemary
- Sage
- Summer savory
- Tarragon
- Thyme

FALL

FRUITS
- Apples
- Cranberries
- Figs
- Grapes
- Mangoes
- Pears
- Persimmons
- Pomegranates
- Quinces

VEGETABLES
- Beets
- Belgian endive
- Bell peppers
- Broccoli
- Brussels sprouts
- Cabbage
- Cauliflower
- Celery
- Eggplant
- Escarole
- Fennel
- Frisée
- Green beans
- Leeks
- Mushrooms
- Parsnips
- Peppers (sweet and spicy)
- Pumpkins
- Red potatoes
- Rutabagas
- Shallots
- Sweet potatoes
- Turnips
- Winter squash
- Yukon gold potatoes

HERBS
- Basil
- Bay leaves
- Parsley
- Rosemary
- Sage
- Tarragon
- Thyme

WINTER

FRUITS
- Apples
- Blood oranges
- Cranberries
- Grapefruit
- Kiwifruit
- Kumquats
- Lemons
- Limes
- Mandarin oranges
- Navel oranges
- Pears
- Persimmons
- Pomegranates
- Pomelos
- Quinces
- Tangelos
- Tangerines

VEGETABLES
- Baby turnips
- Beets
- Belgian endive
- Brussels sprouts
- Celery root
- Escarole
- Fennel
- Frisée
- Jerusalem artichokes
- Kale
- Leeks
- Mushrooms
- Parsnips
- Potatoes
- Rutabagas
- Sweet potatoes
- Turnips
- Watercress
- Winter squash

NUTRITIONAL INFORMATION

HOW TO USE IT AND WHY

At *Cooking Light*, our team of food editors, experienced cooks, and registered dietitians builds recipes with whole foods and whole grains, and bigger portions of plants and seafood than meat. We emphasize oil-based fats more than saturated, and we promote a balanced diet low in processed foods and added sugars (those added during processing or preparation).

Not only do we focus on quality ingredients, but we also adhere to a rigorous set of nutrition guidelines that govern calories, saturated fat, sodium, and sugar based on various recipe categories. The numbers in each category are derived from the most recent set of USDA Dietary Guidelines for Americans, as shown in the following chart. As you look through our numbers, remember that the nutrition stats included with each recipe are for a single serving. When we build recipes, we look at each dish in context of the role it plays in an average day: A one-dish meal that fills a plate with protein, starch, and vegetables will weigh more heavily in calories, saturated fat, and sodium than a recipe for roasted chicken thighs. Similarly, a bowl of ice cream may contain more than half of your daily added sugar recommendation, but balances out when the numbers are folded into a day's worth of healthy food prepared at home.

When reading the chart, remember that recommendations vary by gender and age; other factors, including lifestyle, weight, and your own health—for example, if you're pregnant or breast-feeding or if you have genetic factors such as risk for hypertension—all need consideration. Go to choosemyplate.gov for your own individualized plan.

IN OUR NUTRITIONAL ANALYSIS, WE USE THESE ABBREVIATIONS

sat	saturated fat	**carb**	carbohydrates	**g**	gram	**DV**	daily value
unsat	unsaturated fat	**calc**	calcium	**mg**	milligram		

DAILY NUTRITION GUIDE

	Women ages 25 to 50	Women over 50	Men ages 25 to 50	Men over 50
Calories	2,000	2,000*	2,700	2,500
Protein	50g	50g	63g	60g
Fat	65g*	65g*	88g*	83g*
Saturated Fat	20g*	20g*	27g*	25g*
Carbohydrates	304g	304g	410g	375g
Fiber	25g to 35g	25g to 35g	25g to 35g	25g to 35g
Added Sugars	38g	38g	38g	38g
Cholesterol	300mg*	300mg*	300mg*	300mg*
Iron	18mg	8mg	8mg	8mg
Sodium	2,300mg*	1,500mg*	2,300mg*	1,500mg*
Calcium	1,000mg	1,200mg	1,000mg	1,000mg

*Or less, for optimum health

Nutritional values used in our calculations either come from The Food Processor, Version 10.4 (ESHA Research), or are provided by food manufacturers.

METRIC EQUIVALENTS

The information in the following chart is provided to help cooks outside the United States successfully use the recipes in this book. All equivalents are approximate.

COOKING/OVEN TEMPERATURES

	Fahrenheit	Celsius	Gas Mark
Freeze Water	32° F	0° C	
Room Temp.	68° F	20° C	
Boil Water	212° F	100° C	
Bake	325° F	160° C	3
	350° F	180° C	4
	375° F	190° C	5
	400° F	200° C	6
	425° F	220° C	7
	450° F	230° C	8
Broil			Grill

LIQUID INGREDIENTS BY VOLUME

¼ tsp	=					1	ml
½ tsp	=					2	ml
1 tsp	=					5	ml
3 tsp	=	1 Tbsp	=	½ fl oz	=	15	ml
2 Tbsp	=	⅛ cup	=	1 fl oz	=	30	ml
4 Tbsp	=	¼ cup	=	2 fl oz	=	60	ml
5⅓ Tbsp	=	⅓ cup	=	3 fl oz	=	80	ml
8 Tbsp	=	½ cup	=	4 fl oz	=	120	ml
10⅔ Tbsp	=	⅔ cup	=	5 fl oz	=	160	ml
12 Tbsp	=	¾ cup	=	6 fl oz	=	180	ml
16 Tbsp	=	1 cup	=	8 fl oz	=	240	ml
1 pt	=	2 cups	=	16 fl oz	=	480	ml
1 qt	=	4 cups	=	32 fl oz	=	960	ml
				33 fl oz	=	1000 ml	= 1 l

DRY INGREDIENTS BY WEIGHT

(To convert ounces to grams, multiply the number of ounces by 30.)

1 oz	=	¹⁄₁₆ lb	=	30 g
4 oz	=	¼ lb	=	120 g
8 oz	=	½ lb	=	240 g
12 oz	=	¾ lb	=	360 g
16 oz	=	1 lb	=	480 g

LENGTH

(To convert inches to centimeters, multiply inches by 2.5.)

1 in	=				2.5 cm	
12 in	=	1 ft		=	30 cm	
36 in	=	3 ft	= 1 yd	=	90 cm	
40 in	=				100 cm	= 1m

EQUIVALENTS FOR DIFFERENT TYPES OF INGREDIENTS

Standard Cup	Fine Powder (ex. flour)	Grain (ex. rice)	Granular (ex. sugar)	Liquid Solids (ex. butter)	Liquid (ex. milk)
1	140 g	150 g	190 g	200 g	240 ml
¾	105 g	113 g	143 g	150 g	180 ml
⅔	93 g	100 g	125 g	133 g	160 ml
½	70 g	75 g	95 g	100 g	120 ml
⅓	47 g	50 g	63 g	67 g	80 ml
¼	35 g	38 g	48 g	50 g	60 ml
⅛	18 g	19 g	24 g	25 g	30 ml

INDEX

N

O

P